THE
CANON OF THE MASS

Its History, Theology, and Art

By

Rev. Jerome Gassner,

O.S.B., Ph.D., H.D., S.T.D.

B. HERDER BOOK CO.
15 & 17 SOUTH BROADWAY, ST. LOUIS 2, MO.
AND
33 QUEEN SQUARE, LONDON, W. C.
1950

IMPRIMI POTEST

✠ *Dr. Bernardus Kaelin,*

Abbas Primas

Ex aedibus S. Anselmi, die 6 mai, 1949

IMPRIMATUR

E Vicariatu Urbis, die 7. V. 49.

✠ *Aloysius Traglia*

Archiepus Caesarien. Vicesgerens.

L.S.

Copyright 1949

B. HERDER BOOK CO.

Second Impression

Vail-Ballou Press, Inc., Binghamton and New York

Foreword

THE WORK involved in the preparation of the present volume
on the Canon of the Mass has taken years of study and research and is a valuable contribution to the literature on the
history and theology of the Canon; it is also a notable addition
to works of appreciation of the Canon as a work of art.

Since the book is intended to give the reader a correct understanding and appreciation of the Canon of the Mass, it
will be of great value to priests and students of theology as
well as to the large and increasing number of the faithful who
pray the Mass.

The age of the Canon requires that any useful study of it
be made from the historical point of view. In this book Father
Jerome brings to the reader historical information about the
Canon that ordinarily is accessible only to scholars with suitable library facilities and experience in research. This historical treatment is the best guaranty that the book is not a subjective or sentimental interpretation of the Canon.

Throughout the work there is continual reference to the
scriptural background of the Canon. Again, this approach
serves to explain the Canon and make it understood. It is not
a formal dogmatic treatise on the Holy Eucharist; yet the
historical and scriptural approach will reveal the primordial
theology of the Eucharist.

Father Jerome also presents the Canon as a work of art; in particular as a mosaic in which the several parts are coherently brought together to effect a unity in which there is a proper proportion of parts. And this approach to the Canon is also made to contribute to the better understanding of it.

This work may not be described as an easy book which in a rapid reading gives the reader a ready understanding of the Canon. It contains too much solid matter for such facile digestion. Most readers will find a great deal of new material and will desire to study the book carefully.

The author of this work is a Benedictine monk of Seitenstetten, Austria. After lecturing at St. Gregory's Abbey for six years, he has returned to Rome, where he will resume his lectures at the Benedictine International College there.

MARK BRAUN, O.S.B.
Abbot, St. Gregory's Abbey
Shawnee, Oklahoma

Note

The author, Father Jerome Gassner, O.S.B., has been appointed Postulator general in causes of beatification and also Prosynodal judge at the Roman Curia.

Contents

v

The Roman Canon

Common Preface

V. Forever and ever.

R. Amen.

V. The Lord be with you.

R. And with thy spirit.

V. Lift up your hearts.

R. We have lifted them up to the Lord.

V. Let us give thanks to the Lord our God.

R. It is meet and right to do so.

It is truly meet and right, proper and availing to salvation, that we should always and everywhere give thanks to Thee, holy Lord, Father almighty, ever-living God, through Christ our Lord. Through whom the angels praise Thy majesty, the dominions worship it, the powers are in awe before it. The heavens and the heavenly hosts and the blessed seraphim join together in expressing their joyful happiness. We pray Thee to join our voices with theirs as we sing with humble praise:

Sanctus: Holy, holy, holy Lord God of hosts. Heaven and earth are full of Thy glory. Hosanna in the highest!

Benedictus: Blessed is He that cometh in the name of the Lord. Hosanna in the highest!

Te igitur: Therefore, most merciful Father, we humbly pray

and beseech Thee, through Jesus Christ Thy Son, our Lord, that Thou wilt be pleased to accept and bless these gifts, these offerings, these holy unblemished sacrifices, which we offer to Thee in the first place for Thy holy Catholic Church: that Thou wilt be pleased to keep her in peace, to watch over her, to maintain her in unity, and to guide her throughout the world; together with Thy servant our Pope N., our Bishop N., and all right-believing promoters of the Catholic and apostolic faith.

Commemoratio pro vivis: Remember, O Lord, Thy servants and handmaids N. and N. and all here present whose faith and devotion are known unto Thee; for whom we offer, or who themselves do offer, this sacrifice of praise for themselves and all theirs, for the redeeming of their souls, for their hope of safety and salvation; who dedicate themselves to Thee, the eternal, living, and true God.

Infra actionem: Being in fellowship with and reverently bringing to mind, first, the glorious Mary, ever virgin, Mother of God, and of our Lord Jesus Christ; and then of Thy blessed apostles and martyrs Peter and Paul, Andrew, James, John, Thomas, James, Philip, Bartholomew, Matthew, Simon, and Thaddaeus; of Linus, Cletus, Clement, Sixtus, Cornelius, Cyprian, Lawrence, Chrysogonus, John and Paul, Cosmas and Damian, and of all the saints: through whose good deeds and prayers grant that we may be guarded by Thy providence in all things. Through the same Christ our Lord. Amen.

Hanc igitur oblationem: We therefore pray Thee, O Lord, graciously to accept this our dutiful offering and service and that of all Thy family. Order our days in Thy peace and cause us to be saved from everlasting doom and to be num-

bered among Thy chosen ones. Through Christ our Lord.
Amen.

Quam oblationem: Vouchsafe, O God, to make these offerings
in all respects blessed, consecrated, approved, right, and
acceptable; that it may become for us the body and blood
of Thy most dearly beloved Son, our Lord Jesus Christ.

Qui pridie: Who the day before He suffered took bread into
His holy and venerable hands and, with His eyes raised
toward heaven unto Thee, God, His almighty Father, He
gave thanks to Thee, and He blessed, broke, and gave to
His disciples, saying: Take, and eat ye all of this.
For this is My body.
Likewise, after He had supped, taking this glorious chalice
into His holy and venerable hands, He gave thanks to Thee,
and He blessed and gave to His disciples, saying:
Take, and drink ye all of this.
For this is the chalice of My blood, of the new and eternal
testament, the mystery of faith, which shall be shed for you
and for many unto the remission of sins.
As often as you shall do these things, you shall do them in
memory of Me.

Unde et memores: Wherefore, O Lord, we Thy servants and
all Thy holy people, are mindful of the blessed passion of
the same Christ Thy Son, our Lord, and of His rising from
the shades of death and His glorious ascension into heaven;
and we offer to Thy most excellent majesty, of Thine own
gifts bestowed on us, a pure victim, a holy victim, a spotless victim: the holy bread of everlasting life, and the
chalice of everlasting salvation.

Supra quae: Be pleased to look down upon them with a favorable and gracious countenance, and to accept them as Thou

wast pleased to accept the offerings of Thy righteous servant Abel and the sacrifice of our patriarch Abraham and
that which Thy high priest Melchisedech offered unto
Thee, a holy sacrifice, a spotless victim.

Supplices te rogamus: We humbly beseech Thee, almighty
God, to command that these offerings be carried by the
hands of Thy holy angel to Thy altar on high in the sight
of Thy divine majesty, that all who are partakers at the altar
of the precious body and blood of Thy Son may be filled
with all heavenly blessing and grace. Through the same
Christ our Lord.

Commemoratio pro defunctis: Remember, O Lord, Thy servants and handmaids N. and N. who are gone hence before
us with the sign of faith and sleep the sleep of peace. To
these, O Lord, and to all that rest in Christ we pray Thee
grant a place of refreshment, light, and peace. Through the
same Christ our Lord. Amen.

Nobis quoque peccatoribus: To us also, Thy sinful servants,
who hope in the multitude of Thy mercies, vouchsafe to
grant some part and fellowship with Thy holy apostles and
martyrs: with John, Stephen, Matthias, Barnabas, Ignatius,
Alexander, Marcellinus, Peter, Felicitas, Perpetua, Agatha,
Lucy, Agnes, Cecilia, Anastasia, and all Thy saints. We
pray Thee to admit us into their company, not weighing our
merits, but freely granting us pardon. Through Christ our
Lord.

Per quem haec omnia: By whom, O Lord, Thou dost create,
hallow, quicken, and bless these ever good things and give
them to us.

Per ipsum: By Him and with Him and in Him are to Thee,
God the Father almighty, in the unity of the Holy Ghost
all honor and glory forever and ever. Amen.

CHAPTER I

The Council of Trent on the Canon

THE solemn declarations of the Council of Trent on the Canon of the Mass are contained within its doctrine on the Eucharistic sacrifice.[1]

With regard to the definition on the Eucharistic sacrifice, the Council found itself in a position to which we may apply St. Paul's admonition to Timothy (I Tim. 3:9): "Holding the mystery of faith in a pure conscience." The Council had to preserve, to protect, and to defend the purity of faith and doctrine about the Eucharistic sacrifice against all errors and attacks of the reformers. This intention of the Council is expressed in the introduction to the nine chapters and the corresponding canons on the Sacrifice of the Mass with the implicit quotation from St. Paul (I Tim. 3:9), "that the ancient, complete, and in every way perfect faith and teaching regarding the great mystery of the Eucharist in the Catholic Church may be retained and . . . preserved." With this implicit quotation from I Tim. 3:9, the Council connects the parallel text of I Tim. 3:16: "And evidently great is the mystery of godliness," and demonstrates with the love and admiration of faithful disciples of the Apostle the truth and majesty of the Holy Eucharist as "the true and only sacrifice."

[1] Sess. 22, *Doctrina de sacrificio missae.* Cf. Denzinger, *Enchiridion symbolorum*, ed. 1937, nos. 937a–56.

1

The reformers all denied the sacrificial nature of the Eucharistic oblation. They admitted that it is an act of praise and thanksgiving which may be called a sacrifice in the wider sense as any kind of thanksgiving may be called so. They denied particularly its propitiatory value and declared that it is an empty commemoration (not an objective memorial that contains what it signifies) of the sacrifice on the cross. In their opinion the celebration of Mass with the claim of propitiatory value is a blasphemy against the sacrifice on the cross and derogates from the dignity and value of the bloody sacrifice as the only sacrifice of the New Testament. They condemned the Eucharistic liturgy and called its prayers and ceremonies, which express so forcibly the faith of the Church in the Eucharistic sacrifice, "provocations to impiety," the offering of Masses to the honor of saints an "imposture." They condemned the Roman rite and concentrated their attacks on the sacred Canon, the center and heart of the Eucharistic liturgy, protested against its errors and demanded its abrogation.

The Council answered these accusations "instructed by the light of the Holy Ghost," in the most authoritative form with nine anathemas. In the most dignified language it then summarized the "ancient, complete, and in every way perfect faith and teaching regarding the great mystery of the Eucharist," of the "true and only sacrifice," of the "divine sacrifice." It declared that of all things this sacrifice is the "most holy." The Council defended the Eucharistic liturgy, all the ancient rites approved by the holy Roman Church, particularly the Roman liturgy, as "visible signs of religion and piety," as work of piety "unfolding the majesty of so great a sacrifice." It defended the sacred Canon, the most ancient, most eloquent, most comprehensive expression of the faith of the Church in the Eucharistic sacrifice, and testified to its immunity from errors, to its singular sanctity and piety.

LITURGY IN GENERAL

The reformers argued against the sacrificial nature of the Eucharist from Scripture, particularly from St. Paul, and condemned the Eucharistic liturgy—the primary organ of tradition which testifies most explicitly to the sacrificial nature of the Holy Eucharist—as contrary to Scripture.

The Council met this objection with a refutation from Scripture, particularly from St. Paul. It maintained that the liturgy contains the faithful interpretation of Scripture, that it is of primary dogmatic value containing apostolic tradition.

The argument of the reformers was taken from St. Paul (Heb. 9:28): "So also Christ was offered once to exhaust the sins of many" (cf. Heb. 10:10: "We are sanctified by the oblation of the body of Jesus Christ once"). From this and similar texts they argued to the unity of the New Testament sacrifice as a propitiatory oblation to the exclusion of the Eucharist.

In the course of its argumentation from Scripture regarding the sacrificial nature of the Holy Eucharist, the Council refers twice explicitly to St. Paul with the phrase, "according to the testimony of the Apostle Paul," [2] about the priesthood of Christ exercised in the Eucharistic celebration, and about the sacrificial oblation "to which the Apostle Paul evidently refers, writing to the Corinthians" (I Cor. 10:21).[3]

Demonstrating the propitiatory value of the Eucharistic oblation, the Council [4] refers again to St. Paul (Heb. 4:16) and at this point introduces the liturgy as witness. Therefore in the introduction the Council had alluded to both groups of

[2] *Ibid.*, no. 938.
[3] *Ibid.*
[4] *Ibid.*, no. 940.

arguments, from Scripture and from the liturgy, speaking of its intention to preserve "faith and teaching regarding the great mystery of the Eucharist" in its purity. Now this expression is contained in the very heart of the Eucharistic liturgy where it has the value of an exclamation testifying to the reality of the Eucharist, "the mystery of faith." In this way the Council announced the two main sources for its argumentation: St. Paul and the liturgy.

The Council refers to the liturgy under a double aspect: liturgy as a genuine and faithful interpretation of Scripture; liturgy as the first organ of apostolic tradition.

Both methods are employed in chapter two,[5] about the propitiatory value of the Eucharist. The Council deduces this point from the scriptural arguments about the sacrificial nature presented in chapter one, and concludes with an implicit quotation from the Offertory prayer, "Accept, O holy Father," and declares: "Therefore it is rightly offered not only for the sins, punishments, satisfactions, and other necessities of the faithful who are living, but also for those departed in Christ, but not yet fully purified." This reference to the liturgy the Council understands as an argument from apostolic tradition ("according to the tradition of the apostles").

This method of combining the arguments from Scripture with the arguments from the liturgy as witness of apostolic tradition is applied throughout the whole treatise, introducing here and there explicit and implicit quotations from liturgical texts as explanation, interpretation, and confirmation of arguments taken from Scripture.

The value of the liturgy as the first organ of apostolic tradition regarding the doctrine of the Eucharist is explicitly stated four times: three times about liturgy generally, once

[5] *Ibid.*

about the Eucharistic Canon in particular. Chapter two refers to the liturgy as testimony from apostolic tradition for the Eucharist as propitiatory sacrifice; chapter four [6] states the Canon's immunity from error because of the apostolic tradition contained in it; chapter five [7] defends the ceremonies of the Mass as "visible signs of religion and piety," because they contain elements transmitted "in accordance with apostolic discipline and tradition." Lastly, in the Prolegomenon [8] to the nine anathemas, the Gospel, apostolic tradition (in the liturgy), and the teaching of the Fathers are mentioned as the basis of these pronouncements on the Sacrifice of the Mass, on the liturgy, and the Canon.

The proceedings of the Council of Trent on the Eucharistic sacrifice constitute the most prominent case in history of the appeal of the extraordinary magisterium to liturgy as the most important organ of the ordinary magisterium of the Church. It is the most solemn application of the principle proclaimed in the *Indiculus fidei* of Pope Celestine I [9] (422–32) that liturgy is the rule of faith: "The law of prayer is the law of belief." "Let us then examine the sacraments of the sacerdotal prayers which were given by the apostles to the whole world, and are uniformly carried out in the whole Catholic Church, so that the law of belief may be determined by the law of prayer." [10]

This text is referred to by Pope Pius XI (1922–39): "By it [the liturgy] we are carried up to God, are united to Him, we

[6] *Ibid.*, no. 942.
[7] *Ibid.*, no. 943.
[8] *Ibid.*, no. 947.
[9] *Ibid.*, no. 139.
[10] This passage is found in the eighth of the ten capitula, or paragraphs, attached to Pope Celestine's letter to the bishops of Gaul in the fifth century. Its contents agree with the passage found in *De vocatione gentium* of St. Prosper Aquil. (d. 460), and contain allusions to the Orationes of the Mass of the Presanctified (the last remnant of the ancient *Communis oratio*).

confess our faith and discharge the very grave obligation concerning the benefits received and the helps continually needed. Hence a certain intimate connection between dogma and liturgy, likewise between Christian worship and the sanctification of the people. Therefore Celestine I found the canon of faith expressed in the venerable formulas of the liturgy when he said: 'The law of belief may be determined by the law of prayer.' " [11]

ON THE CANON

The consideration accorded to the Canon by the Council of Trent, the place and extent of the respective statements, contents, and wording of them, show that the sacred Canon is itself the center and heart of the Eucharistic liturgy, its original nucleus, the primary, most ancient, eloquent, and comprehensive teaching from tradition on the Eucharistic sacrifice.

Of the eight chapters about the Eucharist (chapter nine is merely the Prolegomenon of the corresponding canons), the first is exclusively on the institution of the Mass according to Scripture; chapter two presents an argument from Scripture and from the liturgy regarding the propitiatory character of the Mass; chapters three to eight are all on the Eucharistic liturgy; chapter four is exclusively on the Canon; chapter five is partly so.

Of the nine canons corresponding to the doctrine presented in the preceding chapters, two canons are concerned explicitly with the Canon of the Mass: canon six is about the Canon's freedom from error; canon nine also speaks of the Eucharistic Canon.

[11] "Const. apost.," *Divini cultus* of December 20, 1928. Cf. Denzinger, no. 2200.

INSTITUTION OF THE CANON

Chapter four treats of the institution of the Canon by the Church and the fundamental reasons for its institution; about its excellence within the Eucharistic liturgy, about its ancient origin, its immunity from error, its sanctity and piety; about its truth, sacramental power, and aesthetic form; about its constitutive elements: the words of our Lord, traditions of the apostles, and pious institutions of holy pontiffs.

The institution which the Council speaks of was not one single act. It extends from the time of the apostles to the time of St. Gregory I, from the original free improvisations in the form of a paraphrase of the thanksgiving prayer of our Lord at the Last Supper to the state of an unchanging rule. Some quotations may illustrate this development.

Didache, 10, 7: "But permit the prophets to make thanksgiving as much as they desire [after there was proposed some formula in the preceding chapter]. Now concerning the thanksgiving, thus give thanks," etc.

St. Justin, *I Apol.*, 65, 3: "The president . . . makes thanksgiving at length. . . . The president sends up prayers and likewise thanksgiving as far as he has the power." [12]

From this state of charismatic improvisation and free oral tradition, gradually progress is made to written compositions, to certain formulas, until we find a unified liturgy at the end of the sixth century.

Canon 23 of the Third Council of Carthage (397) issued the following decree: "At the celebration at the altar the prayer must be addressed always to the Father [a particular feature of the Roman Canon]. And whosoever would adopt

[12] *PG*, 6, 412.

prayers from somewhere, should not use them before he has compared them with the well-instructed brethren." [13]

The Council of Mileve (402) decreed with its canon 12: "It was accepted also, that prayers or orations, or Masses which were approved in the Council, or traditions or com- mendations or impositions of hands, should be observed by all: nor should there be said any one of them in the Church except those which were composed and approved by the Synod, lest perhaps something against the faith, either by ignorance or even with intention, might be composed." [14] In this decree appears an important motive of institution: abuses, lack of knowledge, heretical tendencies, created a desire for sta- bility in firm formulas prescribed by the Church. Against similar abuses St. Paul already had to intervene (I Cor. 14: 14–17).

Pope Celestine I in the famous passage of the *De gratia Dei indiculus* speaks of a uniform rite (cf. above). His statement indicates two things: the progress made to a stabilized form and the existence of original ideas handed to the Church by the apostles.

Pope Vigilius I (537–55) speaks of an unchangeable rule: "We state that the order of prayers in the celebration of Masses has not to be different at any time, at any feast, but in the same manner always the offerings have to be consecrated. . . . Therefore we have ordained also the text of the canoni- cal prayer itself as added above, which by the providence of God we have received from apostolic tradition." [15]

[13] *PL*, 56, 428.

[14] This decree is referred to in a statement of St. Augustine (*De baptismo contra Donatistas*, VI, 25): "The prayers of many would be corrected daily if they were recited by better instructed. . . . Many break forth in prayers, which are composed not only by talkative, inexperienced persons, but even by heretics. They use them in the simplicity of ignorance, since they are un- able to distinguish whether they are good."

[15] *Letter to Profuturus of Braga* (538); *PL*, 69, 18.

MOTIVES OF INSTITUTION

The fundamental motive for the institution of the Canon is indicated by the Council with the words, "since of all things this sacrifice is the most holy." [16] These words allude to the distortion of the reformers, who said that the Canon erroneously gives the Eucharist a sacrificial character. The Canon does not make the Eucharist a sacrifice, but the Canon was instituted because the Eucharist is a sacrifice, and the most holy sacrifice. The existence and nature of the Canon are a testimony for the sacrificial character of the Mass.

The phrase of the Council, "to the end that it [this sacrifice] might be worthily and reverently offered and received," contains also an allusion to the conditions that led the Church to the legislation of the Council of Carthage and the Council of Mileve, and finally to the act recorded in the letter of Pope Vigilius. The words "be offered and received" refer to the two groups of prayers about the Eucharist as sacrifice and as sacrament.

This is the fundamental reason for the institution of the Canon and also the reason why the Canon excels because of its venerable antiquity, its immunity from every error, and its most singular holiness and piety. The Canon is the center N.B. and heart of the Eucharistic liturgy: it is the original Eucharistic prayer. All the rest of the sacrificial liturgy is of a later date, an amplification and extension of the Canon. The Ordinary of the Mass, the proper of the liturgical cycle, the whole system of the liturgical year, are historically and ideologically additions, arranged in concentric circles around the luminous center of the Canon.

The Council made an explicit statement about the Canon's

[16] Denzinger, no. 942.

immunity from every error and sanctioned this statement with the authority of an anathema. The holiness and piety of the Canon are defended against the calumnies of the reformers, who called its prayers "provocations to impiety." The term "redoleat," i.e., "emanates fragrance," associates with the words the sanctifying power of the Holy Ghost, who elevates to God the minds of the offering priest and of the faithful and safeguards the dignity and reverence of the oblation. The Canon is not merely doctrine and instruction, but is a sacramental, and the greatest sacramental. The holiness and piety of the Canon have their source, according to the Council, in the fact that the constitutive elements of the Canon are words of our Lord, traditions of the apostles, and pious institutions of holy pontiffs.

TEXTS

Chapter 4 (*De canone Missae*): "Since it is becoming that holy things be administered in a holy manner, and of all things this sacrifice is the most holy, the Catholic Church, to the end that it might be worthily and reverently offered and received, instituted many centuries ago the holy canon, which is so free from error that it contains nothing that does not in the highest degree savor of a certain holiness and piety and raise up to God the minds of those who offer. For it consists partly of the very words of the Lord, partly of the traditions of the apostles, and also of pious regulations of holy pontiffs." [17]

Chapter 5 (*De solemnibus Missae sacrificii caeremoniis*): "Since the nature of man is such that he cannot without external means be raised easily to meditation on divine things, holy mother Church has instituted certain rites, namely, that some things in the Mass be pronounced in a low tone and

[17] *Ibid.*

others in a louder tone. She has likewise, in accordance with apostolic discipline and tradition, made use of ceremonies, such as mystical blessings, lights, incense, vestments, and many other things of this kind, whereby both the majesty of so great a sacrifice might be emphasized and the minds of the faithful excited by those visible signs of religion and piety to the contemplation of those most sublime things which are hidden in this sacrifice." [18]

Canon 6: "If anyone says that the canon of the Mass contains errors and is therefore to be abrogated, let him be anathema." [19]

[18] *Ibid.*, no. 943.
[19] *Ibid.*, no. 953.

CHAPTER II

The Canon as Doctrine[1]

THE most important statements of the Council of Trent concerning the doctrinal value of the Canon are contained in the declaration about its immunity from every error; then in the declaration that the Eucharistic liturgy unfolds the majesty of such a great sacrifice and inspires the minds of the faithful to the contemplation of the most sublime things hidden in this sacrifice.[2] The Council further refers to the Canon as doctrine in the declaration that the Mass contains a great instruction of the faithful,[3] and "commands pastors and all who have the care of souls that they, either themselves or through others, explain frequently during the celebration of the Mass some of the things read in the Mass, and that among other things they explain some mystery of this most holy sacrifice, especially on Sundays and festival days." The Council, desiring to have the liturgy explained to the faithful, does not limit its regulations to Sundays and feast days, but says "frequently," with special emphasis, however, on holydays of obligation.

The Canon of the Mass is the first authentic teaching of the Church about the Holy Eucharist. It is the original theology of the Church regarding the Eucharistic mystery, exercised in the way of her ordinary magisterium.

[1] Denzinger, *Enchiridion symbolorum,* ed. 1937, no. 942.
[2] *Ibid.,* no. 943.
[3] *Ibid.,* no. 946.

12

SYMBOL OF FAITH

The Canon is not composed in the method and structure of a theological textbook. It does not present its doctrine in the form of theses and canons. Liturgy is light and life, doctrine and action. The Canon is a confession of faith, a symbol of faith about the Eucharistic mystery. It is doctrine and sacramental, vested in the aesthetic form of a work of art.

Comparing the anaphora of the *Traditio apostolica* of St. Hippolytus with one of the symbols of faith, we see the parallelism in structure. The verb: "I believe" or "we believe" is replaced by "We give Thee thanks"; the object of faith is replaced by the object of thanksgiving. As in the symbols of faith, so in the Eucharistic anaphora there is found the fundamental division according to the three divine persons; there is equally the theological and chronological progress in the enumeration of the benefits of God by creation, redemption, and sanctification. Even the article of faith on the Church has its parallel in the anaphora of the *Traditio apostolica,* when the Church is remembered in connection with the descent of the Holy Ghost at the end of the prayer. The Eastern liturgies have preserved this structure very distinctly, but it is somewhat obscured in the Roman Canon, yet it is not completely suppressed. The Roman Canon as a whole is a great doxology, and in some measure so is each prayer as a smaller unit, emphatically the Sanctus and the final doxology.

The name of the Canon in the Gallican liturgy expresses with the term "contestatio" the character of the Canon as a confession of faith. The introduction of the Sanctus in the Roman Preface (Common Preface, Lent, the Holy Cross, the Trinity, the Blessed Virgin, St. Joseph), "in suppliant confession saying," contains the same idea.

Principles of Development

The supreme principle the Church followed in the composition of the Canon as doctrine, is the happy memory of everything our Lord did and said when He instituted the Blessed
Sacrament, His words and actions transmitted by tradition
and Scripture. Inspired by the desire to do what He did, to
execute faithfully what He commanded us to do, the Church
listened eagerly to each of His words, contemplated their contents, meditated on them to understand what they conveyed
directly and indirectly by associations or allusions, what His
gestures suggested, what time, place, and surroundings indicated. The thanksgiving prayer of Christ in connection with
the hymn of the Pasch is the fundamental basis in the development of the Canon. This development is an organic progress
from implicit truth to its explicit proposition, so that the
history of the Canon is equivalent to the historical development of the Eucharistic dogmas of the first six centuries.

In this dogmatic development two lines of thought are
clearly distinguishable: (a) the unfolding of the mystery of
the Eucharist itself; (b) the Eucharist within the system of
divine mysteries, particularly in its relations to the mystery of
the Blessed Trinity and the mystery of the Incarnation.

The development of the Canon shows the unfolding of the
doctrine of the Eucharist, of its nature and its properties, of
its causes, efficacy, and effect. Therein are explained the relations of the Eucharistic sacrifice to its types in the Old Testament, the relations to the Last Supper, to the sacrifice on the
cross, to the heavenly liturgy.

An important step in the development of the Eucharistic
theology of the Canon is marked with the introduction of the
invocations and their impetratory idea. The invocations ex-

press the propitiatory and impetratory value of the Eucharistic sacrifice, further its efficacy in the way of impetration,
different from the way the rest of the sacraments produce
their effects. To the same line of dogmatic development belongs the introduction of the intercessory prayers. With these
prayers is expressed the idea that the Eucharist is a sacrifice
of petition to be offered for the living and for the dead, for
sins, for punishment for sins, for satisfaction and all kinds of
needs. With the introduction of the *Communicantes* and of
the *Nobis quoque peccatoribus* it is testified that we may offer
the Eucharistic sacrifice to the honor of saints, thanking God
for their victory and imploring their powerful intercession.

The introduction of the angelic choirs and of the procession
of saints calls to our attention that in the Eucharistic celebration with Christ the heavenly high priest, angels and saints
take part. The Eucharist is enacted in heaven, the principal
priest and the oblation have celestial glory in them, heaven
and earth are united in one sacred action.

The gradual development of the Canon reveals also the
dogmatic place of the Eucharist within the sublime network
of the divine mysteries, within the luminous stream of com-
munications and manifestations of the divine life, which
originates in the Blessed Trinity from the Father through the
Son, to the Holy Ghost, is poured out and made manifest
ad extra in the mystery of Christ, and is extended and continued through the Eucharist in the mystical body.

Concerning the mystery of the Blessed Trinity, the Canon
testifies on the one hand that the Eucharist is the perfect worship of the Trinity, on the other hand that Eucharistic consecration, as any divine action *ad extra*, is the common work
of the three divine persons. This dogmatic fact, introduced
in the Canon particularly with the distinction of the invoca-

tions, is an important key for a satisfactory solution of the problem of the epiklesis.

The most beautiful element in its development, however, is the unfolding of the Eucharist in its relations to the mystery of the Incarnation, which overshadowed any other influence of dogmatic thoughts. The glorious idea that the Eucharist is a continuation, an extension, of the mystery of the Incarnation, its great objective memorial, led to the development, of the anamnesis after the Consecration, gave to the Canon the superstructure of a great anamnesis as a whole, has inspired the structure of the liturgical year. The concept of consecration as nativity, passion, resurrection, glorification, and second coming anticipated sacramentally, was of inexhaustible fertility for the development of the Eucharistic hymn.

Canon and Holy Scripture

An important principle in the development of the Canon is the intention of the Church to propose within the Canon a comprehensive summary of Scripture texts from the Old and New Testament about the Eucharistic sacrifice. This intention appears even in the tendency to assimilate the historical narrative and the words of consecration, transmitted by tradition, to the scriptural reports about the institution.

The anaphora of the *Apostolic Constitutions* gives evidence of how great the influence of the paschal Hallel was upon the structure and ideas of the Canon. With the necessary separation of the Church from the Synagogue, the dominating features of the Hallel disappeared more and more. But sufficient evidence remained of the incorporation of the Hallel into the Canon, some texts were reintroduced to testify to these connections.

In chapter one about the institution of the Eucharistic sacrifice [4] the Council of Trent has summarized the prophetic types of Christ's priesthood and of His sacrifice in the Eucharist, therein referring to the priesthood of Melchisedech, to the Jewish Pasch the memorial of the Exodus with its typical significance for the Eucharistic sacrifice as the memorial of the transitus of our Lord from this world to the Father, effective of the Exodus of the faithful from the power of the devil to the kingdom of Christ; further to the prophecy of Malachias, to all the types of the time of the law of nature and of the Mosaic law. Now, all these types and prophecies are incorporated in the Canon. There is the prayer *Supra quae propitio* after the consecration with the reference to the sacrifice of Abel, of Abraham, and of Melchisedech. There are found allusions to the prophecy of Malachias, especially in the prosphora after the consecration, *Offerimus praeclarae majestati tuae*. With the angel of sacrifice in the *Supplices te rogamus* a series of sacrifices of the Old Testament is recalled; with the angelic choirs the great theophanies and the Temple worship are referred to in great perspectives in their typical relation to the Eucharist.

The New Testament is represented within the Canon mostly with two authors, explicitly mentioned by the Council of Trent within its theology of the Eucharist: St. Paul and St. John.

The Council refers twice explicitly to St. Paul: to his doctrine about the priesthood of Christ and about the sacrifice of Christ in the Eucharist.[5] It is primarily the Epistle to the Hebrews with a score of quotations which provides the Council with arguments. There is, however, also a series of quo-

[4] *Ibid.*, no. 930.
[5] *Ibid.*, no. 938.

tations from the First Epistle to the Corinthians and from the Epistle to the Colossians. The spirit and words of St. Paul have molded the character of the Christian liturgy.

Besides St. Paul the Council mentions explicitly St. John,[6] who with two major contributions is represented in the Canon: with Christ's sacerdotal prayer and with the heavenly liturgy described in the Apocalypse. Since the influence of the Apocalypse on the Canon is to be explained in a special part of this work, we limit our study in the present general part to the influence of the sacerdotal prayer.

SPIRIT AND WORDS OF ST. PAUL

An ancient tradition ascribes the origin of the Eastern liturgies to St. Paul, the origin of the Roman liturgy to St. Peter. The Apostle himself testifies to his institutions in connection with his report on the institution of the Eucharist (I Cor. 11:23): "For I have received of the Lord that which also I delivered unto you, that the Lord Jesus, the same night in which He was betrayed, took bread," etc. And then (I Cor. 11:34): "And the rest I will set in order, when I come."

It is true that St. Paul's influence is more discernible in the Eastern liturgy; a characteristic mark of this influence is that all the Eastern liturgies have the narrative about the institution according to St. Paul: "In the night in which He was betrayed," etc. But the history of the Roman Canon shows that St. Paul together with St. John has exercised the most important influence upon its development as a summary of Scripture texts about the Holy Eucharist.

The joyful atmosphere of the Canon, its character as song and as hymn, the rhythmic cadences of spiritual, mystical poetry, and the exalted language are so much molded by St.

---

[6] *Ibid.*, no. 945.

Paul that, according to Paul Cagin's textual analysis of the anaphora of the *Traditio apostolica*,[7] this important Canon can be said to be of quasi-Pauline origin. The spirit of St. Paul is living in the rhythms of the Canon (Eph. 5:19 f.): "Speaking to yourselves in psalms and hymns and spiritual canticles, singing and making melody in your hearts to the Lord; giving thanks always for all things, in the name of our Lord Jesus Christ, to God and the Father." (Cf. Acts 2:46: "Continuing daily with one accord in the temple, and breaking bread from house to house, they took their meat with gladness and simplicity of heart.") It is this spirit which contributed so much to the victory of Christianity. Not only the greatness of its incomparable doctrine, but likewise the spirit of joy and gladness filled the lives of the apostles and the faithful, which could blossom into the enthusiasm for martyrdom. St. Paul himself possessed this spirit to a high degree, so that he himself in his Epistles here and there breaks forth in verses and fragments of hymns (Eph. 5:14; I Tim. 3:16; II Tim. 2:11).

Three major ideas of Pauline origin are transmitted in the Canon. (a) One is the idea of the Eucharist as *annuntiatio*, *proclamatio*, as antitype of the proclamation (Haggadah) at the Pasch, of the death of the Lord; the idea of the celebration of the Eucharist as a memorial according to the command as emphasized by St. Paul (I Cor. 11:25). (b) The mediatorship of Christ the heavenly high priest is one of the ideas that give to the Eucharist its halo of heavenly liturgy. (c) Further, the group of intercessory prayers is based in great part on the text of St. Paul (I Tim. 2:1).

In particular we note the following. The introduction to the Preface has a parallel text in Col. 2:1: the angelic choirs are partly from Rom. 8:38, Eph. 1:21, Col. 1:16. The invoca-

---

[7] Paul Cagin, O.S.B., *L'Eucharistie, Canon primitif de la messe*, Paris, 1912.

tions have received terms from St. Paul: "accepted" (I Tim. 2:23; 5:4); "reasonable," "acceptable" (Rom. 12:1; Phil. 3:3). The term "mysterium fidei" in the middle of the Canon within the words of consecration, with all its wonderful association of the hymn to Christ triumphant, is inherited from St. Paul (I Tim. 3:9, 16). The solemn conclusion of the Canon is a final contribution of the Apostle from Rom. 11:36.

For many texts of the Old Testament found in the Canon, St. Paul has acted as mediator, so for the prayer *Supra quae* with its reference to the priesthood of Melchisedech, the reference to the Jewish Pasch, to the prophecy of Malachias. This influence of St. Paul's Epistles on the Roman Canon is partly direct, partly indirect through the Eastern liturgies.

THE HIGH-PRIESTLY PRAYER, A MODEL OF THE CANON

The influence of Christ's sacerdotal prayer on the structure of the Canon, on the invocations, and on the intercessory prayers is so obvious that it may be called the model of liturgical supplication. The place assigned to this prayer within the liturgy of Christ suggests in itself its incorporation into the Canon: it is the sacerdotal consecration of Christ for His bloody sacrifice. This is the unanimous interpretation of the Fathers. St. Chrysostom: "What is meant by 'I sanctify Myself,' 'I offer sacrifice to Thee'? That he was referring to His sacrifice when He said, 'I sanctify,' is clear from what follows . . . 'since indeed He died for them.'" St. Cyril of Alexandria: "When He says 'I sanctify,' He means this: I offer and dedicate Myself an immaculate victim to God and the Father. For what is dedicated to God is said to be sanctified." St. Thomas follows the Fathers, saying: "I sanctify Myself, that is, I offer Myself in sacrifice."

The character of Christ's sacerdotal prayer as a formal

oblation for His bloody sacrifice appears emphatically if we suppose that it was said in the Temple. It has been a disputed question since the time of the Fathers of the Church, where and when our Lord uttered the discourses of chapters 15–17 of the Gospel of St. John, particularly the sacerdotal prayer of chapter 17. Its close local and temporal association with the Last Supper led some authors to the view that it must be understood as an explanation of the Last Supper and its relation to the sacrifice on the cross.[8] But several reasons suggest that the prayer was uttered in the Temple: e.g., the Temple was open from midnight when Jesus passed by the Temple on His way to Gethsemane; the parable of the vine (John 15) seems to contain an allusion to the Temple, where the porch of the Temple was built, entwined by great golden vines with golden branches and man-size clusters of grapes which must have shone brightly at night in the light of the torches, attracting the eye of everyone passing by; and on an earlier occasion Christ had spoken in the Temple about the parable of the vineyard (Matt. 21:33–42; Mark 12:1–12; Luke 20:9–19). We may imagine that, after the wonderful experience of the apostles at the Last Supper, they looked up with great admiration to the golden shining symbol; and Christ, knowing their thoughts, began: "I am the vine." There are still other parallels to the same conclusion: it was fitting that Christ should conclude His earthly activity in the Temple where He had started His mission (Luke 2:49); some days before a similar subject as that contained in the sacerdotal prayer was mentioned by Christ in the Temple (John 12:28; cf. Luke 21:37). All these reasons and parallels suggest that the prayer was said in the Temple.[9] Descending from the

[8] U. de la Taille, The Mystery of Faith (New York, 1940), p. 121.
[9] Josef Pickl, The Messias (St. Louis, 1946), pp. 117–27.

cenacle, where He had sacramentally anticipated the sacrifice on the cross, Christ entered the Temple for the last time to make the formal oblation for His sacrifice *in specie propria.* The words "For them I sanctify Myself," pronounced in the Temple soon after midnight, declare clearly the sacerdotal intention, the sacrificial oblation. After these words, and because of them, Christ left the Temple and entered upon the Passion (John 18:1): "When Jesus had said these things, He went forth with His disciples over the brook Cedron, where there was a garden."

PARALLELISM OF STRUCTURE

The exegetes usually divide the sacerdotal prayer into three parts: the prayer of Christ for Himself; the prayer for His disciples; the prayer for the followers of the disciples.

This inadequate division neglects the most important element of the prayer, its center and climax in John 17:19: "And for them do I sanctify Myself." Taking account of the specific character of this prayer as the sacerdotal prayer of Christ, as the consecration of Himself, as His formal sacrificial oblation for the bloody sacrifice, this solemn Canon of Christ's sacrifice must be analyzed and interpreted from this center. To this act of sacrificial oblation all the other parts of the prayer are subordinate, are arranged round it in a certain symmetry (vv. 6–10); symmetrically to it corresponds, after the consecration of v. 17, the intercession for the followers of the disciples (vv. 20–22). Beyond this inner circle we see another one in the petition for glorification (vv. 1–5) at the beginning, and corresponding symmetrically; at the other end of the prayer, the petition for glorification of His disciples and their followers (vv. 22–25).

Within the two groups of corresponding prayers several

ideas are distinctly coordinated; most explicitly in the prayer for unity. The prayer of v. 22, "that they may be one, as We also are," has its counterpart in the words of v. 20: "And not for them only do I pray, but for them also who through their word shall believe in Me; that they all may be one, as Thou, Father in Me, and I in Thee." A certain correspondence is in the petition for sanctification of the disciples (vv. 17, 19); in the disposition required (vv. 7, 20).

For the comparison with the Canon we should note the tenderness of affection and overflowing filial devotion of the Savior toward His heavenly Father expressed in the name "Father," repeated five times in the course of the prayer (v. 1, "Father"; v. 5, "O Father"; "holy Father"; v. 21, "Father"; v. 24, "Father"; v. 25, "just Father"). There is finally the analogy between the introduction of Christ's prayer (John 17:1): "And lifting up His eyes to heaven, He said . . ." and the rubrics (of later date than the Canon, but in its spirit): "Sacerdos extendens, elevans aliquantulum et jungens manus, elevansque ad coelum oculos."

The Canon of the Mass is likewise a composition that is focused on a central point. Around the words of consecration which correspond to "For them do I sanctify Myself" are symmetrically arranged the invocations and intercessions. To the petition for glorification (John 17:1–5) corresponds in the Canon the *Te igitur clementissime Pater* with its continuations in the *Hanc igitur* and the *Quam oblationem*. St. Thomas has distinctly felt the connection of the *Quam oblationem* of the Canon with the petition for glorification of the sacerdotal prayer. To the objection that it is superfluous to ask with the *Quam oblationem* for the accomplishment of the consecration, since we know with certitude that the divine power will accomplish it, St. Thomas replies with the words: "It is not unfitting to ask God for something that we know He will most certainly accomplish, just as Christ prayed for His glorification." Christ's prayer for the glorification of His disciples has its parallel in the Canon with the petition for fruitful Communion, "ut quotquot ex hac altaris participatione," etc.

The two prayers of intercession for His disciples and their followers have their parallels in the intercession of the Church for the living and the dead, somewhat also in the commemoration of the saints in the *Communicantes* and in the *Nobis quoque peccatoribus*. In the prayer for the Church the unity and protection is emphasized: "Quam adunare digneris . . . una cum famulo tuo," etc. Christ prays for His disciples because they belong to the Father: "Because they are Thine" (John 17:9). Correspondingly the Canon prays: "for Thy holy Catholic Church . . . together with Thy servant the Pope." Christ prayed for the protection of His disciples: "Holy Father, keep them in Thy name"; the Canon prays for the Church that God may give her "peace and protection"; for the living, "for the good of their souls, for their hope of salvation, and deliverance from all harm." As in the sacerdotal prayer is required a necessary disposition, so likewise in the Canon for the effect of the Eucharistic sacrifice for those "whose faith is known to Thee."

The term "Father" occurs three times in the Canon, once in the entreating connection "clementissime Pater" which reflects the tenderness of affection and filial devotion of the sacerdotal prayer. For the rest the Canon addresses the heavenly Father with "Lord," "eternal, living and true God," "almighty God," to mark the distinction between the Father of the only-begotten Son and the Father of the children of adoption.

In conclusion we refer to several liturgies which have preserved and transmitted to the Roman liturgy the spirit and words of Christ's sacerdotal prayer. The *Didache* (chap. 9) gives thanks for the revelation of the name of God as Christ (John 17:6). The anaphora of Deir-Balizeh is the most ancient document that has in the preconsecratory invocation the petition for glorification: "Fill us also with Thy glory which is with Thee and deign to send Thy Spirit upon these creatures." (Cf. John 17:5.) The anaphora of Serapion uses a similar phrase but replaces the term "glory" with "Thy virtue and communication." The term "virtue" is used in Scripture many times as equivalent to "glory" (cf. II Pet. 1:3): "He hath called us by His own proper glory and virtue." The anaphora of the *Apostolic Constitutions* has before the narrative of the Passion: "He has made manifest Thy name to them who did not know it" (cf. John 17:6). The epiklesis of the Coptic liturgy replaces the term "glory" with "benediction": "Fill, O God, this oblation also with the benediction which is with Thee" (cf. John 7:5).

CHAPTER III

The Canon as a Sacramental

"To the end that it [the Eucharist] might be worthily and reverently offered and received," the Church instituted the holy Canon, "since it is becoming that holy things be administered in a holy manner." [1] The Council of Trent further declares that the Canon radiates in the highest degree holiness and piety, that by it "the majesty of so great a sacrifice is emphasized, and the minds of the faithful excited . . . to the contemplation of those most sublime things which are hidden in this sacrifice." [2] In all these statements it is declared that the Canon is a sacramental, indeed that it is the most excellent sacramental.

THE MOST EXCELLENT SACRAMENTAL

The institution of sacramentals is the right of the Church. The dignity of a sacramental depends, therefore, upon the intention of the Church expressed either by a special declaration, or implicitly expressed in the solemnity of the rite and with the terms of the prayers. The official pronouncements of the Council of Trent, referred to above, and also the solemnity and terms of the Canon, express that it is the most excellent sacramental.

It was the intention of the Church, expressed in the chapter

[1] Denzinger, no. 942.
[2] *Ibid.*, no. 943.

on the Eucharistic Canon, to give the Canon a solemnity and dignity which is in proportion to the worthy and respectful administration, oblation, and reception of the sacrifice. The same idea is expressed with the words referring to the effect produced by the Canon: "It contains nothing that does not in the highest degree savor of a certain holiness and piety." The third reason of the excellent dignity of the Canon is its antiquity. The Church "instituted the Canon many centuries ago." With this phrase we may understand the care and solicitude of the Church in instituting the Canon, preserving it as an unchangeable rule since the sixth century, a fact which is singular in the history of the sacramentals. Lastly the Council mentions as a reason for the holiness and piety of the Canon, that it consists of the very words of the Lord and of traditions of the apostles, and likewise of pious regulations of holy pontiffs.

The Canon has the special dignity among the sacramentals that it contains the very words of Christ. This phrase must not be limited to the words of consecration (besides, the Church did not institute the words of consecration, they are not part of the sacramental). This phrase extends to words contained in the prayers of the Canon which surround the words of consecration. It extends first to the fundamental idea of the whole thanksgiving, of which the Canon is a kind of paraphrase. Concerning this idea we may even say that Christ instituted the Canon. Christ instituted not only the sacraments, but also a series of sacramentals, at least generically, in their fundamental elements. (Cf. Matt. 14:19; 15:36; 19:15; 26:26 f.; Luke 24:30; 24:50; again by His command to the disciples, Matt. 10:8; Mark 6:13; Luke 9:49; 10:17.)

The Canon has a special dignity as a legacy from the apostles. Before any Gospel or Epistle was written, the Church celebrated the Eucharist according to the rite transmitted by the apostles.

The Canon is the work of holy pontiffs. The Council does not mention any pope explicitly. Although the records of the *Liber pontificalis* are not absolutely reliable, especially those of the early centuries, and although we cannot determine exactly the contributions to the Canon by St. Leo I, St. Gelasius I, and St. Gregory I, their names will always be remembered in the history of the Canon together with those of Pope Innocent I and Pope Vigilius I.

THE FATHERS OF THE CHURCH ON THE CANON

The high respect which the Fathers of the Church expressed for the Canon as a sacramental led occasionally to a misinterpretation of its value. In the writings of the Fathers are to be found statements in which the words of consecration and the Canon appear as one consecratory formula.

Origen, *In Matt.*: "The bread is consecrated by the word of God and the prayer." [3] In this and in other expressions are reflected the words of St. Paul (I Tim. 4:4 f.): "For every creature of God is good, and nothing is to be rejected that is received with thanksgiving. For it is sanctified by the word of God and prayer."

St. Athanasius, *Ex sermone ad baptizatos:* "As long as the prayers and invocations are not finished, they [the bread and wine] are nothing but bread and wine. As soon, however, as the great and wonderful prayers are said, then the bread becomes the body, and the chalice becomes the blood, of our Lord Jesus Christ. . . . Let us come to the accomplishing of the mysteries. This bread and this chalice before the prayers and supplications have nothing beyond their proper nature;

[3] *PG*, 13, 948.

as soon, however, as the great prayers and holy supplications are said, the Word descends upon bread and chalice, and His body is there brought about (*et corpus ejus conficitur*)." [4]

St. Gregory of Nyssa, *Oratio cat.:* "This bread is sanctified by the word of God and the prayer." [5]

De sacramentis: "Do you wish to know with what heavenly words it is being consecrated? Receive the words: Make for us, he says, this oblation," etc.[6] In this passage the invocation *Hanc oblationem* is called "heavenly words," which consecrate together with the words of our Lord.

The Council of Rome (1097) demanded from Berengarius the signing of the following statement: "By the mystery of the sacred prayer and the words of our Redeemer . . . bread and wine . . . are substantially changed into the true and proper and vivifying flesh and blood of our Lord Jesus Christ." [7]

We can have no doubt that in such expressions consecratory power is ascribed to the whole Canon. The term "consecratory" is to be interpreted in a wider sense, comprising the consecration effected by the words of Christ as the form of the Eucharistic sacrament and sacrifice, and the consecration effected by the Canon as sacramental. It is precisely because of the high dignity of the Canon as the most excellent sacramental that it is singled out from the rest of liturgical formulas, and because of its proximate preparation for consecration it is mentioned as a unity with the words of Christ. It would be an intolerable exaggeration, contradicted by the Fathers themselves and by a pronouncement of the Church, to say that the Fathers regarded the whole Canon as the form

[4] *PG,* 26, 1325.
[5] *PG,* 45, 97.
[6] St. Ambrose, *De sacramentis,* IV, 5; *PL,* 16, 463.
[7] Denzinger, no. 355.

of the Eucharistic sacrament, or that the Fathers did not know that only the words of our Savior alone would consecrate, or that at the time of the Fathers the exact moment of consecration was not yet defined and understood.

F. Cabrol [8] referred to these expressions of the Fathers. He spoke merely as a historian and did not add any distinction to the term "consecratory power," nor did he take notice that at the same time the Fathers of the Church ascribe consecratory power to the words of Christ exclusively, e.g., *De sacramentis*, IV, 4: "When, however, it has come to the point that the venerable sacrament is to be accomplished, then he [the priest] does not use his own words, but he uses the words of Christ. Therefore the words of Christ accomplish the sacrament." [9]

Some authors interpret this statement of the *De sacramentis* as a development of dogmatic thought, as if before that time prayers like the epiklesis universally would have been considered necessary for consecration as part of the essential form of the Eucharistic sacrament. The pronouncement of the Church in the Council of Trent does not admit of such an interpretation: "This has always been the belief of the Church of God, that immediately after the consecration [i.e., after the words of Christ], the true body and the true blood of our Lord together with His soul and divinity, exist under the form of bread and wine." [10] In the intention of the Council the term "consecration" applies to the words of our Lord.

M. de la Taille [11] criticized the article of Abbot Cabrol. He admits the fluctuation in the meaning of "prex" in the writing

[8] Art. "Amen," *D.A.C.L.*
[9] *De sacramentis*, IV, 4. Cf. St. Thomas, *Summa theol.*, IIIa, q. 78, a. 1 sed contra.
[10] Denzinger, no. 876.
[11] De la Taille, *Mysterium fidei* (Paris, 1919), pp. 469 f.

of the Fathers, and presents a long list of passages from the Fathers wherein both the Canon and the words of our Lord are connected with the consecration, to which he adds the clear distinction in the term "consecration": consecration as transubstantiation and as "liturgical name."

De la Taille's criticism, however, does not do justice to the Canon as the most excellent sacramental, which is the reason why the holy Fathers of the Church have considered the Canon in union with the words of our Lord. Therein appears its high dignity as the most excellent sacramental, which sanctifies proximately priest, faithful, bread and wine, as preparation for the act of transubstantiation.

EFFICACY AND EFFECTS

The Canon has its efficacy, as every sacramental does, *ex opere operantis Ecclesiae,* through the power of the prayer of the Church. This means more than merely *ex opere operantis,* i.e., according to the degree of disposition of the person who administers or receives the sacramental. The sacramentals have an objective dignity that is independent of the disposition of the person who administers or receives them, because they are administered in the name of the Church and through the power of the prayer of the Church.

In analogy to the sacraments, the sacramentals produce the effect they signify. They cannot produce sanctifying grace. They impart actual grace, forgiveness of venial sins; they curb the power of the devil and work many temporal blessings.

The sacred Canon is a complex of sacramentals, all in analogy to the Eucharist, for which they prepare and dispose, sacramentals which sanctify the priest and the faithful, sacramentals which sanctify the bread and wine. In priest and faithful, these sacramentals produce an abundance of grace all in preparation and as disposing for a worthy administration, celebration, and reception of sacrifice and sacrament.[12] By these graces accidentally and in subordination to the efficacy and effects produced by the sacrament *ex opere operato*, the effect of sacrifice and sacrament is increased.

The graces produced in the priest, according to the words of the prayers in the faithful also, are acts of faith in the Eucharistic presence, in the reality of the sacrifice; acts, moreover, of expectant hope, of reverence and admiration for the Eucharistic mysteries; acts of gratitude for the love and mercy of God, for so great a sacrifice, for so great a glory merited for us by the Redeemer; acts of gratitude and admiration, of joy in the particular mystery commemorated in the Preface; acts of reverence before the glory and majesty of God made manifest by the Eucharistic consecration, acts of adoration of the holiness of God. Again there is consciousness of the tremendous mystery accomplished. These graces fill the heart with profound humility, with filial confidence. These prayers renew the intention of the priest, make it actual, purify and intensify intention and devotion, prepare the faithful for the incorporation into the glorious sacrifice of Christ in His mystical body. A fragrance and light of faith, of holiness and piety are radiated by the prayers; these rays of grace penetrate mind and heart, envelop the soul. The priest entering the Canon, finds himself in a higher spiritual atmosphere, radiating light, grace, life. It is the Church that leads him into the holy of holies, communicates to him of her beauty and glory. She sanctifies his voice to sing, to praise, to glorify God, she sanc-

---

[12] Cf. Pius X, *Decree on Frequent Communion* (December 20, 1905): "The sacraments of the New Law, though they take effect *ex opere operato*, nevertheless produce a greater effect in proportion as the dispositions of the recipient are better. Therefore care is to be taken that Holy Communion be preceded by serious preparation and followed by a suitable thanksgiving."

tifies his hands, his eyes, his thoughts and affections, that in a holy manner he may accomplish the most holy sacrifice. It happens spiritually to the priest as it did to Moses when he went up on Mount Sinai (Exod. 24:16, 18): "And the glory of the Lord dwelt upon Sinai, covering it with a cloud . . . and Moses, entering into the midst of the cloud, went up into the mountain." Or when the high priest on the day of propitiation entered the holy of holies, and a flood of light received him at his coming forth from the "glory of God" upon the propitiatory throne (Lev. 16:2). It is the intention of the Church to assimilate the priest to Christ, that he may feel like the Master (Luke 22:15): "With desire I have desired to eat this pasch with you."

The Canon sanctifies the faithful, those especially who attend the sacrifice, those who are remembered; it gives them forgiveness of venial sins, actual faith in the Holy Eucharist, hope and confidence in the propitiatory power of the Holy Sacrifice, and an abundance of temporal graces: peace, concord, health, and protection that they may be able to celebrate and to enjoy the divine mysteries and to become filled with the abundance of all heavenly blessings and graces, flowing from the sacrifice and sacrament.

The Canon sanctifies the oblation. There is to be distinguished a twofold effect to which the prayers before and after the consecration refer in a different way.[13] St. Thomas distinguishes an effect (a) removing impediments, as far as by these blessings the influence and power of the demons is removed; (b) producing a certain disposition ("vel etiam idoneitatem quamdam faciendo ad sacramenti perfectionem"), which prepares the species for the act of transubstantiation. St. Thomas probably thought of the analogy of accidental

---

[13] St. Thomas, *Summa theol.*, IIIa, q. 65, a. 1 ad 6.

changes which precede and prepare for the substantial change in the physical world. The blessings remove the influence of the power of darkness, they remove from matter the consequences of the curse of God and dispose it for the reception of the Word of God. Through the prayers of the Canon, bread and wine are presanctified, purified, made sacred, are completely destined for God.

There is a special difficulty about the postconsecratory blessings over the species. The sacramentals referring to the priest and the faithful can produce their effect at any time, particularly during the time between consecration and Communion, during the time the sacrificial oblation is virtually continued as long as the separated species are present on the altar. But it is different about the sacramentals upon the oblation. The blessings over the species cannot have any effect after the consecration. St. Thomas explains: "These blessings after consecration do not have any effect, but merely commemorate and make manifest, recall to mind the power and efficacy of the Cross and the Passion of Christ." [14]

[14] *Ibid.*, q. 83, a. 5, ad 4.

CHAPTER IV

The Canon as a Work of Art

THE Canon is a magnificent work of art. It is a thanksgiving
hymn, a song of victory with a triumphant melody. It is a
dramatic poem, unfolding in successive events what is accomplished at the moment of consecration. It is a painting,
a mosaic of a spiritual kind. It is a gorgeous architectural
edifice, a work of art proper to the Roman genius.

THE CANON AS A HYMN

Hymns, chants, and psalms were the exemplars of the
Canon; the canticle of Moses is its prototype, the Hallel of the
Jewish Pasch the proximate type. The Gospel narrative leads
us to suppose the recitation of the hymn at the Last Supper
(Matt. 26:30); St. Paul advised (Eph. 5:19; Col. 3:16) and
exhorted to psalms, hymns, and spiritual canticles. The canticle of the Lamb in the Apocalypse has inspired the Eucharistic hymn; the Sanctus of the seraphim and the hymn to
Christ triumphant (I Tim. 3:16) have contributed to its
rhythms, have molded its melody.

The Canticle of Moses is a song of victory produced in two
choirs (Exod. 15:1): "Then Moses and the children of Israel
sung this canticle to the Lord and said: Let us sing to the
Lord: for He is gloriously magnified." When Moses had
ended, his sister Mary continued (Exod. 15:20): "So Mary
the prophetess, the sister of Aaron, took a timbrel in her hand:
35

and all the women went forth after her with timbrels and with dances: and she began the song to them, saying: Let us sing to the Lord, for He is gloriously magnified."

The Hallel of the Jews (Ps. 112–117, 135) is a great hymn, sung in two parts: the first (Ps. 112:1—113:8) before the eating of the pasch; the second (Ps. 113:9—117:29; 135) after the eating of the pasch. It was sung by our Lord with the disciples at the Last Supper (Matt. 26:30): "And a hymn being said, they went out unto Mount Olivet."

St. Paul advises (Eph. 5:19): "Speaking to yourselves in psalms and hymns and spiritual canticles, singing and making melody in your hearts to the Lord; giving thanks always for all things, in the name of our Lord Jesus Christ, to God and the Father"; and again (Col. 3:16): "Teaching and admonishing one another in psalms, hymns, and spiritual canticles, singing in grace in your hearts to God."

The celestial music of the choirs of the Apocalypse has inspired the Eucharistic canticle (Apoc. 14:2): "And I heard a voice from heaven, as the voice of many waters, and as the voice of great thunders; and the voice which I heard was as the voice of harpers, harping on their harps." Apoc. 15:2: "And I saw as it were a sea of glass mingled with fire, and them that had overcome the beast . . . standing on the sea of glass, having the harps of God; and singing the canticle of Moses, the servant of God, and the canticle of the Lamb."

Heaven and earth are united in singing the hymn of the glory of God with the Sanctus and the Benedictus: "We sing the hymn of Thy glory," the Preface concludes. The "mysterium fidei" in the middle of the Canon and the structure of the Anamnesis recall the melodies of the hymn to Christ triumphant recorded by St. Paul in his Epistle to Timothy (I Tim. 3:16).

THE CANON AS A DRAMATIC POEM

The dialogue at the beginning of the Preface introduces the Canon as a drama. Priest and congregation, the angelic choirs, the procession of the saints and Christ, the heavenly high priest in the center, are so many actors in the sacred drama.

There is a dramatic progress in the giving of thanks and in the invocations, both in the direct and in the indirect object: there is the progress in the one to whom thanks are rendered: from the Father, to the Son, to the Holy Ghost. There is the progress in the object for which thanks are rendered (the *Per quem haec omnia* summarizes: "Through whom, O Lord, Thou dost ever create, hallow, fill with life, bless, and bestow upon us all good things"). The progress in the object of the invocation: the *Quam oblationem* asks explicitly for the making of the victim present, the *Supplices te rogamus* and the *Supra quae propitio* ask for the acceptance of the oblation set upon the altar, and finally for the fruit of sacrifice and sacrament "that we may be filled with all heavenly blessing and grace."

This "dramatic theory," proposed by Cardinal Bessarion,[1] is of the greatest importance for the satisfactory interpretation of the postconsecratory invocations: throughout the Canon the dramatic present tense is employed. But the invocations, preconsecratory as well as postconsecratory, are to be referred to the time not *in quo* they are said, but to the time *pro quo*, i.e., to the moment of consecration.

THE CANON A MOSAIC

The Canon is a mosaic of spiritual art. It is a mosaic historically: apostles and martyrs, the Roman pontiffs with the

[1] Bessarion, *De sacramento eucharistiae et quibus verbis Christi corpus conficiatur; PG*, 161, 494–526.

Fathers of the Church, have contributed colors, figures, ideas, and prayers. The Canon is a mosaic of Scripture texts selected from the Old and the New Testament, which make it a comprehensive picture of God's revelation about the Eucharistic sacrifice. But in particular the Canon is a mosaic of the classic period of this early Christian art: the same motives are found in the Canon as in the mosaics of Rome and Ravenna. It is a fact that Canon and mosaics have mutually inspired each other. Further, these identical motives are presented in similar style, concept, and composition. There exists a beautiful relationship between the perennial art of the colored stones and the art of the unchangeable rule.

IDENTICAL MOTIVES

The motive of the *Communicantes* and of the *Nobis quoque peccatoribus,* the glorious Virgin with the procession of saints conceived as the assembly of the twenty-four ancients before the throne of God in the Apocalypse, is the favored subject of the mosaics in the apse of Santa Maria Maggiore in Rome, upon the triumphal arch in the basilica of San Paolo fuori le mura, in Sant Apollinare, and in San Vitale of Ravenna.

Under Pope Sixtus III (432–40) [2] one of the richest mosaic cycles of the early period of that Christian art was executed in Santa Maria Maggiore which echo the acclamations heard in Ephesus (431) when the Blessed Virgin was saluted with the title *Theotokos,* "Mother of God." Pope Sixtus restored the basilica of Liberius from the foundations as a memorial of the Council of Ephesus. Now, the insertion of the name and glorious title of the Blessed Virgin in the Canon, "the glorious and ever virgin Mary, mother of our Lord and God, Jesus Christ," is likewise a memorial of the Council of Ephesus; the

[2] I. Schuster, *The Sacramentary.* London, 1924.

final arrangement of the *Communicantes* with the association of the text of the Apocalypse (Apoc. 4:10) is in assimilation to the famous mosaics.

The work of Sixtus III included the mosaics of the triumphal arch of the basilica of Mary and of the apse. The mosaics of the arch, still extant, represent scenes of the Gospel of the infancy. The mosaics of the apse, now covered with mosaics of the time of Nicholas IV (1288–1292), had pictures honoring Our Lady according to the epigraph of Sixtus III:

Virgin Mary for thee has Xystus built the new Temple
Worthy a work of art, glory and praise to thy womb.
Mother not knowing a man, hast conceived by the Holy Spirit,
Virgin forever art thou, bringing forth our Lord.
Testifying for thee, behold the martyrs assembled,
Carrying in hands their crowns, standing on signs of their deaths.
Sword and fire, wild beasts, drowning and murder with poison—
So many horrors of death—one is the crown of reward.

Virgo Maria, tibi Xystus nova tecta dicavi
Digna salutifero munera ventre tuo.
Te Genetrix ignara viri, tu denique foeta,
Visceribus salvis, edita nostra salus.
Ecce tui testes uteri sibi praemia portant,
Sub pedibus jacet, passio cuique sua,
Ferrum, flamma, ferae, fluvius saevumque venenum.
Tot tamen has mortes, una corona manet.[3]

The central picture must have been the Blessed Virgin with the divine Infant, to whom a procession of martyrs presented their crowns according to the description of the Apocalypse (Apoc. 4:10): "The four and twenty ancients fell down before

[3] Cf. Ricarda Huch, *Preface to Early Christian Mosaics.* New York: Oxford University Press, 1946. Cf. also W. F. Volbach, *The Development and Style of the Early Christian Mosaics.*

Him that sitteth on the throne and adored Him that liveth forever and ever, and cast their crowns before the throne, saying: Thou art worthy, O Lord our God, to receive glory and honor and power."

The same motive has inspired the mosaics on the triumphal arch in San Paolo (almost destroyed by fire): a mosaic by Galla Placidia executed under Pope Leo I, showing the twenty-four ancients standing beside Christ, who has raised His hands in blessing.

The same idea is represented in the richest cycle of mosaics in Ravenna, in Sant Apollinare Nuovo and in Sant Apollinare in Classe. In Sant Apollinare Nuovo, begun under Theodoric, the mosaics are in three tiers, one above the other along the nave. On top are twenty-six square scenes from the Gospels. Below that series the second zone represents thirty-two large figures of saints. In the lowest and most dominating zone are represented Christ with the Madonna, angels, and a splendid procession of martyrs and virgins, inspired as we know positively, by the liturgy of Jerusalem with the association of the apocalyptic scene.

Two other motives of the Canon, the *Supra quae propitio,* and the following prayer, *Supplices te rogamus,* have their parallels in San Vitale of Ravenna (526–47). This splendid work of art represents the climax of early Byzantine style. Space and decoration, architecture and mosaics, form a perfect unity with the liturgy which they serve, which they express and glorify. There appear the three sacrifices of Abel, Abraham, and Melchisedech. The antitype of them is represented in the volutes: the Lamb of God, the sacrifice of the New Testament, borne in a wreath of the most delicate colors and flowers by four angels, an illustration of the prayer: "Almighty God, bid these offerings to be brought by the hands of Thy angel unto Thy altar above, before the face of Thy divine majesty."

PARALLELISM IN ARTISTIC CONCEPT

The art of mosaics replaced expensive rugs. The new technique attracted by the solidity and durability of the material as well as by the brilliant colors of the stones. The first Christian mosaics retained pagan motives and mixed them with ideas from the Eastern synagogues until we find the first purely Christian mosaic in Santa Pudenziana in Rome (end of the fourth century). From then on a tendency to the most sublime spirituality, a supernaturalism, dominates the new art in colors, which reaches its climax in the course of the sixth century.

This aversion to the earthly and human, this aspiration to the supernatural, the impression of a divinity, majestic and infinitely distant, feelings before the sacred, the *mysterium,* before God who inhabits light inaccessible, is achieved by: (a) the representation of the divine in symbols; (b) by strict symmetry; (c) by the brilliance of the colors in stone.

These symbols—Christ's monogram, the Lamb, the throne, the figures themselves, more symbols than men with identical gestures, standing solemnly side by side—seem to say: God is high, too distant to be conceived by a mortal; eternal fire would consume you if you dared to cast your eyes on it.

Strict symmetry removes the incidents and persons represented from the earthly. Christ often occupies the center of the picture, at His sides are symbols of heavenly glory, or disciples, apostles, angels, with identical features and gestures. The gold of the mosaics is, as it were, the celestial atmosphere, the light of glory of the heavenly Jerusalem, where there is no sun, no moon, no stars, because the Lamb itself illuminates the city of God. Surrounded by the light of glory, vested in the colors of the rainbow, the saints step forward in grave transcendental solemnity. The statement of a Russian Christian philosopher of our times exhibits a deep understanding: "It appears never as a dense, massive gold, but it has a kind of etherial-airy cobweb, woven of fine golden rays, radiating from the divinity, illuminating with its shine all the surroundings." [4]

The archaic figures, the rigid lines, the motionless face, deprived of individuality, express the transcendental state of glory. The stiff gestures reflect the ecstasies; the large, wide-open eyes mirror the wonderment and admiration as the gates of paradise are opened to them.

But the chief effect of the mosaics consists in the colors. On stone color acquires a peculiar brilliance not found otherwise. The music of these brilliant colors raises the soul into the sphere of the holy. These colors are splendor never seen, never experienced before; the blue and gold manifest the divine in symbol, the supernatural.

At the time of the perfection of the art of mosaics, symbolism and symmetry became a principle even in the composition and distribution of the colors; the individual cubes decompose the color. Complementary colors are separated, occasionally reunited in the center of the picture, so that the composition, also from the point of view of colors, is balanced and symmetrical.

Such an art of the supernatural was able to influence the unchangeable rule, the most sacred prayer, and expressed the union of heaven and earth in the sacred action. The development of the Canon, especially the ultimate arrange-

[4] E. V. Trubetzoy, *Die religiose Weltanschauung der altrussichen Ikonen Malerei*. Paderborn, 1927.

ment of its prayers, is contemporaneous with the period of highest perfection of the mosaics. The artistic concept of the art of the mosaics became a principle for the structure of the present Roman Canon.

The number of saints in the *Communicantes* and the *Nobis quoque peccatoribus* is symbolical: in the *Communicantes* the number twenty-five consist of the Blessed Virgin and the twenty-four ancients, divided into two groups of twelve each, according to the number of the apostles. After the Consecration the number of saints is fifteen: St. John, the leading figure, corresponding to the Blessed Virgin of the *Communicantes;* the fourteen saints are arranged in two groups of seven, men and women. Some of the saints are fusions of several historical persons, therefore more symbols than individuals.

The principle of symmetry establishes the closest relation between mosaics and Canon: the number of prayers before and after the Consecration, the motives of these two symmetrical groups, even the wording of them, emphasize this idea. There is first the symmetry in the motive of thanksgiving and in the invocations: The Preface is the thanksgiving before the Consecration, the final doxology is the corresponding prayer after the Consecration. "Let us give thanks to the Lord our God, through Christ our Lord." So we begin the Canon, and we conclude: "Through Him and with Him and in Him, is to Thee, God the Father almighty, all honor and glory." The impetratory motive: "Therefore most gracious Father, we humbly beg of Thee and entreat Thee," we pray before the Consecration; "Most humbly we implore Thee, almighty God," comes the echo after the Consecration. The same symmetry can be observed in the prayers of intercession.

This symmetry extends even into the terms and blessing. Such terms, symmetrically arranged, are for instance: "to bless," "to accept." The signs of the cross correspond: three at the beginning and three at the end of the Canon; five immediately before the Consecration and five after it.[5]

If the prayers *Supra quae* and *Supplices te rogamus* are the symmetrical counterpart of the invocations before the Consecration, then their interpretation as invocations for the Consecration and for acceptance of the sacrifice does not offer any difficulty.

If the angel of sacrifice is the symmetrical counterpart of the angels of the Sanctus, then he is a real angel, a created spirit.

Thus the Canon is a magnificent work of art. It is a mosaic of symmetrical structure, extending in concentrix circles from the human words of the thanksgiving hymn in the outer part, from the blessing of the Church and priest in the inner circle, into the reality and actuality of the central core, where the divine Word takes up the same melody, perfecting it to the infinite praise and glory of the heavenly Father. The brilliance of the divine light in the center is analyzed, resolved into the rainbow hues of the prayers surrounding it, the whole being a mosaic of spiritual art of the time of the climax of that marvelous technique of decorating the sanctuary.

[5] Cf. Pius Parsch, *The Liturgy of the Mass* (St. Louis, 1941), p. 193.

CHAPTER V

Names and Limits

THE NAMES

THE names and limits of the Canon are in close relation. Some names refer to the Canon in its present extent from the prayer *Te igitur clementissime Pater* to the final doxology, *Per ipsum, etc.* Others refer to the Eucharistic prayer as far as it includes the Preface as a part. The most ancient names refer primarily to the Preface, which together with the final doxology constitutes the original Canon.

The Canon is prayer and rite, word and action, instruction and sacramental, light and life. These characteristics are expressed in the various terms used to designate the Canon: eucharistia, eulogia, theologia, oratio, actio, agenda, prex, praedicatio, contestatio, immolatio, mysterium, anaphora, and canon.

The most ancient name is *Eucharistia*, i.e., thanksgiving, derived from the "giving thanks" in the narrative of the institution of the Blessed Sacrament (I Cor. 11:24): "And giving thanks, broke, and said: Take ye and eat: this is My body." This term occurs in the *Didache* (9,1): "Concerning the thanksgiving, give thanks thus." [1] St. Ignatius (d. 107) uses this term: "Be careful to use one Eucharist; for there is one

[1] Cf. Harnack, *Die Lehre der Zwoelf Apostel; Texte und Untersuchungen* (Leipzig, 1884), II, 1 f.

45

body of our Lord Jesus Christ and one chalice in the unity of
His blood; one altar as there is one bishop with the priesthood
and deacons." [2] Gradually this term was transferred from the
prayer of thanksgiving to the sacrament itself. St. Justin (d.
167) used the term "Eucharist" already for the sacrament as
a technical term: "We have learned that the food, made a
Eucharist by a word of prayer that comes from Him, from
which our blood and flesh are nourished, by change is the
flesh and blood of the incarnate Jesus." [3]

Eulogia is a synonym of *Eucharistia*. When the term
Eucharistia became the technical term for the Blessed Sacrament, the term *Eulogia* was reserved to designate the unconsecrated bread, distributed among the faithful after the
celebration of the Sacrifice. This term is used in the narratives
of the institution of the Blessed Sacrament as a verb: *eulogesen*
and *eulogesas* with the identical meaning of the verb: *eucha-
ristesen* and *eucharistesas*.

A beautiful term, very expressive of the Canon as doctrine,
is *theologia*. This term is used by Eusebius of Caesarea (d.
340): "The unbloody and reasonable sacrifices, which are
accomplished by the prayers and the ineffable theology." [4]
In the intention of Eusebius the term "theology" seems to
refer primarily to the words of consecration. St. Cyril of Jerusalem (d. 386) calls the Sanctus, "theology": "Sanctus, sanctus, sanctus, etc., for that reason do we say this seraphic theology transmitted to us, that we may communicate in hymnody
with the heavenly hosts." [5]

Oratio as a name of the Canon occurs in St. Justin: "By the

---

[2] *Ad Phil.*, 4.
[3] St. Justin Martyr, *I Apol.*, 66; *PG*, 6, 510.
[4] *De laudibus Constantini*, 16; *PG*, 20, 1425.
[5] *Cat. myst.*, 5; *PG*, 33, 1072.

word of prayer [*oratio*] delivered by Jesus Himself." [6] Origen
uses the same term: "The food which is consecrated by the
word of God and prayer [*oratione*]." [7]

   Prex is a common term for the Canon in the writings of the
Fathers. St. Cyprian (d. 258) says: "Orations and prayers
(*orationes et preces*) accomplish the celebration of the sacrifice." [8] St. Athanasius (d. 373) uses the same term: "Before
the prayers (*preces*) are said, they are nothing but bread and
wine." [9] St. Jerome (d. 420) knows this term: "At their prayers
(*preces*) the body and the blood of Christ are made present." [10] St. Augustine (d. 430) uses the term *Prex mystica:* "It
is consecrated by the mystical prayer." [11] St. Gregory I (d.
604) uses this term: "We say therefore our Lord's prayer
immediately after the prayer (*mox post precem dicimus*)." [12]

   Actio, a name of the Canon which is derived from
gratiarum actio, signifies primarily the sacrificial action, the
entire Eucharistic rite. In the Gelasian Sacramentary is found
the combination, *Canon actionis.* The *Liber pontificalis* (p.
56) uses this term also: "This one [Xystus] has ordained that
within the action the priest should begin and the people should
continue with the singing of the hymn: Sanctus," etc.[13]

   Synonymous with *Actio* is *Agenda,* used by St. Augustine:
"This is the order in which it is to be done (*agendi ordinem*),
observed by the universal Church throughout the world." [14]

   The term *Praedicatio* occurs in the *Liber pontificalis* in

[6] St. Justin Martyr, *op. cit.,* 65; *PG,* 6, 428.
[7] *In Matt.,* 26; *PG,* 13, 949.
[8] *Ep.,* 64, 4; *PL,* 4, 392.
[9] *Sermo ad bapt., PG,* 26, 1325.
[10] *Ep.,* 146, 1; *PL,* 22, 1193.
[11] *De Trin.,* 3, 4; *PL,* 42, 874.
[12] *Ep.,* 9, 12; *PL,* 77, 956.
[13] *Liber pont.* (ed. Duchesne, 1886), I, 56.
[14] *Loc. cit.; Ep.; PL,* 33, 203.

connection with the Canon: "This one [St. Gregory I] has added in the proclamation of the Canon (*in praedicationem Canonis*): Give peace in these our days." [15] According to J. A. Jungmann, S.J.,[16] the term *praefatio* is originally equivalent to *praedicatio* and signifies not only the actual Preface but the whole Canon as the solemn prayer said before the congregation.

Contestatio is a Gallican name for the Eucharistic prayer, which emphasizes its character as a confession of faith. A passage of St. Augustine expresses the same idea: "And you testify that it is worthy and just to say thanks to Him." [17] A synonymous term in the Gallican liturgy is *Contestata. Immolatio missae*, likewise of Gallican origin, specifies the term *Actio.*

Mysterium is found in St. Ambrose (d. 397): "Through the mystery of the sacred prayer they are changed into flesh and blood." [18] With the same meaning this term is used in the much disputed passage of Pope Innocent I (d. 417) in the Epistle *Ad Decentium:* "The priest has to say the prayer . . . and then the names of those to be commemorated are to be mentioned, so that they become mentioned within the mysteries . . . so that by the mysteries themselves we may open the way for the prayers to follow." [19] The Council of Rome (1097) used the same term in the declaration of Berengarius: "I, Berengarius, believe with the heart and confess with the mouth, that bread and wine, put on the altar, are changed substantially into the true and proper and life-giving flesh and blood of our Lord Jesus Christ, by the mystery of the sacred

---

15 *Liber pont.*, I, 312.
16 "Praefatio und Stiller Canon," *ZkTh*, LIII (1929), 66–94.
17 *Sermo* 227; *PL*, 42, 874; *Ep.; PL*, 33, 203.
18 *De fide*, 4, 10; *PL*, 16, 64.
19 *Ep.* 25; *PL*, 20, 553.

prayer and the words of our Redeemer." [20] The term "mystery" quite obviously emphasizes the sacramental character of the Canon.

Anaphora is the term used universally in the Eastern liturgies. It is derived from Scripture, e.g., Heb. 7:27; 13:15: *thysias anapherein,* i.e., "to offer sacrifices." This term was substituted for *eucharistia* in order to emphasize the sacrificial character of the Eucharist.

"Canon" is a specific Roman term for the Eucharistic prayer. The word occurs in Gal. 6:16: "And whosoever shall follow this rule, peace on them and mercy." It was introduced in the beginning of the sixth century to designate the rule for the consecration of the Eucharist. It occurs in the letter of Pope Vigilius (d. 555) to Bishop Profuturus of Braga (538) in connection with the term *prex:* "Therefore we have ordained the text of the canonical prayer as above." [21] St. Aldhelm (d. 709) refers to the additions made in the Canon by St. Gregory I with the words: "Our preceptor and master Gregory has added in the daily Canon, when the solemnities of the Mass are being celebrated," etc.[22] Walafrid Strabo (d. 849) says that the term "Canon" is the specific Roman term for the Eucharistic prayer: "The Action, which the Romans call also Canon." [23] This term is to be translated "rule." But apparently it did not from the very beginning mean "unchangeable rule." It received this significance only in the course of time as a consequence of the law forbidding any change, referred to already in a passage of Pope Vigilius: "We state that we do not change the order of prayers in the celebration of Masses, but in the same manner always we consecrate the offerings

[20] Denzinger, no. 355.
[21] *Ep. ad Profuturum; PL,* 69, 18.
[22] *De laudibus virginitatis; PL,* 89, 142.
[23] *De rebus eccl.,* 22; *PL,* 114, 947.

to God." [24] Pope Vigilius gives as the reason why the text of the Eucharistic prayer must be preserved unchanged, not only its proximate connection with the consecration, but also its apostolic origin: "Which by the mercy of God we have received from apostolic tradition."

THE LIMITS OF THE CANON

In the Eastern liturgies the term "anaphora" applies to the whole Eucharistic prayer extending from the introductory dialogue to the final doxology, to the "Amen" found in the *Didache* (X, 6), of which St. Justin says: "When he [the priest] has ended the prayers and thanksgiving, all the people present cry out, saying, Amen." [25]

In the present Roman Missal the title "Canon Missae" is found after the Sanctus, before the *Te igitur clementissime Pater*. In the Gelasian Sacramentary the title "Incipit Canon actionis" stands before the *Sursum corda*, so that the Canon at that time included the Preface. Ideologically even at present the Preface belongs to the Canon and forms, with the prayers beginning with the *Te igitur clementissime Pater*, one continuous Eucharistic canticle.

Various causes led to the separation of the Preface from the Canon in the Roman and in all Western liturgies. 1. The custom of the Sanctus being sung by the congregation after its intonation by the priest who himself continued the Eucharistic prayer silently, the *Liber pontificalis* ascribes to Pope Sixtus I. 2. The development of the invocations, the insertion of the intercessory prayers with all the changes and rearrangements of this central part which made it a unit by itself in contrast to the original Canon. The ancient Eucharistic prayer

---

[24] *Loc. cit.*
[25] *I Apol.*, 65, 3; *PG*, 6, 510.

with its jubilant tone has a specifically latreutic and Eucharistic character. With the invocations a new element, different in tone and color, was introduced. It is the propitiatory power of the Eucharistic sacrifice and its impetratory efficacy that is emphasized with the humble, imploring supplications of the newly developed central part. 3. The laws that prescribe the Canon as "unchangeable rule" (except insertions in the *Communicantes* and the *Hanc igitur*, corresponding to the variable Prefaces) distinguished it from the Prefaces which vary according to the feast or season. The Leonine Sacramentary has 267 Prefaces, the Gelasian 54, the Gregorian 10 (in its appendix 100), the present Roman Missal 15.

At the time of Pope Leo I, although the Preface was already a composition by itself, it remained externally still united with the rest of the Canon, so that the Gelasian Sacramentary carries the title "Incipit Canon actionis" before the *Sursum corda*. In the Gregorian Sacramentary the Preface is already externally separated from the rest of the Canon. In its first Christmas Mass the Preface is found in the Proper of the feast inserted between the Secret and the Postcommunion. The *Ordo Romanus I* (eighth century) has the rubric: "When they have finished [the Sanctus], the Pontiff rises and goes alone to the Canon." [26] The term "Canon" occurs already with St. Cyprian: "When we stand for prayer, beloved brethren, we have to watch and to attend with the whole heart. . . . For this reason the priest likewise prepares before the prayer the minds of the brethren with a preceding preface, saying: Lift up your hearts." [27] In this text, however, the term "preface" refers only to the dialogue, the introductory portion of the Preface of the Roman Missal. In the meaning of the present

[26] *Ordo Romanus I; PL*, 78, 937–68.
[27] *De Dominica oratione*, 31; *PL*, 4, 557.

Missal, the term is used first in the Gregorian Sacramentary.

The separation of the Preface from the Canon was carried out externally in the latter part of the Middle Ages. The beginning was made with the miniature around the first letter T of the prayer *Te igitur clementissime Pater.* Pope Zacharias, in a letter to St. Boniface, mentions the sign of the cross at this place.[28] The first miniature of the Crucifixion appears in the Sacramentary of Gellonius (eighth century). In the eleventh century the picture of the Crucifixion is by that time independent of the text of the prayer, i.e., from the letter T of the prayer *Te igitur clementissime Pater.*

[28] Cf. L. Eisenhofer, *Handbuch der kath. Liturgik* (Freiburg, 1933), II, 156; F. Cabrol, "Canon romain," *D.A.C.L.*, 1547–1905.

CHAPTER VI

The Preface. The Original Canon

THE name and the present function of the preface do not reveal that it is itself the most ancient element of the Canon, that together with the final doxology it constitutes the original Eucharistic prayer. Although externally reduced to an introduction of the Canon, it has preserved all fundamental ideas and is ideologically so intimately connected with the present Canon that what is now called the Canon has to be explained as the result of the organic unfolding of the ideas proclaimed in the few words of the preface.

The original Canon is the most jubilant hymn of thanksgiving, the most triumphant chant of the glory of God. This Eucharistic canticle *katexochen,* this first song of Christendom, is most sacred in origin and character, most sublime in its ideology, most comprehensive in significance and efficacy. It has incorporated on the one hand the great hymn inspired by the Holy Ghost: the canticle of Moses, the first hymn contained in divine revelation; the Hallel of the Old Testament, the most solemn hymn of the liturgy of the Temple. The original Canon is the continuation of the hymn of the Last Supper, a paraphrase of our Lord's prayer of thanksgiving before the institution of the mysteries of His body and blood. That prayer forms the most sacred nucleus of the Canon. It

53

resounds finally in the melodies of the canticle of the heavenly liturgy, revealed in the Apocalypse. The original Canon is, on the other hand, the model and exemplar for the rest of the most venerable hymns of the liturgy, of Christian antiquity: it has inspired the symbols of faith, the *Gloria in excelsis,* the *Exultet,* the *Te Deum.* It is a delightful study to compare structure and ideas of the symbols of faith with the Canon of the *Traditio apostolica* of St. Hippolytus, with the Eucharistic prayer of the *Apostolic Constitutions* (chap. 8). The etherial joy of the *Gloria* expressed in the exclamations, "We praise Thee, we bless Thee, we adore Thee, we give Thee thanks because of Thy great glory," is inspired by the Eucharistic canticle. The *Exultet,* this majestic proclamation of Easter, this jewel of the liturgy, is filled with profound theology, radiant with youthful enthusiasm, flowing in the most solemn rhythms, resounding in the most jubilant cadences. This Canon with preface has transmitted to us much of the ancient form of the Eucharistic prayer. The *Te Deum,* the solemn verses of which resound like so many harps, representing all the voices of the Universe, is in its first ten verses taken from the anaphora of the liturgy of Jerusalem; verses 11–13 and 24–26 are inspired by the *Gloria.*

For an adequate interpretation of the Preface as the original Canon it is indispensable to analyze first the scriptural background, to follow its historical development from the canticle of Moses as the prototype, from the Hallel as its immediate type; to understand its dependence on the heavenly liturgy described in the Apocalypse, which reflects the earliest Christian liturgy and has served as an inspiration for its further development. A review of ancient liturgies and present Oriental rites gives evidence of this dependence. Upon such a scriptural and historic background we have to visualize the Preface of the present Roman Missal synoptically with all its variations in the course of the liturgical year in order to understand its meaning, to evaluate its import. Thus we shall realize the profound significance as well as the beauty and dignity of the Christian thanksgiving. We will view it as the most worthy worship of the heavenly Father, as thanks most universal in the object for which thanks are rendered, for creation, redemption, and sanctification, being in itself a new creation, a continued redemption, an extension and intensification of sanctification. It is most universal in the subjects rendering thanks, uniting priest and faithful with the ministering angels, the Church on earth with the Church in heaven through Christ the eternal High Priest. It is a giving of thanks most significant and most efficacious, incorporated into the hymn of glory of infinite dignity with which the Word of God glorifies the Father from eternity to eternity.

The Prototype of the Canon

The deliverance of the Israelites from the servitude in Egypt, the passage through the Red Sea, the victory over Pharaoh and his hosts, and the entry into the Promised Land are all types of the redemption of mankind from the servitude of sin, for our Lord's passion, for His victory over the devil and his hosts, for His transitus from this world to the Father, for His glorification and for the entry of the blessed into the heavenly paradise. This relation of type and antitype determines the parallelism in contents and structure of the thanksgiving hymn of Moses and its continued memorial in the thanksgiving of the Jews with the Hallel, with the thanksgiving of Christ and its continued memorial in the Eucharistic canticle of the Christians; lastly, with the thanksgiving hymn of the triumphant Church and of the angels with Christ in heaven.

Scripture points out the connection between the canticle of Moses and the Hallel on the one hand, and, on the other hand, the thanksgiving hymn of the blessed in heaven with explicit quotations, with the parallelism in ideas and structure. Our Lord Himself established the connection of His thanksgiving with the thanksgiving of the Hebrews by the celebration of His Eucharistic Pasch within the celebration of the Jewish Pasch; He linked His thanksgiving with the Hallel. The Church, being conscious of these relations, has reproduced them in her own Eucharistic canticle.

The canticle of Moses and the Hallel of the Jews are connected with each other: the first is the original thanksgiving hymn; the second is its developed form in the annual memorial celebration. There are, however, certain differences: the canticle of Moses is a thanksgiving without a sacrifice, or rather a thanksgiving to be completed with the sacrifice on Mount Sinai. The Hallel is a sacrificial hymn celebrating simultaneously the deliverance from Egypt and the institution of the Old Testament with a sacrifice on Mount Sinai. The canticle of Moses is partly prophetic, so far as the journey through the desert is still ahead, the entry into the Promised Land is still hoped for. The Hallel, on the other hand, gives thanks for all divine benefactions at a time when the Promised Land has long been in secure possession of the chosen people. But the canticle of Moses and the Hallel are equally triumphant, victorious, Eucharistic hymns, both foreshadow the victory of Christ over sin and the devil, His glorious entry into heaven, the victory of His saints, and their triumphant entrance into the heavenly paradise.

The Hallel refers with explicit quotations to the canticle of
Moses as its model: verse 14 of psalm 117 quotes the canticle
of Moses (Exod. 15:2) explicitly: "The Lord is my strength
and my praise; and He is become salvation to me." Further,
Ps. 113:1–8 and Ps. 135:10–22 of the Great Hallel, each repeat
the narrative of the canticle of Moses.

The Apocalypse refers to the canticle of Moses as a type
for the Eucharistic hymn of the triumphant Church with the
words (Apoc. 15:2 f.): "I saw as it were a sea of glass mingled
with fire: and them that had overcome the beast and his
image and the number of his name standing on the sea of
glass, having the harps of God: and singing the canticle of
Moses, the servant of God, and the canticle of the Lamb."

Besides these explicit quotations, there is the parallelism
in ideas and structure. We find in the canticle of Moses and in
the Hallel: an introduction with an exhortation to thanksgiving, a conclusion with a doxology. The one to whom thanks
are given is God in His nature and attributes; the object for
which thanks are rendered is the great works of God by creation, providence, redemption.

ANALYSIS OF THE CANTICLE OF MOSES (EXOD. 15:1–18)

The introduction to the canticle, "Let us sing to the Lord,"
is specified with the object: "for He is gloriously magnified;
the horse and the rider He hath thrown into the sea," which
gives the canticle the character of a paean of victory. The
terms expressive of exuberant joy and of thanksgiving and
praise contain significant allusions: thus verse 2, "The Lord
is . . . my praise," i.e., the Lord is the object of my praise.
The Hebrew term *simr-ja* used in this verse is equivalent to
hallelu-ja; both are combinations with the abbreviation of the
Hebrew name of God (the Tetragrammaton): Jahve-ja. In

the exclamations, "I will glorify Him. . . . I will exalt Him," with which Moses is speaking as the representative of his nation, there is contained an allusion to the future worship in the Temple in Jerusalem. The Chaldean version of the verb "glorify" means: "I shall build into a sanctuary." Now the propitiatory throne of the holy of holies is a kind of triumphal chariot, a visible memorial of the victory of God over Pharaoh and his hosts (Ps. 67:18; I Par. 28:18; Ezech. 1; cf. Cornelius a Lapide on Exod. 25:18).

The canticle is divided into two parts according to the one to whom thanks are given, and according to the object for which thanks are rendered: (a) God is glorified in His attributes of omnipotence, justice, holiness, and mercy; (b) thanks are given for the great works of liberation and redemption. The two parts are connected with each other, so far as the works of God reveal his attributes.

God is praised first generally in verse 1: "for He is gloriously magnified," and in verse 7, which speaks of "the multitude of Thy glory." The first attribute of God to be praised specifically is His omnipotence (v. 2): "The Lord is my strength"; (v. 3): "The Lord is as a man of war: Almighty is His name"; v. 11: "Who is like to Thee among the strong, O Lord"; v. 16: "In the greatness of Thy arm." The second attribute praised is the justice of God (v. 7): "Thou hast sent Thy wrath"; v. 8: "and with the blast of Thy anger"; v. 10: "Thy wind blew." The third attribute is sanctity (v. 11): "Who is like to Thee, glorious in holiness?" The fourth is mercy (v. 2): "He is become salvation to me"; v. 13: "In Thy mercy Thou hast been a leader to the people which Thou hast redeemed."

The works of God for which thanks are rendered are (a) the events of the past from the departure out of Egypt up to the time of victory over the Pharaoh (vv. 1–12); (b) the

events of the future from the shores of the Red Sea to the
journey ahead through the desert and the victorious occupation of the Promised Land (vv. 13–17). The first part is presented in its negative and positive aspects: destruction of the
Egyptians, salvation of the Israelites. The defeat of Pharaoh
is proclaimed with seven statements, each concluding with
an identical or equivalent phrase: "they were drowned in the
sea." These repetitions bring to mind the stupendous event,
the sound of the waters, the fierceness of the enemy, his
chariots and horsemen as types of the demons; they impress
with the amazement about the sudden and decisive liberation,
the greatness and completeness of the victory, admiration,
jubilation, and gratitude. The salvation of the Israelites is
proclaimed with two statements: (a) in contrast to the first
proclamation of the fate of the Egyptians (v. 2): "The Lord
is my strength and my praise: and He is become salvation to
me"; (b) as a conclusion of the seven statements about the
Egyptians (v. 13): "In Thy mercy Thou hast been a leader
to Thy people which Thou hast redeemed." This statement
serves simultaneously as introduction to the prophetic procla-
mations. With three statements the fate of the enemy nations
is described. These events are foretold in the perfect tense,
expressing the confidence in the fulfillment of these prophecies: (a) sorrow took hold of the inhabitants of Philisthiim
(v. 14); (b) all the inhabitants of Chanaan became stiff (v.
15); (c) the enemies became immovable as a stone (v. 16).
Thanks are rendered for the saving of the Israelites with v.
13 b: "and in Thy strength Thou hast carried them to Thy holy
habitation." Again in v. 17, where "Thy holy habitation" is
specified with three terms which open a wide perspective,
the glorious vision of type and antitype united: the Temple
of Jerusalem as future center of the theocracy combined with

the vision of the heavenly Jerusalem: (a) "Thou shalt bring them in, and plant them in the mountain of Thy inheritance"; (b) "in Thy most firm habitation, which Thou hast made, O Lord"; (c) "Thy sanctuary, O Lord, which Thy hands have established." It is a prophetic vision of the entering of the faithful into the Church; of the journey of the saints from this life into heaven, opened by the entrance of Christ into the kingdom of His Father.

The canticle concludes with an exclamation equivalent to a doxology: "The Lord shall reign forever and ever."

TEXT AND STRUCTURE

INTRODUCTION

v. 1a: Then Moses and the children of Israel sung this canticle to the Lord, and said: Let us sing to the Lord, for He is gloriously magnified. (The seven conclusions mentioned above are here indicated by italics.)

PART I

LIBERATION FROM EGYPT

v. 1b   The horse and the rider *He hath thrown into the sea.*

v. 2   The Lord is my strength and my praise: and He is become salvation to me.

He is my God and I will glorify Him: the God of my father, and I will exalt Him.

v. 3   The Lord is a man of war: Almighty is His name.

v. 4   Pharaoh's chariots and his army *He hath cast into the sea:*

His chosen captains *are drowned in the Red Sea.*

v. 5   The depths have covered them: they *are sunk to the bottom like a stone.*

v. 6   Thy right hand, O Lord, is magnified in strength: Thy right hand, O Lord, hath slain the enemy.

v. 7   And in the multitude of Thy glory Thou hast put down Thy adversaries:
Thou hast sent Thy wrath, *which hath devoured them* like stubble.

v. 8   And with the blast of Thy anger the waters were gathered together.
The flowing water stood: the depths were gathered together in the midst of the sea.

v. 9   The enemy said: I will pursue and overtake; I will divide the spoils, my soul shall have its fill.
I will draw my sword; my hand shall slay them.

v. 10 Thy wind blew, and the sea covered them; *they sunk as lead in the mighty waters.*

v. 11 Who is like to Thee, among the strong, O Lord?
Who is like to Thee, glorious in holiness, terrible and praiseworthy, doing wonders?

v. 12 Thou stretchedst forth Thy hand:
And *the earth swallowed them.*

Part II

Introduction into the Promised Land

Prologue

v. 13 In Thy mercy Thou hast been a leader to the people which Thou hast redeemed:
and in Thy strength Thou hast carried them to Thy holy habitation.

Victory over the Chanaanites

v. 14(a) Nations rose up and were angry:
sorrows took hold on the inhabitants of Philisthiim.

v. 15(b) Then were the princes of Edom troubled, trembling
seized on the stout men of Moab.

All the inhabitants of Chanaan became stiff.

v. 16(c) Let fear and dread fall upon them in the greatness
of Thy arm;

let them become unmovable as a stone, until Thy
people, O Lord, pass by:

until this Thy people pass by, which Thou hast possessed.

Entry into the Promised Land

v. 17(a) Thou shalt bring them in, and plant them in the
mountain of Thy inheritance;

(b) in Thy most firm habitation which Thou hast made,
O Lord:

(c) Thy sanctuary, O Lord, which Thy hands have established.

Ecphonesis

v. 18   The Lord shall reign forever and ever.

CHAPTER VII

The Hallel, the Proximate Type of the Canon

IN the tender words of our Savior with which He began the Last Supper, the connection of the Jewish Pasch with the Eucharistic sacrifice as type and antitype is alluded to (Luke 22:15): "With desire I have desired to eat this pasch with you before I suffer." St. Paul, writing to the Corinthians about the year 57 concerning Easter, exclaims (I Cor. 5:7): "Christ our Pasch is sacrificed," and puts into these words the exultant joy he experienced with the celebration of the paschal mysteries. The term "Pasch" means for St. Paul the sacrifice of Christ as antitype of the Jewish Pasch, implying also the memorial of it, and sacramental Pasch. The Council of Trent has summarized these relations of type and antitype in the chapter about the institution of the Eucharistic sacrifice: "Having celebrated the ancient Passover which the multitude of the children of Israel sacrificed (Exod. 12:1 ff.) in memory of their departure from Egypt, He instituted a new Passover, namely, Himself, to be immolated under visible signs by the Church through the priests in memory of His own passage from this world to the Father, when by the shedding of His blood He redeemed and delivered us from the power of darkness and translated us into His kingdom" (Col. 1:13).[1] The

---

[1] *Denzinger*, no. 938.

63

departure from Egypt symbolizes the *transitus* of Christ from this world to the Father and the "translation of us into the kingdom of the Son of His love." With both the Eucharist is connected as the sacramental antitype, and as the anticipation of our translation into the kingdom. This complex of ideas makes the Hallel the immediate type of the Eucharistic canticle of the Church.

NAME AND LITURGY OF THE HALLEL

The term "Hallel" signifies "All glory to God." The Hebrew term is a combination of the verb *allelu* ("all hail, all glory in the highest") with *ja* ("who is"), the abbreviation of the Tetragrammaton. It occurs first in Tob. 13:21 f., in the description of the glory and joy in heaven: "The gates of Jerusalem shall be built of sapphire and of emerald, and all the walls thereof round about of precious stones. All its streets shall be paved with white and clean stones: and Alleluja shall be sung in its streets." About twenty psalms were given the title Alleluja, because they begin or close with this word. The passage from Tobias is reflected in the fourfold Alleluja of the heavenly liturgy, described in the Apocalypse, chapter 19.

At the celebration of the Jewish Passover the Hallel [2] was introduced in the way ordained by Moses according to the command of God (Exod. 12:26): "And when your children shall say to you: What is the meaning of this service?" With these words a son of the house, or someone else, asked for the explanation of the paschal rites. Then the head of the paschal table related the story of the departure from Egypt and explained the significance of each dish served at the Pasch according to the order (Exod. 12:27): "You shall say to them:

[2] Cf. F. X. Poelzl, *The Passion and Glory of Christ.* Tr. by C. C. Martindale, p. 36. New York, 1919.

It is the victim of the passage of the Lord, when He passed over the houses of the children of Israel in Egypt, striking the Egyptians, and saving our houses." Exod. 13:8: "And thou shalt tell thy son in that day, saying: This is what the Lord did to me when I came forth out of Egypt." Exod. 13:14: "And when thy son shall ask thee tomorrow, saying: What is this? Thou shalt answer him: With a strong hand did the Lord bring us forth out of the land of Egypt, out of the house of bondage."

Following these explanations the singing of the Hallel was introduced: "Therefore it is our duty to thank, praise, laud, extol, exalt, magnify, bless, honor, and worship Him who hath done all these things for our fathers and for ourselves: He hath brought us out of bondage into freedom; out of oppression to joy, out of mourning to festal gladness, out of darkness to great light, and out of servitude to redemption; therefore let us sing before Him a new song, Alleluja."

In response to this invitation all present sang the first part of the Hallel (Ps. 112:1–113:8). At certain words the cup of wine (second cup) was raised and then replaced on the table. When the psalms were sung, the cup was drunk (called the cup of Haggadah). Then followed the eating of the pasch. When the meal was finished, the third cup of wine was mixed, called the "cup of blessing," because it was taken immediately following the prayer after the meal. The blessing concluded with an invocation of the coming of the Messiah: "May the All-merciful make us worthy of the days of the Messiah and of the life of the world to come." Then the fourth cup was mixed, and the second part of the Hallel (Ps. 113:9—117:29) was sung. After the hymn the fourth cup (called the cup of the Hallel) was taken. To the fifth cup corresponded the Great Hallel (Ps. 135). The Great Hallel had to be sung also at the slaughter of the paschal lamb. It was prescribed (Exod. 12:5 ff.) that the lambs should be slain at sunset on the 14th of Nisan: "And it shall be a lamb without blemish, a male of one year: according to which rite also you shall take a kid. And you shall keep it until the fourteenth day of this month: and the whole multitude of the children of Israel shall sacrifice it in the evening." It was custom to begin the slaughter at about the third hour in the afternoon, as soon as the evening sacrifice had been offered, for on that day this took place earlier than usual.[3] With a trumpet the sign was given from the pinnacle of the Temple to begin the killing of the lambs in the forecourt of the Temple. The priests took part in the immolation, standing in two rows to catch the blood in bowls, which were passed from hand to hand to the altar of sacrifice and poured out at its base. During these ceremonies Levites chanted the Great Hallel to the sound of trumpets.

The Hallel and the Canticle of Moses

The Hallel is the continuation of the canticle of Moses, its developed and amplified form. A series of explicit quotations, an identity of ideas and parallelism in structure, give evidence of these connections, as demonstrated below.

Hallel, Ps. 117	Canticle of Moses, Exod. 15
V. 14: The Lord is my strength and my praise: and He is become my salvation.	V. 2a: The Lord is my strength and my praise: and He is become my salvation.
V. 16: The right hand of the Lord hath wrought strength: the right hand of the Lord hath exalted me:	V. 5: Thy right hand, O Lord, is magnified in strength: Thy right hand, O Lord, hath slain the enemy.

[3] Cf. Josephus, *Bellum jud.*, VI, 9.

the right hand of the Lord
hath wrought strength.

V. 21b: and art my salva-
tion.

V. 28: Thou art my God,
and I will praise Thee; Thou
art my God, and I will exalt
Thee. . . . Thou art become
my salvation.

V. 2a: and He is become
salvation to me.

V. 2b: He is my God, and I
will glorify Him: the God of
my Father, and I will exalt
Him.

The first part (Ps. 112:1—113:8) of the Hallel. Psalm 112 is a song of thanksgiving, expressing Israel's gratitude over the restoration from Babylonian captivity; like the Egyptian servitude, a type of the captivity of mankind by the devil. The invitation for thanksgiving (v. 1), "Praise the Lord, ye children: praise ye the name of the Lord," recalls the invitation of Moses (Exod. 15:1), "Let us sing to the Lord." It is specified with a prophetic word about the Eucharist, contained in the great prophecy of Malachias, alluded to by St. Paul and incorporated into the Canon (vv. 2 f.): "Blessed be the name of the Lord: from henceforth now and forever. From the rising of the sun unto the going down, My name is great among the Gentiles: and in every place there is sacrifice and there is offered to My name a clean oblation." With these let us compare the following. Mal. 1:11: "From the rising of the sun unto the going down, My name is great among the Gentiles: and in every place there is sacrifice and there is offered to My name a clean oblation"; Eph. 5:20: "Giving thanks always for all things, in the name of our Lord Jesus Christ, to God the Father"; Canon, Preface: "It is meet indeed and just, . . . always and everywhere to give thanks." Following the invitation to thanksgiving, two reasons are presented: (a)

God's exaltation (vv. 4 f.): "The Lord is high above all nations: and His glory above the heavens. Who is as the Lord our God, who dwelleth on high?" (b) God's condescension (vv. 6–9): "And looketh down on the low things in heaven and in earth? Raising up the needy from the earth: and lifting up the poor out of the dunghill."

Ps. 113:1–8 is the particular illustration of God's exaltation and condescension in the redemption of Israel from Egypt. In analogy to the canticle of Moses in vv. 1 f., the theme is proposed: the liberation from Pharaoh and the introduction into the Promised Land. In vv. 4–8 some particular events are recorded: the passage through the Red Sea, the passage through the Jordan (vv. 3, 5); the earthquake on Mount Sinai (vv. 4, 6 f.; cf. Exod. 19:18); the miracle of the water from the rock (v. 8; cf. Exod. 17:1–7; Num. 20:1–13).

ANALYSIS OF THE HALLEL

The Hallel (Ps. 112–117) and the Great Hallel (Ps. 135) are each a complete composition. The Great Hallel, a repetition and abbreviation of the Hallel, widens its view to include the creation of the world in the object of praise and thanksgiving.

The five psalms of the Hallel are distinguishable into three parts: (a) Ps. 112:1—113:8 was sung before the paschal meal. Ps. 112 is a song of God's exaltation and condescension; Ps. 113:1–8 is a hymn to the glory and power of God as revealed in the Exodus. (b) Ps. 113:9–26 and psalms 114 and 115 constitute the second part, which is introduced with a profession of faith in God and His help. These described the extreme trial of the Psalmist with a cry for help and with the promise of a thanksgiving sacrifice (Ps. 114). The prayer has been

heard, and Ps. 114 is an expression of thanks with the preparation of a Eucharistic sacrifice in the Temple. (c) The third
part comprises psalms 116 and 117 and is the most jubilant
part of the Hallel, the most explicit prophecy of the redemption by Christ and the anticipated thanksgiving for it. Psalm
117 is fittingly the Easter psalm of the Church, the model of
the *Exultet,* and the most direct type of the Eucharistic canticle of the Church.

TEXT AND STRUCTURE OF PART I

Invitation to praise (Ps. 112:1–3)
generally (v. 1): Praise the Lord, ye children: praise ye the
name of the Lord.
always (v. 2): Blessed be the name of the Lord: from henceforth now and forever.
everywhere (v. 3): From the rising of the sun unto the going
down of the same, the name of the Lord is worthy of praise.
Object of praise
generally (Ps. 112:4–9)
exaltation of God (vv. 4 f.): The Lord is high above all
nations: and His glory above the heavens. Who is as the
Lord our God, who dwelleth on high:
condescension (vv. 6–9): and looketh down on the low
things in heaven and in earth? Raising up the needy from
the earth: and lifting up the poor out of the dunghill: that
He may place him with princes: with the princes of His
people. Who maketh a barren woman to dwell in a house,
the joyful mother of children.
particularly (Ps. 113:1–8)
theme: When Israel went out of Egypt, the house of Jacob
from a barbarous people: Judea was made His sanctuary,
Israel His dominion.

events
> v. 3: The sea saw and fled: Jordan was turned back.
> v. 4: The mountains skipped like rams: and the hills like the lambs of the flock.
> v. 5: What ailed thee, O thou sea, that thou didst flee? And thou, O Jordan, that thou wast turned back?
> v. 6: Ye mountains, that ye skipped like rams, and ye hills, like lambs of the flock?
> v. 7: At the presence of the Lord the earth was moved: at the presence of the God of Jacob.
> v. 8: Who turned the rock into pools of water, and the stony hill into fountains of waters.

THE SECOND PART OF THE HALLEL,
Ps. 113:9—115:18

The first section of this second part (Ps. 113: 9–26) forms the transition from the first part, imploring God that He may continue to show His glory as in the past so in the future with the protection of His people "of Israel, of the house of Aaron, of all who adore the true God"; that He may show His mercy toward His people, and His power against the idols.

TEXT AND STRUCTURE OF Ps. 113:9–26 [4]

Introduction (v. 9): Not to us, O Lord, not to us: but to Thy name give glory.
attributes of God (vv. 10 f.)
mercy: For Thy mercy,
faithfulness: and for Thy truth's sake: lest the Gentiles should say: Where is their God?
true God: But our God is in heaven:
power: He hath done all things whatsoever He would.

[4] Some editions of the Psalms number verses 9–26 as 1–18.

against idols (vv. 12–16): The idols of the Gentiles are silver and gold, the works of the hands of men. They have mouths and speak not: they have ears and hear not: they have noses and smell not. They have hands and feel not, they have feet and walk not: neither shall they cry out through their throat. Let them that make them become like unto them: and all such as trust in them.

God's protection (vv. 17–23)

in the past: The house of Israel hath hoped in the Lord: He is their helper and their protector. The house of Aaron hath hoped in the Lord: He is their helper and protector. They that fear the Lord have hoped in the Lord: He is their helper and their protector. The Lord hath been mindful of us, and hath blessed us. He hath blessed the house of Israel, He hath blessed the house of Aaron. He hath blessed all that fear the Lord, both the little and great.

in the future: May the Lord add blessings upon you: upon you and upon your children. Blessed be you of the Lord, who made heaven and earth.

conclusion (vv. 24–26): The heaven of heaven is the Lord's: but the earth He hath given to the children of men. The dead shall not praise Thee, O Lord: nor any of them that go down to hell. But we that live bless the Lord: from this time now and forever.

Ps. 114 AND 115

In the Hebrew text these psalms are joined in one. They present one complete group of ideas. A great temporal affliction of the composer has inspired them. Delivered from pain and sorrow, the Psalmist offers a sacrifice of thanksgiving. St. Basil, St. Chrysostom, St. Jerome, and St. Augustine [5] interpret

[5] Cf. Cornelius a Lapide, *In Pss.* 114–115.

these two psalms about the spiritual man desirous of eternal salvation. They apply these psalms to Christ and the Christians, to redemption and the Eucharistic thanksgiving sacrifice. The Church has accepted this interpretation and inserted several quotations of psalm 115 in the Ordinary and Canon of the Mass.

TEXT AND STRUCTURE OF PS. 114

Introduction (vv. 1 f.): I have loved because the Lord will hear the voice of my prayer. Because He hath inclined His ear unto me: and in my days I will call upon Him.

affliction (vv. 3 f.): The sorrows of death have encompassed me: and the perils of hell have found me. I met with trouble and sorrow: and I called upon the name of the Lord. O Lord, deliver my soul.

God's mercy and justice (vv. 5 f.): The Lord is merciful and just, and our God showeth mercy. The Lord is the keeper of little ones: I was humbled, and He delivered me.

exhortation (vv. 7 f.): Turn, O my soul, into thy rest: for the Lord hath been bountiful to thee. For He hath delivered my soul from death; my eyes from tears, my feet from falling.

conclusion (v. 9): I will please the Lord in the land of the living.

PSALM 115

In gratitude for the great mercy of God a sacrifice of thanksgiving is offered. The introduction of this psalm recalls the great affliction, the liberation from it, and the promise of a sacrifice of thanksgiving.

St. Paul refers to this psalm in II Cor. 4:13 and understands it as the thanksgiving of Christ and of the Church redeemed

by Christ and glorified with Him: "But having the same spirit
of faith, as it is written: I believed, for which cause I have
spoken; we also believe, for which cause we speak also: knowing that He who raised up Jesus will raise us up also with
Jesus and place us with you."

The solemnity and dignity of the sacrifice of thanksgiving
are emphasized with repetitions: the idea of v. 4: "I will take
the chalice of salvation: and I will call upon the name of the
Lord," is taken up again in a variant with v. 8: "I will sacrifice
to Thee the sacrifice of praise: and I will call upon the name
of the Lord." The sacrifice is the fulfillment of the promise of
v. 5: "I will pay my vows to the Lord before all His people,"
which is repeated with v. 9: "I will pay my vows to the Lord
in the sight of all His people." In v. 5 the fulfillment may be
understood with a sacrifice on earth, in v. 9 with a thanksgiving
before all the blessed in heaven.

The vv. 3 and 4 became the prayer before the drinking of
the chalice: "What shall I render to the Lord for all the things
that He hath rendered to me? I will take the chalice of salvation; and I will call upon the name of the Lord." The vv. 5
and 8 are part of the commemoration of the living in the
Canon of the Mass: "I will pay my vows to the Lord" (who
pay their vows to the eternal living God); "I will sacrifice to
Thee the sacrifice of praise" (who offer unto Thee this sacrifice of praise).

TEXT AND STRUCTURE OF Ps. 115

Transition from Ps. 114

Ps. 115:1–3: I have believed, therefore have I spoken: but
I have been humbled exceedingly. I said in my excess:
Every man is a liar. What shall I render to the Lord for
all the things that He hath rendered to me?

thanksgiving (vv. 4 f.): I will take the chalice of salvation: and I will call upon the name of the Lord. I will pay my vows to the Lord before all His people.

motive (vv. 6 f.): Precious [not easily permitted] in the sight of the Lord is the death of His saints. O Lord, for I am Thy servant: I am Thy servant, and the son of Thy handmaid. Thou hast broken my bonds.

repetition of thanks (vv. 8 f.): I will sacrifice to Thee the sacrifice of praise, and I will call upon the name of the Lord. I will pay my vows to the Lord in the sight of all His people. In the courts of the house of the Lord, in the midst of thee, O Jerusalem.

Psalms 116 and 117 form the climax of the hymn of the Pasch. They proclaim prophetically the universality of salvation by Christ. The prophetic character of psalm 116, which is merely the introduction to psalm 117, is testified by St. Paul (Rom. 15:9, 11): "But that the Gentiles are to glorify God for His mercy, as it is written: . . . Praise the Lord, all ye Gentiles: and magnify Him, all ye people." Psalm 117 is Messianic according to the testimony of our Lord Himself (Matt. 21:42): "Jesus said to them: Have you never read in the Scriptures: The stone which the builders rejected, the same is become the head of the corner? By the Lord this has been done; and it is wonderful in our eyes." St. Peter in Acts 4:10 f. (cf. I Pet. 2:7): "Our Lord Jesus Christ of Nazareth. . . . This is the stone which was rejected by you the builders, which is become the head of the corner." St. Paul in Rom. 9:33: "As it is written: Behold I lay in Sion a stumblingstone and a rock of scandal. And whosoever believeth in Him shall not be confounded." For the Church and her liturgy it is the Easter psalm, it has inspired the *Exultet*, it is the great and solemn prophecy of the words "through Christ our Lord."

TEXT AND STRUCTURE OF PS. 116

Invitation for praise (v. 1): Praise the Lord, all ye nations [Gentiles]: praise Him, all ye people [Jews].
object of praise (v. 2): For His mercy is confirmed upon us: and the truth of the Lord remaineth forever.

PSALM 117

The connection of this psalm with the canticle of Moses is expressed with several quotations in v. 14 (cf. Exod. 15:2), v. 16 (cf. Exod. 15:6), v. 21 (cf. Exod. 15:2). The canticle of Moses speaks of salvation in general terms: Exod. 15:2: "The Lord is become salvation to me," and Exod. 15:13: "In Thy mercy Thou hast been a leader to the people which Thou hast redeemed: and in Thy strength Thou hast carried them to Thy holy habitation." In psalm 117 this leadership and redemption are explained and unfolded as Passion, Resurrection, entrance into the sanctuary, approach to the altar for the Eucharistic sacrifice.

In v. 1 the invitation to praise is repeated, and the object of praise is proclaimed again: "Give praise to the Lord, for He is good: for His mercy endureth forever." The invitation is extended to the same groups as those enumerated in Ps. 113:17–19: to the house of Israel, to the house of Aaron, to them that fear the Lord. The object of praise is specified in groups separated from each other with a new invitation to praise the Lord. The vv. 5–18 describe the liberation from grave affliction, a type of the servitude of sin and the devil, as well as of the passion of Christ. In vv. 19–21 the description of the object is interrupted with a new invitation to praise at the moment the procession has arrived at the gates of the Temple: "Open ye to me the gates of justice: I will go in to them, and give praise to the Lord. This is the gate of the Lord: the just shall enter into it. I will give glory to Thee because Thou hast heard me: and art become my salvation." This procession is itself a dramatic prophecy of the "transitus" of our Lord from this world to the Father, His entry into heaven for His glorious sacrifice of thanksgiving, sacramentally represented in the Eucharist. The vv. 22–23 describe redemption in the person of the Messiah, by His coming, by His resurrection. The glory of this revelation is so great that the prophet interrupts his narrative with an exclamation (theme of the introduction of the *Exultet*): "This is the day which the Lord hath made: let us be glad and rejoice therein." Verses 25–27 are acclamations to the Messiah as He is coming in incarnation, as He is entering for His sacrifice, as He is ascending into His glory, as He is coming the second time at the end of our days: "O Lord, save me: O Lord, give good success. Blessed be he that cometh in the name of the Lord. We have blessed you out of the house of the Lord. The Lord is God, and He hath shone upon us."

With an exhortation to celebrate the festival day at the altar of sacrifice (v. 27): "Appoint a solemn day with shady boughs, even to the horn of the altar," the reason for praise is repeated thrice with words of the prophet speaking in his own person (v. 28): "Thou art my God, and I will praise Thee; Thou art my God, and I will exalt Thee. I will praise Thee because Thou hast heard me and art become my salvation." With v. 29 (repetition of v. 1), the invitation is a last time extended to all men.

Text and Structure of Ps. 117

Invitation to praise
> generally (v. 1): Give praise to the Lord, for He is good: for His mercy endureth forever.

specified (vv. 2–4): Let Israel now say, that He is good: that His mercy endureth forever. Let the house of Aaron say, that His mercy endureth forever. Let them that fear the Lord now say, that His mercy endureth forever.

object of thanksgiving

redemption (vv. 5–18): In my trouble I called upon the Lord: and the Lord heard me and enlarged me. The Lord is my helper: I will not fear what man can do unto me. The Lord is my helper: and I will look over my enemies. It is good to confide in the Lord, rather than to have confidence in man. It is good to trust in the Lord, rather than to trust in princes. All nations compassed me about; and in the name of the Lord I have been revenged on them. Surrounding me they compassed me about: and in the name of the Lord I have been revenged on them. They surrounded me like bees, and they burned like fire among thorns: and in the name of the Lord I was revenged on them. Being pushed I was overturned that I might fall: but the Lord supported me. The Lord is my strength and my praise: and He is become my salvation. The voice of rejoicing and of salvation is in the tabernacles of the just. The right hand of the Lord hath exalted me: the right hand of the Lord hath wrought strength. I shall not die, but live: and shall declare the works of the Lord. The Lord chastising hath chastised me: but He hath not delivered me over to death.

interruption at the gates of the Temple (vv. 19–21): Open ye to me the gates of justice: I will go in to them, and give praise to the Lord. This is the gate of the Lord, the just shall enter into it. I will give glory to Thee because Thou hast heard me: and art become my salvation.

the redeemer (vv. 22–23): The stone which the builders

rejected: the same is become the head of the corner. This
is the Lord's doing: and it is wonderful in our eyes.

interruption with invitation to joy (v. 24): This is the day
which the Lord hath made: let us be glad and rejoice
therein.

acclamations to Christ (vv. 25–27): O Lord, save me: O
Lord give good success. Blessed be he that cometh in the
name of the Lord. We have blessed you out of the house
of the Lord. The Lord is God, and He hath shone upon us.
Appoint a solemn day, with shady boughs, even to the
horn of the altar.

conclusion (vv. 28 f.): Thou art my God, and I will praise
Thee: Thou art my God, and I will exalt Thee. I will
praise Thee because Thou hast heard me, and art become
my salvation. O praise ye the Lord, for He is good; for
His mercy endureth forever.

PSALM 135

The seventh and last psalm of the paschal hymn, called the
Great Hallel, was sung at the immolation of the paschal lambs
by the priests in the Temple and at the paschal supper when
the fifth cup of wine was served. It is a summary of psalms
112–117 with some additions, specifications, and amplifications. Common to it with the Hallel is the invitation to praise
God (vv. 1–3), thanks for His works (v. 4), for the redemption from Egypt (vv. 10–15), for the introduction into the
Promised Land (vv. 16–22), for the redemption for which the
liberation from Egypt was merely a type (vv. 22 f.). Additions appear in the invitation with an allusion to the Blessed
Trinity addressed with a threefold invitation to thanks. The
mercy of God is emphatically the object of thanks with the
verse: "For His mercy endureth forever," repeated as a refrain

after each verse. The works of God are enumerated in three groups: works of creation (vv. 5–9), of providence (vv. 10–22), and of redemption (vv. 23 f.). A particular idea is contained in verse 25: "Who gives food to all flesh." The literal meaning of this verse would be, that even those who are not stricken with affliction as the prophet was, have nevertheless reason and the duty to thank God for His support of their lives. There is certainly contained in the spiritual interpretation of this psalm another allusion to the Eucharistic sacrament. Gustav Bickel thinks that at the words of verse 25 our Lord instituted the Holy Eucharist.

TEXT AND STRUCTURE OF PS. 135

Introduction (vv. 1–3): Praise the Lord, for He is good: for
  His mercy endureth forever. Praise ye the God of gods:
  for His mercy, etc. Praise ye the Lord of lords: for, etc.
object of praise (vv. 4–25)
  generally (v. 4): Who alone doth great wonders: for His
    mercy, etc.
  specified
    creation (vv. 5–9): Who made the heavens in under-
      standing: for, etc. Who established the earth above
      the waters; who made the great lights: the sun to rule
      the day: the moon and the stars to rule the night:
    providence (vv. 10–22): who smote Egypt with their
      first-born:
    who brought out Israel from among them:
    with a mighty hand and with a stretched-out arm:
    who divided the Red Sea into parts:
    and brought out Israel through the midst thereof:
    and overthrew Pharao and his host in the Red Sea:
    who led His people through the desert:

who smote great kings:
Sehon kind of the Amorrhites:
and Og king of Basan:
and He gave their land for an inheritance:
for an inheritance to His servant Israel.

redemption (vv. 23–25): For He was mindful of us in
our affliction:
and He redeemed us from our enemies:
who giveth food to all flesh.

conclusion (vv. 26 f.): Give glory to the God of heaven:
for, etc. Give glory to the Lord of lords: for his mercy
endureth forever.

CHAPTER VIII

The Liturgy of the Apocalypse

THE liturgy of the Apocalypse serves as witness to the earliest Christian liturgy and model and inspiration for its further development.[1] As antitype of the Old Testament liturgy it has incorporated the canticle of Moses, the Hallel of the Pasch; it presents the ideas and terms of the liturgy of the Temple in Jerusalem with its courts, the holy of holies, the sacrifices of light and incense and of the lamb; the altar and propitiatory throne; the adoring angels, the twenty-four priests in sacred vestments, the high priest entering the sanctuary, the glory of God appearing upon the propitiatory throne. The celestial worship has, on the other hand, the character of the New Testament liturgy: it is celebrated on Sunday (Apoc. 1:10): "I was in the spirit on the Lord's day"; Christ is the celebrating High Priest (Apoc. 1:13): "And in the midst of the seven golden candlesticks, one like to the Son of man, clothed with a garment down to the feet, and girt about the paps with a golden girdle"; the victim is received in heaven (Apoc. 5:6): "And I saw: and behold in the midst of the throne and of the four living creatures, and in the midst of the ancients, a Lamb standing as it were slain"; the prayers offered and accepted are the prayers of the Christians (Apoc. 8:3 f.): "And another angel came and stood be-

[1] Cf. J. M. Nielen, *The Earliest Christian Liturgy.* Tr. by Patrick Cummins, O.S.B. (St. Louis, 1941), p. 401.

fore the altar, having a golden censer: and there was given to
him much incense, that he should offer the prayers of all
saints upon the golden altar which is before the throne of
God. And the smoke of the incense of the prayers of the saints
ascended up before God from the hand of the angel." The
twenty-four ancients intone a song of praise with allusions to
the Eucharistic canticle of the Church (Apoc. 11:17): "We
give Thee thanks, O Lord God Almighty. . . ."

In the present chapter we examine the liturgy of the Apocalypse concerning its dependence on the canticle of Moses
and on the Hallel. Direct quotations inserted from the canticle of Moses and the Hallel into the text of the Apocalypse
and a comparison of the structure of the heavenly worship
with the structure of the canticle and of the Hallel prove this
dependence. Its dependence on the liturgy of the Temple in
Jerusalem will be discussed in the question about the origin
of the liturgical Sanctus. Its relations to the earliest Christian
liturgy as witness and model will likewise be the particular
subject in the chapters about the Sanctus, about the *Communicantes,* and about the angel of sacrifice.

THE APOCALYPSE AND THE CANTICLE OF MOSES

There are found three quotations, allusions to the canticle
of Moses in the thanksgiving hymn of the triumphant Church.

Apoc. 15:3: "And singing the canticle of Moses, the servant
of God, and the canticle of the Lamb."

Apoc. 15:2: "And I saw as it were a sea of glass mingled
with fire, and them that had overcome the beast, and his
image, and the number of his name, standing on the sea of
glass, having the harps of God" (cf. Exod. 15:1: "And they
saw the Egyptians dead upon the sea shore, and the mighty
hand that the Lord had used against them and the people

feared the Lord, and they believed the Lord, and Moses His servant. Then Moses and the children of Israel sung this canticle to the Lord").

Apoc. 15:3 f.: "Great and wonderful are Thy works, O Lord God Almighty . . . who shall not fear Thee, O Lord, and magnify Thy name? For Thou art holy" (cf. Exod. 15:11: "Who is like Thee, among the strong, O Lord? Who is like to Thee, glorious in holiness, terrible and praiseworthy, doing wonders?").

THE HALLEL OF HEAVEN

The Hallel of the Pasch is a sevenfold hymn composed of seven psalms expressive of the fullness of joy, of thanks, of praise. Likewise the hymn of glory in heaven is sevenfold (Apoc. 7:11 f.; cf. 5:11 f.): "And all the angels stood round about the throne and the ancients and the four living creatures. And they fell before the throne upon their faces and adored God, saying: Amen. Benediction and glory and wisdom and thanksgiving, honor and power and strength, to our God, forever and ever. Amen."

Twice the act of adoration is introduced with a phrase similar to the introduction of the Hallel at the Pasch (Apoc. 5:11): "Thou art worthy, O Lord our God, to receive glory and honor and power"; (Apoc. 5:12): "The Lamb that was slain is worthy to receive power and dignity and wisdom and strength and honor and glory and benediction." The introduction of the Hallel: "Therefore it is our duty to thank, praise, laud, extol, exalt, magnify, bless, honor and worship Him who has done all these things for our fathers and for ourselves. . . ."

The invitation to praise in Apoc. 19:5 is worded according to the invitations of the Hallel (Apoc. 19:5): "And a voice came out from the throne saying: Give praise to our God, all ye His servants; and you that fear Him, little and great." The parallel texts of the Hallel are Ps. 112:1: "Praise the Lord, ye servants: praise ye the name of the Lord." Ps. 113:13b: "He hath blessed all that fear the Lord, both little and great." Ps. 116:1: "Praise the Lord, all ye nations: praise Him all ye people."

The final victory of Christ is celebrated in heaven with the singing of a fourfold Alleluja, and it is joined by all servants of God throughout the universe (Apoc. 19:1): "I heard as it were the voice of much people in heaven, saying: Alleluja." (Apoc. 19:3): "And again they said: Alleluja." Next join the twenty-four ancients and the cherubim (Apoc. 19:4): "And the four and twenty ancients and the four living creatures fell down and adored God that sitteth upon the throne, saying: Amen. Alleluja." Then follow all the servants of God (Apoc. 19:6): "And I heard as it were the voice of a great multitude, and as the voice of many waters, and as the voice of great thunders, saying: Alleluja." The number four of the choirs enumerated may indicate the universality of extension of this praise. In Apoc. 5:13 the same extension is indicated with the fourfold doxology: "And every creature, which is in heaven, and on the earth, and under the earth, and such as are in the sea, and all that are in them: I heard all saying: To Him that sitteth on the throne, and to the Lamb, benediction and honor and glory and power forever and ever." This fourfold division indicates the four (all) regions of the earth, and analogically the regions (all) of the universe.

The singing of the Alleluja in heaven is concluded with the glorious verse of the Hallel (Ps. 117:24): "This is the day which the Lord hath made: let us be glad and rejoice therein."

Apoc. 19:7: "Let us be glad and rejoice and give glory to Him."

Structure of the Heavenly Liturgy

The canticle of Moses was intoned by Moses and sung by the Hebrews in two choirs, by men and women (Exod.15:1, 20 f.): "Then Moses and the children of Israel sung this canticle to the Lord and said: Let us sing to the Lord, for He is gloriously magnified. . . . So Mary, the prophetess, the sister of Aaron, took a timbrel in her hand: and all the women went forth after her with timbrels and with dances: and she began the song to them, saying: Let us sing to the Lord, for He is gloriously magnified."

The Hallel was intoned by the head of the paschal table and sung by alternating groups. Psalm 117 particularly was composed to be sung by two choirs; verses 19–29 are a dramatic colloquy between the prophet, the priests, and the people. At verse 19 the procession had arrived at the gates of the Temple and requested: "Open ye to me the gates of justice." The priests inside the doors may have answered (v. 20): "This is the gate of the Lord: the just shall enter into it."

The liturgy of the Apocalypse is arranged in several choirs. The four cherubim intone the Trisagion (Apoc. 4:8): "And they rested not day and night, saying: Holy, Holy, Holy, Lord God Almighty, who was and who is and who is to come." The hymn of glory is followed by the twenty-four ancients (Apoc. 4:9 f.): "And when those living creatures gave glory and honor and benediction to Him that sitteth on the throne, who liveth forever and ever: the four and twenty ancients fell down before Him . . . and adored Him . . . saying: Thou art worthy, O Lord our God, to receive glory and honor and power" (threefold because of the thrice "Holy" of the angels).

The adoration of the Lamb is carried out in choirs following one another (Apoc. 5:8; 11:13): the four living creatures; the twenty-four ancients; many angels round about the throne and the living creatures and the ancients; every creature that is in heaven and on earth and under the earth, and such as are in the sea, and all that are in them.

The singing of the Alleluja proceeds in an analogous order: (a) Apoc. 19:1: "The voice of much people in heaven [angels], saying: Alleluja." (b) Apoc. 19:4: "And the four and twenty ancients." (c) "And the four living creatures." (d) Apoc. 19:6: "The voice of a great multitude, and as the voice of many waters, and as the voice of great thunders, saying: Alleluja."

The praise is offered to the Blessed Trinity, alluded to in the thrice "Holy" (Apoc. 4:8); in the three terms (Apoc. 19:1): "Salvation and glory and power is to our God." It is offered to the Father and to the Lamb (Apoc. 5:13): "To Him that sitteth on the throne and to the Lamb, benediction and honor and glory and power, forever and ever."

The attributes of God which are praised are: (a) omnipotence (Apoc. 4:8): "Holy, Holy, Holy, Lord God Almighty"; (Apoc. 11:17): "We give Thee thanks, O Lord God Almighty"; (b) holiness; (c) eternity. In the sevenfold praise a series of attributes is summarized, reminiscent of the attributes mentioned in the canticle of Moses and in the Hallel.

The object for which thanks are rendered are: (a) creation (Apoc. 4:11): "Thou art worthy, O Lord our God, to receive glory and honor and power. Because Thou hast created all things: and for Thy will they were and have been created"; (b) redemption (Apoc. 5:9): "Thou art worthy, O Lord our God . . . because Thou wast slain and hast redeemed us to

God in Thy blood, out of every tribe and tongue and people and nation: and hast made us to our God a kingdom and priests."

The object of the heavenly canticle is redemption prefigured with the passage through the Red Sea, in its reality as the entrance of the faithful by baptism into the Church, the "transitus of Christ" from this world to the Father, the "transitus" of the saints from this earth into heaven, the nuptials of the Lamb.

CHAPTER IX

Traditional Ideas in
Ancient and Eastern Liturgies[1]

THE ancient and Eastern liturgies testify to the influence of the canticle of Moses and of the Hallel of the Pasch upon the Eucharistic hymn of the New Testament. They give evidence that the heavenly liturgy of the Apocalypse is both a mirror of the earliest Christian liturgy and an important factor for its characteristic development.

We find in ancient and Eastern liturgical texts ideas, terms, and structure of the canticle of Moses and of the Hallel. There is found the formula of invitation to thanksgiving; God is glorified in His attributes. God is thanked for the works of creation and redemption. There are found many explicit quotations from these Old Testament hymns in ancient Eucharistic anaphoras.

The inherited ideas, however, contained in the canticle of Moses and in the Hallel, but there veiled in figures and symbols, are now perfectly unfolded, directly revealed. There is in the great Hallel (Ps. 135:1–3) merely an allusion to the mystery of the Blessed Trinity. In the Christian liturgy the triune God is explicitly glorified. In the Eucharistic liturgy of the New Testament is celebrated the "transitus" of Christ

[1] Cf. Renaudot, *Liturgiarum orientalium collectio* (Frankfurt, 1947); F. E. Brightman, *Liturgies Eastern and Western* (Oxford, 1896); Donald Attwater, *Eastern Catholic Worship* (New York, 1945); S. Salaville, *An Introduction to the Study of Eastern Liturgies* (London, 1938).

to the Father, not merely in figure and symbol, as promise and prophecy, but in truth. Fully conscious that the memorial of the incarnate Word is the worship in spirit and in truth, fully conscious also that in the Eucharistic memorial is perfectly accomplished the prophecy of the canticle of Moses, "I will glorify Him," "I will build into a sanctuary," the Christian liturgy assigns to figure and type a minor place, a proportionate subordinate place.

It is further the ideology of the heavenly liturgy as described in the Apocalypse which gives to the Christian liturgy its marked distinction, which gives to the Eucharistic canticle the aura of heavenly glory. It is a heavenly liturgy with Christ the heavenly High Priest, with the ministry of the angels, accomplished in heaven, a divine victim, a glorified sacrifice, offered upon the heavenly altar, accepted upon the throne of God.

It is the time of fulfillment, of reality and consummation, in which the Christian thanksgiving is celebrated. There is therefore felt throughout the Christian liturgies the eschatological spirit, more explicit in the ancient anaphoras and in the Eastern liturgies than in later composition and in the Roman Canon.

These statements can be verified with a review of the ideas and structure of the Eucharistic prayer of the *Didache,* with passages from the First Epistle of St. Clement, with the Canon of the *Traditio apostolica* of St. Hippolytus, with the liturgy of the *Apostolic Constitutions,* with the liturgy of St. James, and with the Byzantine liturgy. In the present chapter we confine our study to the influence of the Old Testament hymns upon ideas and structure of the Eucharistic canticle of the Church, and to the difference between the Christian Eucharistic hymn and the canticle of Moses and between the Hallel in the presentation of the mystery of the Blessed Trinity and of the mysteries of the incarnate Word. The character of the Christian liturgy as heavenly liturgy will be analyzed in connection with the question about the introduction of the Sanctus and the angelic choirs into the Canon.

THANKSGIVING PRAYER OF THE *Didache*

Without prejudice to the disputed character of the thanksgiving prayer of the *Didache*—whether it is a Eucharistic thanksgiving (without the words of consecration), or merely a prayer at the celebration of the Agape—it cannot be denied that it contains ideas and the structure of an anaphora. It is the earliest liturgical text after those recorded in Scripture. The influence of the Jewish ritual is evident. The blessing for bread and wine is modeled on the Jewish prayers for blessing bread and wine on the Sabbath. There is no established rule in the manner of thanksgiving (chap. 10): "But permit the prophets to make thanksgiving as much as they desire."

The Hallel is referred to with two explicit quotations. The concluding doxology (X, 6), "Hosanna to the God of David," recalls Ps. 117: 25: "O Lord, save me: O Lord, give good success." The passage (X, 4), "Thou gavest food and drink to men for enjoyment," recalls the text of the Great Hallel, Ps. 135:25: "Who giveth food to all flesh." God is given praise in His omnipotence: "Thou Master almighty"; "Before all thanks we thank Thee that Thou art mighty." God is thanked for creation: "Thou, Master almighty, didst create all things."

There is, however, a marked difference in the manner in which God is addressed and in the terms with which thanks are given for redemption. The prayer is explicitly addressed to the Father: "We thank Thee, our Father." Redemption is thanked for with many terms: "For life and knowledge which

Thou madest known to us through Jesus Thy servant." "For Thy holy name which Thou didst cause to tabernacle in our hearts, and for the knowledge and faith and immortality." The passage, "Thou gavest food and drink to men for enjoyment," is interpreted "for spiritual food and drink and life eternal." There is already the word "through Jesus Christ" used as a liturgical formula, repeated five times in the course of the prayer in close connection with the doxology. This doxology itself, "To thee be the glory forever," and "For thine is the power and glory forever," occurs seven times in this prayer. The sevenfold doxology has four times the phrase, "To Thee be the glory forever," twice, "for Thine is the power and the glory forever"; once, "Hosanna to the God of David" (cf. II Tim. 4:18; Heb. 13:21; II Pet. 3:18; Apoc. 1:6).

Eschatological ideas appear in the prayer for the Church and in the conclusion: "Even as this broken bread was scattered over the hills and was gathered together and became one, so let the Church be gathered together from the end of the earth into Thy kingdom." "Gather it from the four winds, sanctified for Thy kingdom which Thou hast prepared for it." "Let grace come, and let this world pass away" (cf. I Cor. 16:22; Apoc. 22:20).

TEXT AND STRUCTURES OF THE *Didache*, IX–X

Before Communion: Now concerning the thanksgiving, thus give thanks. First concerning the cup: We thank Thee, our Father, for the holy vine of David Thy servant, which Thou madest known to us through Jesus Thy servant. To Thee be the glory forever.

And concerning the broken bread: We thank Thee, our Father, for the life and knowledge which Thou madest known to us through Jesus Thy servant; to Thee be the glory forever. Even as this broken bread was scattered over the hills and was gathered together from the ends of the earth into Thy kingdom; for Thine is the glory and the power through Jesus Christ forever.

But let no one eat or drink of your thanksgiving, but those who have been baptized into the name of the Lord; for concerning this also the Lord hath said, Give not that which is holy to dogs.

after Communion: But after you are filled, thus give thanks: We thank Thee, holy Father, for Thy holy name which Thou didst cause to tabernacle in our hearts, and for the knowledge and faith and immortality which Thou madest known to us through Jesus Thy servant; to Thee be the glory forever.

Thou, Master almighty, didst create all things for Thy name's sake; Thou gavest food and drink to men for enjoyment, that they might give thanks to Thee; but to us Thou didst freely give spiritual food and drink and life eternal through Thy servant.

Before all things we thank Thee that Thou art mighty; to Thee be the glory forever.

Remember, Lord, Thy Church, to deliver it from all evil and to make it perfect in Thy love, and gather it from the four winds, sanctified for Thy kingdom which Thou hast prepared for it; for Thine is the power and the glory forever.

Let grace come, and let this world pass away. Hosanna to the God of David.

If anyone is holy, let him come; if anyone is not, let him repent.

Maran-atha. Amen. But permit the prophets to make thanksgiving as much as they desire.

First Epistle of St. Clement to the Corinthians
(about 96–98)

This Epistle, written to pacify a schism in the Church of Corinth, was esteemed so highly that it was read publicly in the churches like an epistle of the apostles. There appears clearly the idea of the Christian liturgy as one celebrated with the angels in heaven. The object of thanksgiving is creation and the various benefactions of God in nature; then the grace in Jesus Christ. The high priesthood of Christ exercised in the Eucharist is emphatically praised.

precept of thanksgiving (38, 4): Since we have all these things from Him, we must give thanks for all things in Him, to whom be glory forever and ever. Amen.

heavenly liturgy (34, 6): The Scripture says: Ten thousand waited on Him, and a thousand thousand served Him and cried: Holy, holy, holy, Lord of hosts, every creature is full of Thy glory (Dan. 7:10; Isa. 6:3; cf. Apoc. 5:9). And we guided by our conscience, gathered together in one place, cry to Him continually as with one voice that we become sharers in His great and glorious promises.

priesthood of Christ (61): We confess Thee, who alone canst give us these and more good things, by Jesus Christ the high priest and protector of our souls.

doxology: Through whom be glory and majesty, to Thee now forever and ever and for ages and ages. Amen.

Prayer of St. Polycarp (d. 156)

Heavenly high priest, Christ: Therefore for everything I praise Thee, I bless Thee, I glorify Thee through the eternal and celestial high priest, Jesus Christ, Thy beloved Son, through whom is glory to Thee with the Holy Spirit Himself, now and in future ages. Amen.

St. Justin (d. about 157)

Freedom in thanksgiving (*Apol.*, 67): The president . . . offers prayers and thanksgiving according to his ability.

object (*Dial.*, 41): Eucharist, the celebration of which our Lord Jesus Christ prescribed in remembrance of the suffering which He endured on behalf of those who are purified in soul from all iniquity, in order that we may at the same time thank God for having created the world, with all things therein, for the sake of men and for delivering us from the evil in which we were, and for overthrowing utterly principalities and powers by Him who suffered according to His will. He then speaks of those Gentiles, namely, us, who in every place offer sacrifices to Him, i.e., the bread of the Eucharist, affirming both that we glorify His name, and that you profane it. . . . Now it is evident that in this prophecy (Isa. 33:13–19) allusion is made to the bread which our Christ gave us to eat in remembrance of His being made flesh for the sake of His believers, for whom also He suffered; and the cup which He gave us to drink, in remembrance of His own blood with giving thanks.

Trinity (*Apol.*, 67): And for all things wherewith we are supplied, we bless the Maker of all things through His Son Jesus Christ and through the Holy Ghost.

Traditio Apostolica (about 220)

The anaphora of the *Traditio apostolica*, considered by many the original form of the Roman Canon, is one continuous thanksgiving prayer. There is found the introductory dialogue. The object of thanksgiving is creation and redemption.

The mediation of Christ in both, in creation and in redemption, is emphasized. Consecration takes place in the middle of the prayer which now shows distinctly Trinitarian structure. The mysteries of the life of Christ commemorated in the middle portion are the following: the incarnation, conception, crucifixion, death, and resurrection of Christ. The final doxology is Trinitarian.

TEXT AND STRUCTURE

Introduction: The Lord be with you; and all say: And with thy spirit. Lift up your hearts. We have them (lifted) unto the Lord. Let us give thanks to the Lord. It is meet and just.

thanks to the Father: We render thanks unto Thee, O God, through Thy beloved Son Jesus Christ, whom in these last times Thou didst send to us as Savior and Redeemer and the angel of Thy will; who is Thy inseparable Word, through whom Thou didst make all things and in whom Thou wast well pleased; whom Thou didst send from heaven into the Virgin's womb, and who, conceived within the womb, was made flesh and was demonstrated to be Thy Son, being born of the Holy Spirit and a virgin; who, fulfilling Thy will and preparing for Thee a holy people, stretched forth His hands as He suffered that He might release from suffering those who have believed in Thee; who when He was delivered to the voluntary passion, that He might abolish death and rend the bonds of the devil and tread down hell and enlighten the just and establish the ordinance and demonstrate the resurrection, taking bread, giving thanks to Thee, said: Take ye and eat: this is My body which is broken for you. Likewise also the chalice, saying: This is My blood, which is shed for you; when you do this, do it unto My commemoration. Mindful, therefore,

of His death and resurrection, we offer Thee bread and
the chalice, thanking Thee because Thou hast found us
worthy to stand before Thee and minister unto Thee. And
we beg that Thou send Thy Holy Spirit upon the oblation
of holy Church, gathering into one all the saints who partake
that they may be filled with the Holy Spirit unto the
strengthening of their faith in truth, that we may praise and
glorify Thee through Thy Son Jesus Christ, through whom
glory and honor be unto Thee, the Father and the Son with
the Holy Spirit in Thy holy Church now and world without
end. Amen.

THE LITURGY OF THE APOSTOLIC CONSTITUTIONS, VIII

The *Apostolic Constitutions* are a compilation by a Syrian
writer at the end of the fourth century. Although there is no
evidence that the liturgy described in Book VIII is the liturgy
of the apostolic age, there are found so many parallels between it and the writings of the early Fathers of the Church
that we must admit that it contains much liturgical matter of
the early Church.

The anaphora recorded in Book VIII has preserved better
than any other liturgy the structure of the Hallel: God is
glorified in His attributes. He is thanked for the work of creation, and for His providence in the history of the Exodus with
the enumeration of a long series of events.

The mystery of the Trinity is proclaimed in the introduction
(blessing), in the entire structure of the prayer, and in the
concluding doxology.

The mystery of the Incarnation occupies the central portion
with a series of events enumerated from the conception to the
ascension. Christ is introduced as mediator in creation, as
high priest in redemption.

The introduction of the angelic choirs within the prayer, the frequent doxologies with terms reminiscent of those found in the Apocalypse, indicate its influence and the character of the heavenly liturgy.

TEXT AND STRUCTURE

Introduction: The grace of Almighty God, and the love of our
 Lord Jesus Christ, and the fellowship of the Holy Ghost,
 be with you all.
 It is very meet and right before all things to sing a hymn
 to Thee.
attributes of the Father: Who art the true God
 who art before all things,
 from whom the whole family in heaven and earth is named,
 who only art unbegotten
 and without beginning
 and without a ruler and without a master,
 who standest in need of nothing,
 who art the bestower of everything that is good,
 who art beyond all cause and generation,
 who art always and immutably the same,
 from whom all kings came into being, as from their proper
  original,
 Thou art eternal knowledge, everlasting sight,
 unbegotten hearing, untaught wisdom,
 the first by nature,
 the measure of being,
 beyond all number,
 who didst bring all things out of nothing into being
mediation of the Son: by Thy only-begotten Son,
 but didst beget Him before all ages by Thy will, Thy power,
 and Thy goodness without any instrument;

the only-begotten Son,
God the Word,
the living wisdom,
the first-born of every creature,
the angel of good counsel,
Thy high priest,
the King and Lord of every intellectual and sensible crea-
    ture,
who was before all things,
creation: by whom were all things,
    for Thou, O eternal God, didst make all things by Him,
    and through Him it is that Thou vouchsafest Thy suitable
providence: providence over the whole world.
Exodus: Thou didst divide the sea and bring the Israelites
        through,
    didst drown and destroy the Egyptians.
Thou didst sweeten the bitter water with wood;
Thou didst bring water out of the rock of stone;
Thou didst rain manna from heaven;
Thou didst afford them a pillar of fire;
Thou didst declare Josue to be the general of the army;
Thou didst divide Jordan and dry up the rivers of Etham;
Thou didst overthrow walls without instruments:
    for all these things, glory be to Thee, O God Almighty.
angelic choirs: Thee do the innumerable hosts of angels, arch-
        angels, thrones, dominions, principalities, authorities,
        and powers,
Thy everlasting armies, adore.
The cherubim and the six-winged seraphim
together with thousand thousands of archangels and ten
        thousand times ten thousand of angels,
incessantly, and with constant and loud voices,

and let all the people say it with them: Holy . . .
Trinity: For thou art truly holy, and most holy, the highest
and most highly exalted forever.
Holy also is Thy only-begotten Son our Lord,
who in all things ministered to His God and Father,
both in Thy various creation
and Thy suitable providence
has not overlooked lost mankind.
Incarnation: He was pleased by Thy good will to become man,
to be a sacrifice,
who was a high priest.
He appeased Thee,
He was made in the womb of a virgin.
He manifested His name to those that knew it not.
He was delivered to Pilate.
He arose from the dead.
He was taken up into heaven, and is sat down on the right.
Consecration: Being mindful, therefore, of those things that
He endured for our sake, we give Thee thanks, O God
Almighty, not in such manner as we ought, but as we are
able and fulfill His constitution. For in the same
night . . .
anamnesis: Being mindful, therefore . . .
we offer to Thee, our King and our God,
giving thanks through Him, that Thou hast thought us
worthy to stand before Thee, and to sacrifice to Thee.
epiklesis: And we beseech Thee that Thou wilt mercifully
look down upon these gifts, and do Thou accept them
to the honor of Thy Christ and send down upon this
sacrifice Thy Holy Spirit
that He may show this bread to be the body of Thy
Christ . . .

partakers may be filled with the Holy Ghost

may be made worthy of Thy Christ, may obtain eternal life.

intercession: We further pray unto Thee, O Lord, for Thy
holy Church,

for the holy presbytery,

for the king and all authority,

for all those holy persons who have pleased Thee from the
beginning of the world . . .

Thou wilt keep us all in piety and gather together in the
kingdom of Thy Christ.

doxology: For to Thee belong all glory and worship and
thanksgiving, honor, and adoration,

the Father, with the Son and to the Holy Ghost. . . .

THE LITURGY OF ST. JAMES

The liturgy of St. James, called after St. James the "brother
of the Lord" and first bishop of Jerusalem, follows the main
lines of the liturgy of the *Apostolic Constitutions*. It existed
already in the fourth century, but received some added details later. It was finally compiled during the second half of
the fifth century, after being completely developed in Jerusalem. It is the second source of early liturgies next to the
Apostolic Constitutions.

In this liturgy are found the same reminiscences of the
Hallel: the introduction to the thanksgiving. God is praised
in His attributes; He is thanked for the works of creation,
providence, and redemption. There is again remembered a
long series of events of the Exodus.

The Blessed Trinity is mentioned in the introduction, in
the Sanctus, in the entire structure of the anaphora, and in
the final doxology.

The mystery of the Incarnation is presented in the middle,

with the events of redemption in chronological order after the history of creation, and Christ is praised as mediator in creation and redemption.

The character of the heavenly liturgy is expressed with the Sanctus.

TEXT AND STRUCTURE

Introduction: The love of the Lord and Father,
   the grace of the Lord and Son,
   and the fellowship and the gift of the Holy Spirit be with you all.
   It is becoming and right . . . to praise Thee, to sing to Thee, to bless Thee, to worship Thee, to glorify Thee, to give Thee thanks. . . .
attributes: Maker of every creature visible and invisible,
   treasure of eternal good things,
   fountain of life and immortality,
   God and Lord of all;
Sanctus: whom the heavens of heaven praise and all the hosts of them,
   the sun and the moon and all the choirs of the stars . . .
   Jerusalem, the heavenly assembly and church of the first-born that are written in heaven . . .
   angels, archangels, thrones, dominions, principalities, authorities, dread powers,
   and the many-eyed cherubim, and the six-winged seraphim,
   with a loud voice singing the victorious hymn of Thy majestic glory
   crying aloud, praising, shouting, and saying: Holy . . .
Trinity: Holy to the Father . . .
   holy also Thy only-begotten Son . . .
   holy also Thy Holy Spirit.

attributes: Holy art Thou almighty, all-powerful,

creation: who didst make man from earth after Thine own
image . . .

redemption: afterwards didst send forth Thine only-begotten
Son Himself.

epiklesis: Have mercy on us, O God, according to Thy great
mercy and send forth on us, and on these offered gifts,
Thy all-holy Spirit.

The sovereign and quickening Spirit

He may sanctify this bread and this cup

that they may be to all that partake of them for remission of
sins, etc.

The Byzantine Liturgy

Derived from the liturgy of St. James, it is the most im-
portant of all the present Eastern liturgies. It is the rite of the
Orthodox Church and is the most widely spread among the
Catholic liturgies after the Roman liturgy.

The introduction is identical with the one in the *Apostolic
Constitutions*. God is praised in a series of attributes. Thanks
are given for the work of creation and redemption. The works
of providence in the history of the Hebrews are eliminated.

The mystery of the Blessed Trinity is presented in the introduction, in the act of thanksgiving, in the Sanctus, in the
concluding doxology, and in the entire structure of the anaphora.

Cherubikon and Sanctus express its character as a heavenly
liturgy.

Introduction: It is meet and right to worship the consubstantial and undivided Trinity, the Father, the Son, and the
Holy Ghost . . .

thanksgiving: to sing to Thee, to bless Thee, to praise Thee,
    to give thanks to Thee, to worship Thee . . .
attributes: for Thou art God,
  unspeakable, unsearchable, unseen, beyond our under-
    standing, eternally the same.
creation: Thou didst bring us from nothing into being,
redemption: Thou didst raise us when we had fallen,
    Thou didst leave nothing undone to bring us to heaven and
    to Thy kingdom which is to come.
Trinity: We give thanks to Thee
    and to the only-begotten Son
    and to the Holy Spirit,
Sanctus: while there stand about the legions of archan-
    gels . . .
  we too with all those blessed hosts cry out and say: Sanctus.
consecration: (surrounded by anamnesis of the mysteries of
    the life of Christ)
epiklesis: We pray and beseech and implore Thee to send
    down Thy Holy Spirit upon us and upon these gifts.
doxology: To Thee do we give glory and thanks and worship
    Father, Son, and Holy Ghost,
  now and forever, world without end.

CHAPTER X

The Roman Preface

THE Roman Preface appears upon the broad historical background of the Old Testament hymns, of the ancient and Eastern liturgies, as the clear crystallization of the essential, traditional ideas. Brevity and conciseness, simplicity and realistic spirit, systematic structure and architechtonic symmetry are its proper qualities as a work of the Latin genius. Most of the long series of motives of thanksgiving are eliminated and reduced to brief, representative formulas. Of all the motives of thanksgiving from creation, from providence, from redemption, the common preface has left the simple formula: *"semper et ubique gratias agere."* The particular motives, however, are not completely suppressed. Although eliminated from the sacrificial Canon, the motives from creation and from providence in the history of the Old Testament, are preserved in the most solemn sacramentals of the liturgical year, composed in the form of anaphoras. They are retained in the Proper of Holy Saturday, in the *Exultet,* in the *Benedictio fontis.* As a result of both, of the tendency for brevity and of the development of the historical aspect of the work of redemption in the liturgical year, the motives from redemption are distributed upon the feasts of the year. This is the marked distinction of the Roman liturgy. It is a system of great dimensions and wide perspectives.

The Roman Preface has likewise preserved the brightness

and brilliance of the spirit of the heavenly liturgy of the ancient Christian anaphora. Sanctus and Benedictus with the jubilation of the angelic choirs resound daily and throughout the year in the Roman Preface, delicately differentiated appropriate to the liturgical season. Considered synoptically there appears in all the variants of the annual cycle that which is founded on specific ideas in the glory of Eastern liturgies.

The analysis of the Roman Preface, considered in the variants of the present Roman Missal, can follow the clearly distinguishable parts: Introduction (dialogue), the object to which thanks are rendered (the attributes of God), act of thanksgiving, the priesthood of Christ, the motives of thanksgiving (object for which thanks are given), the ministry of the angels, Sanctus, Benedictus.

The Dialogue

The dialogue between priest and congregation, this introduction of the Preface, this preface to the Preface [1] is an amplified form of the "Let us sing to the Lord" of the canticle of Moses, of the "Praise, ye servants, the Lord" of the Hallel, of the "Give praise to our God, all His servants" of the Apocalypse.

In the amplified form of a dialogue, the invitation to thanksgiving is found first in the Canon of the *Traditio apostolica* of St. Hippolytus, in the anaphora of the *Apostolic Constitutions*. St. Cyprian knew it, and St. Cyril of Jerusalem [2] refers to it.

The "The Lord be with you" takes the place of the blessing

[1] St. Cyprian, *De Dominica oratione*, chap. 31 (*PL*, 4, 557): "When we rise to pray, we must be careful to give our attention wholeheartedly to the prayers we say. Every thought of the world or of earthly things must retire into the background, so that the soul may contemplate nothing but the content of the prayers. Therefore the priest recites a foreword before the prayer, preparing the hearts of the brethren, by saying: Sursum corda, etc."

[2] *Cat. myst.*, V, 4–5 (*PG*, 33, 1072).

mentioned in *Apostolic Constitutions* (8, 12), found universally in the Eastern liturgies: "The grace of Almighty God, and
the love of our Lord Jesus Christ, and the fellowship of the
Holy Ghost, be with you all."

"Lift up your hearts" is probably taken from Jeremias (Lam.
3:41): "Let us lift up our hearts with our hands to the Lord
in the heavens." An equivalent idea is expressed by the prophet
in verse 25 of the same chapter: "The Lord is good to them
that hope in Him, to the soul that seeketh Him." St. Cyprian
interprets the *"Sursum corda"* (in the passage cited above),
by saying it should remind the faithful that they should think
of nothing but God. St. John Chrysostom [3] says: "In that hour
thou shalt not know how to have any business; thou shalt not
think to be still upon this earth. A person must be of stone,
who at that hour believes he is still on earth and does not rather
believe he is singing with the choir of angels. With them thou
hast sent up to God the mystical song, with them thou hast
offered to God the triumphant hymn." St. Thomas [4] explains
that higher attention and more profound devotion than at any
other sacred rite is required, because the Eucharistic sacrament is the most excellent sacrament; it is offered by the priest
in communion with the faithful, it is further offered for all.

"Let us give thanks to the Lord our God." This invitation
for thanksgiving is at the same time a formulation and declaration of the intention. To make this intention clearly understood, distinctly resolved, the priest called for attention in
the "Lift up your hearts."

"It is meet and just." These words echo the introduction of
the Hallel by the head of the paschal table: "Therefore it is
our duty to thank, praise, laud, extol, magnify," etc. (cf. Apoc.

[3] *Hom. 24 in II Cor.*
[4] *Summa theol.,* IIIa., q. 83, a. 4 ad 5.

4:11; 5:9, 12). The multiplication of terms indicates the solemnity of the act, the majesty of God to whom thanks are rendered, the infinite dignity of the Eucharistic thanksgiving. It is an act according to the dignity of God, and most becoming and dignifying for men. It refers to the high obligation to be fulfilled and to the sacred object of thanksgiving. The terms are almost synonyms except the last, which refers to grace and heavenly blessings that men derive from the Eucharistic sacrifice, as the result of the thanksgiving.

The Act of Thanksgiving

The act of thanksgiving is specified with several verbs, with appositions about place and time, with the object to whom thanks are offered, and with the object for which thanks are given.

A review of the different prefaces shows the following verbs as substitutes for "giving thanks": "to sing a hymn of glory" (Nativity, Epiphany, Easter, Ascension, Apostles, Requiem, Sacred Heart, Christ the King); "to praise, to adore, to exult and celebrate, to confess suppliantly" (Lent, Holy Cross): "to exult with profusion of joy" (Pentecost); "to confess, to adore, to praise" (Trinity).

The Common Preface has summarized and concentrated all objects for which thanks are offered in the phrase "*Semper et ubique.*" It is the idea of the Hallel (Ps. 112:2 f.): "Blessed be the name of the Lord; from henceforth now and forever. From the rising of the sun unto the going down of the same." The same idea is repeated in the prophecy of Malachias (1: 11): "For from the rising of the sun even to the going down, My name is great among the Gentiles: and in every place there is sacrifice and there is offered to My name a clean oblation." St. Paul took up this idea in a phrase which is the

immediate source of the words of the Preface (Eph. 5:20):
"Giving thanks always for all things, in the name of our Lord
Jesus Christ, to God the Father."

God and His Attributes

The thanksgiving is addressed to "the holy Lord, the omnip-
otent Father, the eternal God." The Roman Preface is a confession of faith in the mystery of the Blessed Trinity. The
entire Roman Canon is a great doxology that is addressed
to the Trinity. The terms with which God is invoked, the
structure of the Canon, and the final doxology prove this
statement. In the first invocation the term "Holy Lord" is
immediately specified with the personal term "Father Almighty." The mediation of Christ is explained as one of a
divine person: "through Christ our Lord." The first invocation after the Sanctus addresses God as "the most merciful
Father" through "Jesus Christ Thy Son our Lord." The last
invocation before the Consecration concludes with entreating
words: "that it may become for us the body and blood of Thy
most beloved Son, our Lord Jesus Christ." Both, Father and
Son, are mentioned in the *Unde memores,* in the *Supplices te
rogamus.* In the many clauses of the prayers the mediatorship
of Christ is expressed as that of a divine person, "through
Christ our Lord." The structure of the Canon, in analogy to
the structure of the ancient and Eastern anaphoras, is Trinitarian: there are prayers of thanksgiving and invocations before the Consecration, invocations and thanksgiving after the
Consecration. The Consecration itself with the narrative of
institution, constitutes a third group of prayers. Most explicitly, however, the Eucharistic prayer is designated as the
worship of the Blessed Trinity through the final doxology.
What is in the course of the preceding prayers presented in a

logical and theological progress from the Father, through the Son, in the Holy Spirit, or to the Father through the Son, in the Holy Spirit, is in the final doxology summarized: "Through Him and with Him and in Him, is to Thee, God the Father Almighty, in the union of the Holy Ghost, all honor and glory." The Canon is one prayer; the final doxology refers to the entire Eucharistic canticle.

There is, however, a difference between the Roman way of professing and proclaiming the mystery of the Blessed Trinity within the Eucharistic canticle, and the method of the Eastern liturgies. The Byzantine liturgy declares in the dialogue: "It is meet and just to worship the consubstantial and undivided Trinity, the Father, the Son, and the Holy Ghost." It says again within the anaphora: "We give thanks to Thee and to Thy only-begotten Son and to Thy Holy Spirit." In the Sanctus: "Holy and all-holy art Thou with thine only-begotten Son and the Holy Ghost."

The Trinitarian formula of the Roman Preface and of the entire Roman Canon is not "to the Father and to the Son and to the Holy Ghost" as in the Eastern anaphoras, but "to the Father, through the Son, in the Holy Ghost." The use of this formula within the Eucharistic prayer was sanctioned at the Third Council of Carthage (997) [5] with canon 23: "In the prayers no one should mention the Father instead of the Son, or the Son instead of the Father. And in the service at the altar, the prayer has to be addressed to the Father." Several reasons may have prompted this regulation. It is certainly a result of the Trinitarian disputes of the fourth century. On the other hand, the Roman liturgy retains an ancient tradition. In close adherence to the example of our Lord, who addressed His thanksgiving to His Father, the *Didache* and the *Traditio*

[5] *PL*, 56, 428.

apostolica directs the thanksgiving prayer exclusively to the Father. St. Thomas [6] adds this reason: "In the same order the thanksgiving has to ascend to God, in which the graces descend to us from God, namely, 'through Jesus Christ.' " In this formula it appears that the order of divine processions is reflected in the Eucharistic mystery. The order in which the divine persons are referred to in the mystery of the Incarnation has its analogy in the act of Consecration. It is finally the emphasis on the high priesthood of Christ when the Eucharistic prayer is exclusively directed to the Father through Christ. The Preface of the Trinity follows the same pattern: "to give thanks to Thee, holy Lord, Father Almighty, eternal God, who with Thy only-begotten Son and the Holy Ghost," etc. The only exception is the Preface of Apostles, which is addressed to Christ, not in the form of a thanksgiving, but as a petition for the protection of His representatives on earth by Him as Supreme Shepherd.

The attributes of God mentioned in the Roman Preface are holiness (holy Lord), omnipotence (almighty Father), eternity (eternal God). Throughout the rest of the Canon are mentioned: mercy (therefore most merciful Father), omnipotence (We humbly beseech Thee, almighty God). In the three terms of the Preface is contained an allusion to the Trinity of the divine persons. The first attribute is holiness: the Eucharistic hymn is an act of religion, an act of profession of the absolute holiness of God. In the sacerdotal prayer our Lord turned to His Father with the words (John 17:11): "Holy Father, keep them in Thy name whom Thou hast given Me." Now, the Canon is modeled after the sacerdotal prayer of Christ. The second term, omnipotence, is used twice in the course of the Eucharistic prayer. It is the attribute mentioned

[6] *In Ep. ad Rom.*, c. 1, lect. 5.

in the first place in the canticle of Moses and in the Hallel. Eucharistic consecration is an act of the divine power. Eternity is *per appropriationem* an attribute proper to the First Divine Person, who is without origin, not proceeding from another person. It intensifies the concept "Father," to whom the Eucharistic canticle is directed.

CHAPTER XI

The Priesthood of Christ

THE intention of the Church with the words of the Preface, "through Christ our Lord," is this: through Christ the heavenly High Priest the Eucharistic sacrifice is offered to God the Father. The Eucharistic hymn is Christ's hymn of glory with which the divine Word glorifies the eternal Father. It is the truth which the Council of Trent has pronounced with the statement: "The victim is one and the same, the same now offering by the ministry of priests who then offered Himself on the cross." [1]

Christ offering as the heavenly High Priest in the Eucharistic sacrifice, is foretold in the Hallel (Ps. 115: 13, 17, 19): "I will take the chalice of salvation"; "I will sacrifice to Thee the sacrifice of praise"; "in the courts of the house of the Lord, in the midst of thee, O Jerusalem." Our Savior at the Last Supper spoke of the exercise of His high priesthood in heaven (Matt. 26:25; Mark 14:25; Luke 22:16): "And I say to you, I will not drink from henceforth of this fruit of the vine, until the day when I shall drink it with you new in the kingdom of My Father." After the resurrection, in the state of glory, Christ, the principal priest, celebrates the Eucharist in the kingdom of the Father.

The words "through Christ our Lord" are filled with the spirit of St. Paul. Christ the heavenly High Priest is St. Paul's

[1] Denzinger, no. 940.

favorite idea (Rom. 5:1 f.): "Let us have peace with God, through our Lord Jesus Christ: by whom also we have access through faith into this grace wherein we stand: and glory in the hope of the glory of the sons of God." Rom. 5:11: "We glory in God, through our Lord Jesus Christ." Heb. 7:24 f.: "He, because He continues forever, has an everlasting priesthood. Therefore He is able at all times to save those who come to God through Him." St. Paul emphasizes the heavenly high priesthood of Christ so much that it seems as if Christ became High Priest only with His glorification (Heb. 5:5): "So Christ also did not glorify Himself, that He might be made a high priest." Heb. 7:26: "For it was fitting that we should have such a high priest, holy, innocent, undefiled, separated from sinners, and made higher than the heavens." Heb. 9:11 ff.: "But Christ, being come a high priest of the good things to come, by a greater and more perfect tabernacle . . . entered once into the holies, having obtained eternal redemption."

This emphasis on the heavenly high priesthood of Christ in the Epistles of St. Paul, contained in the term of the Preface "through Christ our Lord," which is repeated seven times in the course of the Canon (three times before the Consecration, four times after the Consecration, the seventh time in the most solemn way in the final doxology, introduced with the "per quem haec omnia"), has its reasons. There are two stages to be distinguished in the priesthood of Christ: the one reflects the priesthood of Aaron, the other the priesthood of Melchisedech in two respects: with reference to the external state; with reference to the priestly functions.[2]

1. Christ on earth was (a) a priest in a mortal body, subject to a passion and death and as such similar to the priests of the

[2] Cf. J. M. Scheeben, *Handbuch der kathol. Dogmatik* (Freiburg i. B.), III, 429 ff.

order of Aaron, although offering in the "eternal spirit" (Heb.
9:14), and having the divine power of eternal life, but hidden
within; (b) Christ on earth functioned as a lay offerer, hand-
ing over to the priest the victim to be offered, although He
acted at the same time as the receiving priest offering the gift
of mankind; (c) lastly He functioned on earth like the priests
of the order of Aaron, offering a bloody sacrifice and seeking
reconciliation, although at the same time He was finding and
giving peace. In all these functions Christ appears as an
earthly priest, although He was in fact acting as heavenly
High Priest, heavenly by His origin from the Father, by His
dignity at the right hand of the Father where He enjoyed in
spirit the glory of the Son of God.

2. Only in heaven does Christ appear externally in His
specific glory and power; only in heaven and from heaven He
exercises the lasting functions of His priestly power: until
the end of time He functions as principal priest of the Eucharistic sacrifice.

The truth of the statement that Christ is the principal priest
in the oblation of the Eucharistic sacrifice seems to require
that Christ not only virtually (through the actual oblation at
the Last Supper, actual once and for all) consecrates in all the
Eucharistic sacrifices (an opinion defended by M. de la
Taille), but that Christ with a special act of the will concur
in every consecration (actually).

Various Motives for Thanksgiving

Great is the pageant of motives for thanksgiving listed in
the canticle of Moses, in the Hallel, and in the ancient and
Eastern liturgies. The Israelites gave thanks for the great
works of God in the Exodus, for the passage through the Red
Sea, the drowning of the Pharao and his hosts, for the guid-

ance through the desert, for the victory over the enemy re-
sisting their entrance to the Promised Land, its final
occupation. The same motives are remembered in the Hallel,
together with the motives from creation and with many other
motives from divine providence, and all are figures and types
of redemption.

In the *Didache* thanks are given for creation, for food and
drink, for spiritual food and drink and life eternal; for the
holy vine of David, for life and knowledge "which Thou
madest known to us through Jesus Thy servant." The Epistle
of St. Clement gives thanks for all things: "Since we have all
these things from Him, we must give thanks for all things to
Him." Then there are enumerated the various benefits of God
in nature, by creation, and in the order of grace. St. Justin
gives thanks "for all things wherewith we are supplied, we
bless the Maker of all." He mentions particularly the benefits
of creation and redemption: "The Eucharist, the celebration
of which our Lord Jesus Christ prescribed . . . in order that
we may thank God for having created the world, with all
things therein, for the sake of men and for delivering us from
the evil in which we were, and for overthrowing utterly principalities and powers." The *Traditio apostolica* gives thanks
"unto God through Christ through whom Thou didst make all
things and whom Thou didst send . . . that He might release from suffering those who have believed in Thee." The
liturgy of the *Apostolic Constitutions* thanks for creation, for
the acts of providence, for grace. The Byzantine liturgy has
condensed all motives to the brief formula: "Thou didst bring
us from nothing into being, Thou didst raise us when we had
fallen; and Thou didst leave nothing undone to bring us to
heaven and to Thy kingdom which is to come."

In the Leonine Sacramentary there are found 267 prefaces

with a variety of motives of historical interest, sometimes with almost personal allusions. In the Gelasian Sacramentary the number of prefaces is reduced to the common preface and 53 proper prefaces. The Gregorian Sacramentary has the number further restricted to 10, all of them found in the present Roman Missal, with the addition of five, added since the time of the Gregorian Sacramentary: the preface of the feast of the Blessed Virgin, added by Urban II (1088–99); the prefaces of St. Joseph, of the Requiem Mass, of the Sacred Heart, and of Christ the King, all of them added in recent times. We limit our study to those found in the present Missal and explain the variants in connection with the corresponding insertions in the *Communicantes* and in the *Hanc igitur*.

The elimination of the motives from creation and from providence in the Old Testament and the restriction of the motives to those from redemption may have several reasons; it was when the Gregorian Sacramentary took shape that the Canon remained definitely "the unchangeable rule." At the same time the number of prefaces was restricted to ten in order to prevent too many changes in that prayer so closely connected with the Canon; to give to the introduction of the Canon something of the dignity of an unchangeable rule. That the remaining motives were restricted to motives from redemption has its reason in the motive of our Lord in the institution of the Holy Eucharist: as the objective memorial of redemption. It is St. Justin who first speaks of the connection of the two lines of ideas: the Eucharist as a memorial, and the Eucharist as a thanksgiving. *Dial.*, 41: "Eucharist the celebration of which our Lord Jesus Christ prescribed in remembrance of the suffering which He endured on behalf of those who are purified in soul from all iniquity, in order that we may at the same time thank God for having created the world, with all things therein, for the sake of men and for delivering us from the evil in which we were, and for over-throwing utterly principalities and powers by Him who suffered according to His will." *Dial.*, 70: "Now it is evident that in this prophecy (allusion is made) to the bread which our Christ gave us to eat, in remembrance of His being made flesh for the sake of His believers, for whom also He suffered; and to the cup which He gave us to drink, in remembrance of His own blood, with giving of thanks."

In the thought of St. Justin the Eucharistic sacrifice is a memorial not only of the passion of our Lord, although in an excellent manner of the Passion, but of the mystery of the Incarnation generally: "in remembrance of His being made flesh for the sake of His believers, for whom also He suffered." Understanding the Eucharist as an objective memorial of the mystery of the Incarnation, it is consequently an objective memorial of all the mysteries of the life of Christ, all the motives of thanksgiving from redemption are remembered in an objective memorial. The variants of motives remembered in the course of the liturgical year in the various prefaces, are an unfolding of the contents of the Eucharistic objective memorial.

In connection with the special motives of the proper prefaces, there are differences regarding the mediation of Christ, variants in the *Communicantes* and in the *Hanc igitur*, according to which the proper prefaces can be distinguished into different groups. Seven prefaces do not mention the mediation of Christ (Trinity, Nativity, Epiphany, Easter, Sacred Heart, Christ the King, Apostles); seven mention the mediation partly before the special motive (Ascension, Pentecost,

Requiem), partly after the special motive (Lent, Holy Cross, Blessed Virgin, St. Joseph). Five prefaces have assigned an insertion in the *Communicantes* (Nativity, Epiphany, Easter, Ascension, Pentecost); three have assigned an insertion in the *Hanc igitur* (Holy Cross on Holy Thursday, Easter, Pentecost).

The mediation of Christ is omitted whenever it would cause confusion in connection with mysteries of the life of the Savior, as on Nativity, Epiphany, Easter, Sacred Heart, Christ the King. The mediation of Christ does not refer to these mysteries commemorated, but to the giving of thanks. The mediation of Christ is likewise omitted on the feast of the Blessed Trinity. The special motive on this feast refers to the object to whom the thanksgiving is offered: to the Father with the Son and the Holy Ghost. It would sound confusing to offer to the Son "through Jesus Christ" our Lord. On the feasts of the apostles the Preface is addressed to Christ as an invocation for His protection, and the same excludes the modifying phrase "through Christ our Lord." The insertions in the *Communicantes* emphasize the greatness of the mystery of our Lord commemorated: Nativity, Epiphany, Easter, Ascension, Pentecost. The variants of the *Hanc igitur* apply to the special intention with which the Eucharist is offered as a sacrifice of petition. The prayer *Hanc igitur* is understood as *Oratio post nomina,* the prayer after the recitation of the names of those for whom the sacrifice is offered: on Holy Thursday, in the *Communicantes* there is commemorated the mystery of the betrayal of our Lord, in the *Hanc igitur* the institution of the Eucharist itself is remembered. On Easter and Pentecost the Holy Sacrifice is especially offered for the neophytes, who are mentioned in the proper *Hanc igitur.*

NATIVITY

". . . eternal God. Since by the mystery of the Word made flesh a new ray of Thy glory has appeared to the eyes of our souls; that while we know God visibly, we may be drawn after Him to the love of things invisible. . . ." *Communicantes:* "celebrating the most holy day, on which the undefiled virginity of the blessed Mary has borne the Savior to this world." The proper part in this preface reveals the derivation of the feast of the Nativity from the feast of Epiphany with the words, "a new ray of Thy glory has appeared." Only the passage of the *Communicantes* refers specifically to the temporal birth of the Savior.

EPHIPHANY

". . . eternal God. Because when Thy only-begotten Son appeared in the substance of our mortal flesh, He restored us by the new light of His immortality." *Communicantes:* "celebrating the most holy day, on which Thy only-begotten, co-eternal with Thee in Thy glory, appeared visibly in a body which is truly of our flesh." More than any other proper preface it commemorates not merely a single event of the life of our Lord, but the entire mystery of the Incarnation with all its redemptive events. It indicates that the Eucharist is the objective memorial of the entire *Opus redemptionis.*

LENT

". . . eternal God, who by this bodily fast dost extinguish our vices, elevate the mind, and bestow on us virtue and its rewards: through Christ our Lord." In this preface the object of thanksgiving is redemption applied in effect.

Holy Cross

". . . eternal God, who hast ordained that the salvation of mankind should be wrought on the wood of the cross: that whence death came, thence life might arise; and that He who overcame by the tree, might also by the tree be overcome." *Communicantes* (on Holy Thursday): "celebrating the most holy day on which our Lord Jesus Christ was betrayed for us." *Hanc igitur:* "in memory of the day on which our Lord Jesus Christ delivered to His disciples for celebration the mysteries of His body and blood." It is the passion of our Lord on the cross in particular which is commemorated in the proper preface of Passiontide. On Holy Thursday the particular motive of the betrayal and the institution of Holy Eucharist is added, the one in the *Communicantes,* the other in the *Hanc igitur.*

Easter

"It is truly meet . . . to praise Thee, O Lord, at all times, but chiefly on this day when Christ our Passover was sacrificed for us. For He is the true Lamb who hath taken away the sins of the world. Who by dying has destroyed our death, and by rising again has restored us to life." *Communicantes:* "celebrating the most holy day of the resurrection of our Lord Jesus Christ in the flesh." *Hanc igitur:* "This oblation . . . which we offer also for those whom Thou hast deigned to regenerate by water and the Holy Ghost, granting them forgiveness of all sins." The immediate inspiration of the proper part of the Preface came from St. Paul (I Cor. 5:7): "For Christ our Pasch is sacrificed." This glorious word connects the Old Testament Pasch and its Hallel with that of the New

Testament and its Alleluja. The passage, "who by dying has destroyed our death, and by rising again has restored us to life," indicates that the New Testament Pasch is the objective memorial of both, of death and resurrection. The *Communicantes* singles out the particular mystery of the feast, Resurrection. In the *Hanc igitur* the special intention with which the Eucharist is celebrated as a sacrifice of petition applies to the neophytes.

THE ASCENSION

". . . through Christ our Lord. Who after His resurrection appeared openly to all His disciples, and in their presence ascended into heaven, to make us partakers of His divinity." *Communicantes:* "celebrating the most holy day on which our Lord Thy only-begotten Son placed at the right of Thy glory our frailty united to Him." The two articles of faith, "ascendeth into heaven" and "sitteth at the right hand," are distributed in the Preface and the *Communicantes,* which follow one another.

PENTECOST

". . . through Christ our Lord. Who ascending above all the heavens, and sitting at Thy right hand, did send down the promised Holy Spirit upon the children of adoption." *Communicantes:* "celebrating the most holy day of Pentecost, on which the Holy Ghost appeared to the apostles under the form of innumerable tongues." *Hanc igitur* (the same as on Easter). In the Preface it is the action of Christ sending down the promised Spirit; in the *Communicantes* it is the appearance of the Holy Ghost following the action of Christ in logical order.

TRINITY

The specifying motive of this Preface is not in the object for which thanks are offered, but in the object to whom thanks are rendered. This proper Preface implies, however, as the special motive for which thanks are given the revelation of the mystery of the Blessed Trinity. The act of thanksgiving is specified as: "we believe of Thy glory," act of faith, confession of faith: "in the confession of a true and eternal divinity"; act of adoration: "equality in the majesty be adored." This preface is the most solemn proclamation of the Trinitarian idea in the Eucharistic sacrifice. It is a summary of the treatise on the mystery of the Blessed Trinity, resembling in the terminology the *Symbolum Athanasianum*.

". . . eternal God. Who together with Thy only-begotten Son and the Holy Ghost, art one God and one Lord: not in a singularity of one Person, but in a trinity of one substance. For what we believe of Thy glory as Thou hast revealed, the same we believe of Thy Son, and of the Holy Ghost, without any difference or distinction. That in the confession of the true and eternal Deity may be adored a distinction in the Persons, a unity in the essence, and an equality in the majesty."

PREFACE OF THE BLESSED VIRGIN

". . . eternal God. And on the feast of Blessed Mary, ever Virgin, we should praise, bless, and glorify Thee. Who, by the overshadowing of the Holy Ghost, conceived Thy only-begotten Son; and, the glory of her virginity still remaining, brought forth the eternal light into the world, Jesus Christ our Lord. By whom," etc. It is again the mystery of the Incarnation which is thanked for. The mystery is considered in the active aspect of conception by the Blessed Virgin through the activity of the Holy Ghost.

PREFACE OF ST. JOSEPH

". . . eternal God. And that we should with due praise magnify and glorify Thee on the feast of blessed Joseph. Who, a righteous man, was given by Thee to be the spouse of the Virgin Mother of God: and as a faithful and prudent servant was appointed over Thy family: that with a father's care he should guard Thy only-begotten Son, who was conceived by the overshadowing of the Holy Ghost. Jesus Christ our Lord. Through whom," etc. This preface is composed in a manner analogous to the Preface of the Blessed Virgin and follows its ideas and relations to the mystery of the Incarnation. The special motive in both these prefaces follows immediately the invocation of the heavenly Father, and the mediation follows the special motive in a new sentence. The reason for this grammatical structure is the same as for the omission of the mediation of Christ in the prefaces commemorating the mysteries of the life of the Savior.

PREFACE OF THE APOSTLES

This is the only preface not addressed to the Father. It is not in the form of a thanksgiving, but in the form of a petition. In the wording of this petition appears clearly the influence of the high-priestly prayer (with the difference that the precae is addressed to Christ the eternal pastor): "It is truly meet and just, right and salutary, that we should suppliantly implore Thee, O Lord, that Thou, our eternal Shepherd, wouldst not forsake Thy flock; but that Thou shouldst, through Thy blessed apostles, keep it under continual protection, so that it may be governed by those whom Thou hast appointed its vicars and pastors." Cf. John 17:11 f.: "Holy Father, keep them in Thy name whom Thou hast given Me. . . . While I was with them, I kept them in Thy name. Those whom Thou gavest Me have I kept; and none of them is lost." John 17:15: "I pray not that Thou shouldst take them out of the world, but that Thou shouldst keep them from evil." We should note that this Preface is addressed to "the Lord, one eternal Shepherd."

PREFACE OF THE DEAD

The resurrection of Christ as efficient and exemplary cause of resurrection and immortality for which thanks are offered.

". . . through Christ our Lord. In whom the hope of a blessed resurrection is shown to us, that they who are saddened by the certain necessity of dying be comforted by the promise of eternal life to come. For the life of Thy faithful, O Lord, is changed, not taken away; and the abode of this earthly sojourn being dissolved, an eternal dwelling is prepared in heaven."

PREFACE OF THE SACRED HEART

The special motive of thanksgiving is the mystery of the opening of the Sacred Heart by the lance. John 19:34: "But one of the soldiers with a spear opened His side, and immediately there came out blood and water." This mystery is interpreted with an accommodation of Ps. 35:9: "And Thou shalt make them drink of the torrent of Thy pleasure," and with Matt. 11:28 f.: "Come to Me, all you that labor and are burdened, and I will refresh you . . . and you shall find rest to your souls."

". . . eternal God. Who didst will that Thy only-begotten Son hanging on the cross should be pierced by the soldier's lance, that the heart thus opened, the sanctuary of divine bounty, should pour out on us an abundance of mercy and grace; and, as it never ceases to burn with love of us, it may be for the devout a haven of rest, and for the penitent an everlasting refuge of salvation."

PREFACE OF CHRIST THE KING

The feast of Christ the King is somehow a duplicate of the feast of Epiphany. Whereas the feast of Epiphany is rightly considered the feast of the Oriental Church within the Roman liturgy, the feast of Christ the King is Roman by origin and character: it concludes at the end of the liturgical year the cycle of the feasts of our Lord. Its dominant idea is the establishment of the universal kingdom of Christ, who by the Incarnation was anointed and constituted eternal priest and universal king, who by His sacrifice on the cross has exercised the priesthood and has entered into the possession of this kingdom. The feast has some eschatological character, since the kingdom of Christ is to be consummated with the second coming. The anointing of Christ as high priest and king (Ps. 44:8) is alluded to: "God, thy God, hath anointed thee with the oil of gladness above thy fellows." The universality of the kingdom of Christ is expressed with seven terms: kingdom of truth, life, sanctity, grace, justice, love, peace.

". . . eternal God. Who hast anointed Thy Son, our Lord Jesus Christ, the eternal high priest and King of all things, with the oil of gladness; that offering Himself on the altar of the Cross as an immaculate host and peace offering, He might complete the mysteries of man's redemption."

CHAPTER XII

The Sanctus

THE last part of the Preface about the angelic choirs is the introduction to the Sanctus. The insertion of this passage of the Eucharistic prayer is in close connection with the insertion of the Sanctus. Both are, therefore, fittingly explained under one title.

A series of problems is connected with the introduction of the Sanctus. Its origin and the time of the actual insertion constitute a much disputed historical question. The exegetical analysis of its scriptural background is a study of great dimensions, extending from the Book of Exodus to the Apocalypse. The intention of the Church with the Sanctus as part of the Canon, based on these studies, implies a series of dogmatic truths.

ORIGIN

Two documents contain explicit statements about the introduction of the Sanctus into the Eucharistic prayer: the *Liber pontificalis* and the decrees of the Council of Vaison (529). The former ascribes the insertion of the Sanctus to Pope Sixtus I (115–25 ?): "This one has ordained that within the action (at that time the Preface was considered a part of the Canon) the priest should intone and the people should continue to sing the hymn: Sanctus, sanctus, sanctus," etc.[1] The

[1] *Liber pont.*, I, 128.

Council of Vaison [2] decreed that the Sanctus be sung not only on solemn feasts but at every Mass, even in Lent and at funerals. The authority of the *Liber pontificalis* is doubtful in the records of early date. The decree of the Council of Vaison concerns the extension of the liturgical use of the Sanctus, but not its original insertion in the Mass.

DIFFERENT OPINIONS

Dom Cagin,[3] Abbot Cabrol,[4] and Cardinal Schuster [5] accept the statement of the *Liber pontificalis* with some reservations, regarding the Sanctus not as an original part of the Canon, but as the first interpolation, inserted probably toward the middle of the second century by Pius I (140–54). The chief reason for the opinion of these scholars is the absence of the Sanctus from an important group of ancient liturgies: it is not found in the Canon of the *Traditio apostolica* by St. Hippolytus, in *Testamentum Domini*, in the Abyssinian *Anaphora of Our Lord*. Since the Canon of the *Traditio apostolica* is regarded by these authors as the common source of all liturgies, the Sanctus, which is missing there, they believe cannot be an original element. Abbot Cabrol says cautiously, that the Sanctus, at least originally, was not found in the present place. Cardinal Schuster thinks it was inserted by Pope Pius I.

Another school of liturgists is inclined to admit its apostolic origin. In the first place, the argument from the *Traditio apostolica*, etc., is not too strong. Throughout the first three centuries the text of the Eucharistic prayer was not definitely

[2] Hefele-Leclercq, *Histoire des conciles*, II, 1114 (can. 3).
[3] *Canon primitif de la messe, ou Formulaire essentiel et premier de toutes les liturgies* (Paris, 1906), p. 329.
[4] *Les origines liturgiques* (Paris, 1906), p. 329.
[5] *The Sacramentary* (London, 1924), I, 110.

determined. The *Didache* (chap. 14) says: "But let the prophets give thanks as much as they will." Likewise St. Justin declares (*I Apol.*, chap. 67): "The president sends up prayers and likewise thanksgiving, as far as he has the power." Consequently the evidence taken from some early liturgies would merely show that the Sanctus was not in universal liturgical use. Further, so far as the original Roman liturgy is concerned, we have no absolute evidence that the Canon of the *Traditio apostolica* is the original Roman Canon. Lastly, we find traces of the Sanctus in the *Testamentum Domini,* since the angels are mentioned there; probably even the Canon of the *Traditio apostolica* shows some allusion to the ministry of the angels with the expression *adstare coram te,* a phrase used in Scripture to designate the excellent ministry of the angels close to the throne of God.

The Sanctus is found in all the rest of ancient and Eastern liturgies, and the early Fathers testify to its liturgical use. The most important document is a passage in the first Epistle of St. Clement to the Corinthians (96–98). On the basis of these testimonies and of the fact that the Sanctus (in the form as it is found in the earlier liturgies, without the Benedictus) is used in the present practice of the synagogue (in the morning service for Sabbaths, and in the Hallel), some authors conclude that it is a heritage from the Old Testament liturgy of the Passover.

Against the argument from the Epistle of St. Clement and from the liturgy of the synagogue, A. Fortescue [6] and B. Botte [7] and others object: A. Fortescue reminds us "that these comparisons are with later Jewish forms. It is quite likely that

[6] *The Mass; a Study of the Roman Liturgy* (New York, 1922), p. 72.
[7] *Le Canon de la messe romaine.* Louvain, 1935.

much of the Passover ritual [8] that we know from these later documents existed already in the time of our Lord; but we should remember that there is an element of uncertainty." Against the authority of the Epistle of St. Clement it is objected that its quotation of the Sanctus does not prove that the Sanctus was part of the liturgy. It reflects merely the general attitude in prayer of the early Christians.[9]

The following review of ancient and Eastern liturgies, and of texts of the early Fathers will show that the Sanctus is certainly of ancient origin. The critical study of the passage of the Epistle of St. Clement, the comparison of it with the text in the different liturgies, and with the liturgy of the Apocalypse, all will show that it is a liturgical text, that consequently the Sanctus as a part of the liturgy has its origin in the apostolic age.

TESTIMONY OF THE LITURGIES

"Heavenly liturgy" is the most adequate term we have for describing the character of the Eastern liturgies. This liturgy is enacted in the kingdom of heaven, in the temple of heaven, upon the heavenly altar, before the God of glory, celebrated through Christ, the heavenly High Priest glorified. The sacred action is developed as an approach of man to God, as an entering into the sanctuary of heaven, as a standing before the heavenly altar, as an ascending into the glory of God. On the other hand, the Eastern liturgy interprets Consecration

[8] A. Baumstark, "Trishagion und Geduscha," *Jb. L. W.*, III (1923), 18–32. Cf. W. O. E. Oesterley, *Jewish Background of the Christian Liturgy* (Oxford 1925), pp. 144–47; Ismar Elbogen, *Der jued. Gottesdienst*, Leipzig, 1913.

[9] Gregoir, "Le Sanctus et l'Agnus Dei" in *Courses et conférences des semaines liturgiques*, XII (1929), 161–75.

and Communion as a manifestation of the glory of God, as a theophany.

In this ideology of the Eastern liturgy the choirs of angels, the angelic ministry, and the seraphic hymn of the Sanctus have their important place. The vision of Isaias (chap. 6) with the seraphim and the Sanctus has inspired the concept of the Eastern liturgy to such an extent that the consecrated host is called "anthrax," i.e., live coal, and the Holy Communion is understood as antitype of the scene of Isaias (6: 6 f.): "And one of the seraphim flew to me, and in his hand was a live coal, which he had taken with the tongs off the altar. And he touched my mouth, and said: Behold this hath touched thy lips, and thy iniquities shall be taken away, and thy sins shall be cleansed."

In the *Apostolic Constitutions* (chap. 8) the angels are twice mentioned: first, at the beginning as the first creatures, again much later, probably in connection with Isaias in the list of benefits of divine providence: "For all these things, glory be to Thee, O Lord Almighty. Thee do the innumerable hosts of angels, archangels, thrones, dominations, principalities, authorities, and powers, Thy everlasting armies, adore. The cherubim and the six-winged seraphim, with two covering their feet, with two their heads, and with two flying, say together with thousand thousands of archangels and ten thousand times ten thousands of angels, incessantly, and with continual and loud voices, and let all the people say it with them: Holy," etc.

The fragment of Deir-Balizeh has also the Sanctus. Only some words about the seraphim are preserved. It adds, "the heaven is full of Thy glory." [10]

[10] Cf. Didymus, *De Trinitate; PG,* 39, 364; St. Cyril of Alex., *De fide ad Theodosium; PG,* 76, 1133.

The anaphora of Serapion has the angelic choirs with the Sanctus: "Thee assist thousands of thousands and ten thousands of ten thousands of angels, archangels, thrones, dominations, principalities, powers. Thee assist two most honored seraphim with six wings, with two covering their face, with two covering the feet, with two flying and sanctifying. Accept with them also our sanctifying by saying: Holy, holy, holy, Lord of hosts. Heaven and earth are full of Thy glory. Full is heaven, full is the earth of Thy magnificent glory, Lord of glories. Fill likewise this sacrifice with Thy glory and Thy communication."

In the liturgy of St. James the angelic choirs are introduced twice: the first time in the so-called *Cherubikon* with the singing of Alleluja at the prayer of incense at the beginning of the liturgy of the faithful; the second time with the Sanctus in the anaphora.

Cherubikon: "Let all mortal flesh be silent, and stand with fear and trembling, and meditate nothing earthly within yourself: for the King of kings and Lord of lords, Christ our God, comes forward to be sacrificed and to be given for food to the faithful; and thousands of angels go before Him with every power and dominion, the many-eyed cherubim, and the six-winged seraphim, covering their faces, and crying aloud the hymn, Alleluja, alleluja, alleluja."

Anaphora: "Whom the heavens of heavens praise, and all the host of them. Jerusalem the heavenly assembly and Church of the first-born that are written in heaven . . . angels, archangels, thrones, dominations, principalities, and authorities, and dread powers and the many-eyed cherubim and the six-winged seraphim . . . with loud voice singing the victorious hymn of Thy majestic glory, crying aloud, praising, shouting, and saying: Holy," etc.

The liturgy of St. James uses the term "live coal" in the prayer of incense and in the prayer for Holy Communion: "Sovereign Lord Jesus Christ . . . who didst freely offer Thyself a blameless sacrifice . . . the coal of double nature, that didst touch the lips of the prophet." "The Lord will bless us, and make us worthy with the pure touching of our fingers to take the live coal."

The Cherubikon of the Byzantine liturgy: "We who mystically represent the cherubim and join with them in singing the thrice holy hymn to the lifegiving Trinity, let us lay aside all the cares of this life . . . for we are now to receive the King of all, who comes escorted by unseen hosts of angels, Alleluja, alleluja, alleluja." The Sanctus: "We give thanks also for that Thou art pleased to accept this service from our hands, while there stand about Thee legions of archangels and myriads of angels, cherubim and seraphim, six-winged and many-eyed, who, borne aloft upon their wings, sing, cry out, and shout the triumphal song, saying: Holy," etc. "We too with all those lesser hosts, O Master, lover of men, cry out, saying: Holy," etc.

WITNESS OF THE FATHERS

According to an ancient and frequently expressed patristic tradition, the angels who participated in the work of redemption from beginning to end, are also present and take part in the celebration of the Eucharistic mysteries. They quote the Sanctus as part of the liturgy.

Clement of Alexandria (d. 215): "The song is a hymn to the King of all things, the maidens sing psalms, the angels praise Him, the prophets teach. O truly holy mysteries!" [11] *Stromata:* "Ever give thanks to God, as do the creatures

[11] *Cohortatio ad Gentes; PG,* 8, 237–46.

(*animalia;* cf. Apoc.), who praise Him with hymns, of whom Isaias speaks in an allegory." [12]

Tertullian (d. 220): "Certainly it is right that God should be blessed by all men in every place and at all times for the due memory always of His benefits . . . to whom that court of angels does not cease to say, Holy, Holy, Holy. Wherefore we, fellows of the angels if we deserve to be, learn that heavenly voice toward God and the duty of future glory already here." [13]

Origen (d. 255) speaks of the liturgical Sanctus in his commentary on Isaias: "The coming of my Jesus is announced. Therefore is the whole earth now full of His glory." [14]

Novatian alludes to the Sanctus. After a list of benefits which are manifestly reminiscent of the *Apostolic Constitutions* (chap. 8), he says: "Hence He sits above the cherubim, and under His throne are the animals that have power above the others." [15]

St. Chrysostom: "The priest is himself at that solemn moment surrounded by angels, and the choir of the heavenly powers unite with him; they occupy the entire space around the altar, to honor Him who lies there as sacrificed." [16] He then describes a vision in which was seen a multitude of angels who, robed in dazzling white garments, with heads deeply bowed, surrounded the altar, as warriors standing in the presence of their king.

[12] *Stromata; PG,* 9, 512.
[13] *De oratione; PL,* 1, 1156.
[14] *In Isaiam hom.,* 1, 2; *PG,* 13, 222.
[15] *De Trinitate; PL,* 3, 899.
[16] *De sacerdotio,* VI, 4.

St. Clement of Rome: First Epistle to the Corinthians, chap. 34 (*cir.* 96–98)

"Let us consider the whole multitude of His angels, how they stand ever ready to minister His will. For the Scripture saith: Ten thousand times ten thousand stood around Him, and thousands of thousands ministered unto Him, and cried, Holy, holy, holy, the Lord of Sabaoth: the whole creation is full of His glory. And let us therefore, conscientiously gathering together in harmony, cry to Him earnestly, as with one mouth, that we may be made partakers of His great and glorious promises."

Some authors deny that this passage contains an allusion to the liturgical Sanctus and think that it shows merely the primitive Christian spirit, the close association of our way of praising God with the way of the angels. But a critical textual study of this passage confirms the view that it is an allusion to the Sanctus of the liturgy: first, because it contains an implicit quotation from St. Paul (I Cor. 11:18–20) about disturbances at the celebration of the Eucharist; secondly, because it alludes to the Apocalypse and the description of the angelic choirs common with the Apocalypse and all the liturgies.

St. Clement of Rome wrote his Epistle to the Corinthians to settle differences like those which occasioned St. Paul's First Epistle to the Corinthians. St. Paul wrote (I Cor. 11: 18–20, 33 f.): "For first of all I hear that when you come together in the church, there are schisms among you; and in part I believe it. . . . When you come therefore together into one place, it is not now to eat the Lord's supper. . . . Wherefore, my brethren, when you come together to eat, wait for one another . . . that you come not together unto judgment."

The words of St. Clement contain the same idea: "And let us therefore, conscientiously gathering together in harmony. . . ."

The combining of the choirs of angels as they are found in the different theophanies of the Old Testament is a feature common to the passage from the Epistle of St. Clement with all the liturgies and of both of them with the angelic choirs of the Apocalypse.

St. Clement combines the angels of the theophany of Daniel with the seraphim of Isaias.

I Cor., chap. 34	Dan. 7:10
Ten thousand times ten thousand stood around Him, and thousands of thousands ministered unto Him and cried Holy, holy, holy.	Thousands of thousands ministered to Him, and ten thousand times a hundred thousand stood before Him.

Isa. 6:3

And they cried one to another, and said: Holy, holy, holy, the Lord God of hosts, all the earth is full of His glory.

The *Apostolic Constitutions* (chap.8) combines the seraphim of Isaias with the cherubim of Ezechiel, with the hosts of Daniel, with the angelic choirs mentioned in the Epistles of St. Paul, and alludes to the angels of the Apocalypse: "For all these things, glory be to Thee, O Lord Almighty. Thee do the innumerable hosts of angels, archangels, thrones, dominations, principalities, authorities, and powers (Col. 1:16, Thine everlasting armies) adore. The cherubim and the six-winged seraphim, with two covering their feet, with two their heads . . .

(Isa. 6:3), together with thousand thousands of archangels, and ten thousand times ten thousand of angels (Dan. 7:10), incessantly, and with continual and loud voices (Apoc. 4:8, 19), and let all the people say it with them: Holy," etc.

The anaphora of Serapion combines the angels of Daniel and of Isaias with the choirs of St. Paul.

The liturgy of St. James has the cherubim of Ezechiel (*Cherubikon*) combined with the seraphim of Isaias and alludes to the bands of angels in St. Luke, to the choirs of St. Paul, and to the angelic hymn of the Apocalypse: "Christ our God comes forward to be sacrificed and to be given to the faithful; and bands of angels go before Him (Luke 2:13; Apoc. 19:10) with every power and domination (Col. 1:16), the many-eyed cherubim (Ezech. 10:12), and the six-winged seraphim (Isa. 6:2), crying aloud the hymn Alleluja, Alleluja, Alleluja (Apoc. 19:5)."

The vision of the Apocalypse presents the heavenly liturgy as a combining of the theophanies of the Old Testament, of Moses, of Isaias, Ezechiel, and Daniel. Likewise the angelic choirs of all of them minister at the throne of God seen in the Apocalypse. Sanctus and Alleluja are united just as in some of the Eastern liturgies. Such parallel texts (cf. below: The Liturgy of the Apocalypse as Theophany) are: seraphim (Isa. 6:1; Apoc. 4:2); Sanctus (Isa. 6:3; Apoc. 4:8); cherubim (Ezech. 10:1; Apoc. 4:6–8); thousands of angels (Dan. 7: 10; Apoc. 5:11).

The expression, "as with one mouth," seems to be a particular allusion to Apoc. 19:6: "And I heard as it were the voice of a great multitude, and as the voice of many waters, and as the voice of great thunders, saying Alleluja." The *Apostolic Constitutions* (chap. 8) uses the phrase, "with continual and loud voices."

These parallelisms permit us to conclude that there is a common idea and a common source to all these texts. These comparisons suggest that the passage from the Epistle of St. Clement about the angels and the Sanctus contains an allusion to the liturgical Sanctus; that all the liturgies with the passage from the Clementine Epistle are inspired by the same idea which unites all the angelic choirs in the Apocalypse. The Apocalypse has certainly inspired the development of the heavenly liturgy in the concept of the Eastern rites. The Sanctus of the Apocalypse may in itself even then reflect the liturgical practice of the apostolic age.

CHAPTER XIII

Scriptural Background

THE liturgical Sanctus with the introduction of the angelic choirs is in itself an exquisite mosaic of Scripture texts. The scriptural background of this glorious passage is a combination of the most beautiful revelations, of the grandest visions, of the most dramatic scenes from the Old and the New Testament. It is a painting with all the colors of heavenly glory, it is a texture of voices, of words, of tones of heaven and earth, it is a symphony of the human with the divine.

In the analysis of the scriptural background we present as an introduction the spirit of the psalms, and then explain the influence of ideas of St. Paul and of the Apocalypse. Through St. Paul and the Apocalypse the great visions of the Old Testament with the choirs of angels and heavenly hymns have contributed to the glory of our liturgy.

THE SPIRIT OF THE PSALMS

The idea of concelebration of men with angels, the close association of our way of praising God with the way of the angels, is an idea often met with in the psalms.

Psalm 102 is a beautiful psalm of thanksgiving to God for His mercies. It begins (vv. 1 f.): "Bless the Lord, O my soul; and let all that is within me bless His holy name. Bless the Lord, O my soul; and never forget all He hath done for thee." It concludes (vv. 20 f.): "Bless the Lord, all ye angels; you that are mighty in strength, and execute His words, hearkening to the voice of His orders. Bless the Lord, all ye His hosts; you ministers of His that do His will."

Ps. 137:1: "I will praise Thee, O Lord, with my whole heart: for Thou hast heard the words of my mouth. I will sing praise to Thee in the sight of the angels."

Psalm 148:1 f.: "Praise ye the Lord from the heavens; praise ye Him in the high places. Praise ye Him, all His angels; praise ye Him all His hosts."

Even Ps. 115:18 of the Hallel, if it is interpreted about the heavenly Jerusalem, would imply the angels, although they are not explicitly mentioned: "I will pay my vows to the Lord in the sight of all His people; in the courts of the house of the Lord, in the midst of thee, O Jerusalem."

IDEAS OF ST. PAUL

In the Common Preface, in the Preface of Lent, of the Holy Cross, of the Blessed Virgin, and of St. Joseph, the angelic choirs are introduced with the phrase: "through Christ our Lord, through whom the angels praise Thy majesty." With this phrase the idea is expressed that the angels join in the Eucharistic praise through Christ their head. This is an idea of St. Paul. The division of the angelic choirs in the various Prefaces is partly from St. Paul. The concept of the Eucharistic celebration as theophany, implied in the liturgical Sanctus, is likewise found in St. Paul.

CHRIST, HEAD OF THE ANGELS

The epistles to the Ephesians and to the Colossians contain the teaching of St. Paul about the primacy of Christ over the entire creation. They are a compendium of Christology; they represent St. Paul's most sublime writings relative to the person and dignity of Christ. Within this doctrine are found the chapters (Eph. 1:20; Col. 1:16–20) about Christ as head of the angels. The Church made use of these truths in the introduction of the angelic choirs in the Preface. It constitutes the particular application of the principle that Christ is the head of the angels, when the angels are believed to concelebrate with the Church on earth, to minister unto Christ in the Eucharistic sacrifice, to give thanks and glory to God through Christ our Lord with the Eucharistic canticle.

In Eph. 1:19–23 the exaltation and supremacy of Christ is proclaimed over the whole universe, over the angelic world, then over the Church: "And what is the exceeding greatness of His power toward us, who believe according to the operation of the might of His power, which He wrought in Christ, raising Him up from the dead and setting Him on His right hand in the heavenly places [in heavenly things]. Above all principality and power and virtue and dominion and every name that is named, not only in this world, but also in that which is to come. And He hath subjected all things under His feet and hath made Him head over all the Church, which is His body and the fullness of Him who is filled all in all."

Still more specific, the primacy of Christ is presented in Col. 1:16 f: "For in Him were all things created in heaven and on earth, visible and invisible, whether thrones or dominations or principalities or powers: all things were created by Him and in Him. And He is before all, and in Him all things consist."

The idea that all things consist in Christ is most specifically expressed with the term "re-establish, reconcile (anakephalaiosis)" in Col. 1:20: "And through Him to reconcile all things unto Himself, making peace through the blood of His cross, both as to the things that are on earth, and the things that are in heaven."

As head, Christ is the source of all graces throughout the universe, of all the supernatural gifts through which there is bestowed capacity to give adequate glory to God. The term "reconcile," so far as it applies to the angels, means for them Christ's mediation of grace and glory unto them. This, however, does not mean redemption of the fallen angels, nor does it imply or suppose that originally all grace of the angels is merited by Christ, still less that Christ was from the beginning the efficient cause of the grace of the angels; neither does it necessarily imply that grace was given to the angels originally in view of Christ, so far as the glory of Christ would have been the final cause of the grace of the angels. It suffices to say that with the entrance of the mystery of the Incarnation into the designs of divine providence, grace and glory of the angels had to come into organic relationship and dependence on Christ. The possession of grace and glory of the angels through Christ, based on the communion with Christ, was made more perfect, was made an organic possession, a possession of right.

St. Thomas [1] expresses this truth with the words: Christ is "universal principle for the entire genus of those who have grace"; He is "the cause of all graces found in the intellectual creatures."

This communion in the life of grace and glory with Christ, in supernatural vital activity, applies particularly to the acts with which the angels glorify the "Father of lights," to the acts of praise and thanksgiving. This means that they minister to Christ in the sacrifice of thanksgiving; thus they are en-

[1] *Summa theol.*, IIIa, q. 7, a. 9.

abled, in Christ and through Christ, to offer to the Father an adequate thanksgiving of infinite dignity.

The Choirs of Angels

Both passages from the Epistle to the Ephesians and from the Epistle to the Colossians were sources for the groups of angels in the various prefaces. Not all the angelic choirs enumerated in the prefaces are taken from the Epistles of St. Paul (seraphim, from Isa. chap. 6; cherubim, from Ezech. chaps. 1 and 10); the angels and archangels are mentioned here and there in Scripture; cf. I Pet. 3:22: "Who is on the right hand of God . . . being gone into heaven, the angels and powers and virtues being made subject to Him.

a) Prefaces of the Nativity, Epiphany, Easter, the Ascension, the Sacred Heart, Christ the King, the Apostles: angels, archangels, thrones, dominations, all heavenly hosts.

b) Prefaces of Lent, the Holy Cross, the Blessed Virgin, St. Joseph, Common Preface: angels, dominations, powers, heavens, heavenly virtues, blessed seraphim.

c) Preface of Pentecost: heavenly virtues, angelic powers.

d) Preface of the Trinity: angels, archangels, cherubim, seraphim.

The groups supplied by St. Paul from the Epistle to the Ephesians are: principalities, powers, virtues, dominations; from the Epistle to the Colossians: thrones (dominations, principalities, powers); from the Epistle to the Philippians came (Phil. 2:10): "that are in heaven." St. Paul does not enumerate them in a fixed order; nor did he intend to give a complete list of the choirs of angels. This fact may have influenced the liberty with which the Church enumerates these choirs, some here, others there, rather representative groups than a complete enumeration.

EUCHARIST AS THEOPHANY

The most glorious, most profound, and central idea intended with the liturgical Sanctus, expressed with the concelebration of men and angels in the Eucharistic hymn, is the analogy of the Eucharistic celebration with the theophanies of the Old Testament, the figurative and typical relation of them to the Eucharistic tabernacle, further the idea that the Eucharist is the sacramental anticipation of the beatific vision. These ideas confessed by the Church with the Sanctus of the liturgy, are transmitted by St. Paul and by the Apocalypse.

In the antithesis between Sinai and Sion of the Epistle to the Hebrews, St. Paul points out at the same time the difference between the Old Testament and the new dispensation, between the worship and sacrifice of the Mosaic law and the worship and sacrifice initiated on Sion by Christ. The terms, however, used for the New Testament worship—Sion and heavenly Jerusalem—imply at the same time the typical relation of the glory of the Temple of Jerusalem and its holy of holies, to the Eucharistic sanctuary.

Heb. 12:18–24: "For you are not come to a mountain that might be touched, and a burning fire, and a whirlwind, and darkness, and storm. And the sound of a trumpet, and the voice of words, which they that heard excused themselves, that the word might not be spoken to them. For they did not endure that which was said: and if so much as a beast shall touch the mount, it shall be stoned. And so terrible was that which was seen, Moses said: I am frighted, and tremble. But you are come to mount Sion, and to the city of the living God, the heavenly Jerusalem, and to the company of many thousands of angels, and to the Church of the first-born, who are written in the heavens, and to God the judge of all, and to the spirits of the just made perfect, and to Jesus the mediator of the new testament, and to the sprinkling of blood which speaketh better than that of Abel."

It is to be noted that the words "the company of many thousands of angels" contain an allusion to the theophany of Dan. 7:9 f.: "I beheld till thrones were placed, and the Ancient of days sat: his garment was white as snow, and the hair of his head like clean wool: his throne like flames of fire: the wheels of it like a burning fire. A swift stream of fire issued forth from before him: thousands of thousands ministered to him, and ten thousand times a hundred thousand stood before him." This passage contains also an allusion to the propitiatory throne in the holy of holies with the cherubim and over them hovering the fire, the "Glory of God," the *Majestas Domini,* just as the words "the sprinkling of blood" contain an allusion to the great sacrifice on the day of propitiation, when the high priest entered the holy of holies and sprinkled the blood of the victim around the propitiatory throne. The Temple worship was a glorious worship. But it is far surpassed by the worship in the heavenly Jerusalem, in the Sion of the supper room in its transcendent beauty and glory, for which the worship in the Temple was merely a material shadow, a figure, a type, to be replaced by the worship "in spirit and in truth."

The Sanctus of the Apocalypse

More than any other part of Scripture, the Sanctus of the Apocalypse in its great context has molded the Christian liturgy to a "heavenly liturgy." The liturgy of the Apocalypse which has influenced the development of the universal liturgy of the New Testament may be understood in both meanings: the liturgy reflected in the Apocalypse as well as the liturgy revealed in it. It is not excluded that the Apocalypse reflects a liturgical practice of the apostolic age which was transmitted to the Churches by tradition. It is, on the other hand, a fact that the liturgy deposited in the Apocalypse has influenced the further development of Christian liturgy, particularly in the concept of "heavenly liturgy."

For an adequate appreciation of the influence of the Sanctus of the Apocalypse on the liturgical Sanctus of the Church, four ideas of the liturgy of the Apocalypse have to be considered.

1. The heavenly liturgy of the Apocalypse connects Sanctus, Hallel, and thanksgiving to one song of glory. Sanctus, Hallel, and thanksgiving are as equivalents substituted for one another.

2. The liturgy of the Apocalypse is described as a theophany, combining the features of the great theophanies of the Old Testament as the fulfillment of all of them in their prophetic character.

3. The liturgy of the Apocalypse is revealed as concelebration of angels, priests, saints; of the Church triumphant with the Church militant, of heaven and earth.

4. The liturgy of the Apocalypse in common with the theophanies of the Old Testament is visualized with the features and colors of the liturgy of the Temple in Jerusalem. The Jerusalem worship is the central idea. The heavenly liturgy is seen in the figures of the golden altar, the holy of holies, the propitiatory throne, the adoring angels, the "glory of God." It is seen as the ultimate fulfillment of the revealed words, "I shall build into a sanctuary," and of the explanation of them (Exod. 25:8): "And the Lord spoke to Moses, saying: And they shall make Me a sanctuary: and I will dwell in the midst of them."

SANCTUS, THANKSGIVING, HALLEL

The Eucharistic hymn is a sublime combination of the Hallel of the Old Testament with the Sanctus of heaven and a song of sacramental thanksgiving. The scriptural background, model and exemplar for this artistic texture of revealed ideas, is the liturgy of the Apocalypse. In the chapter about the influence of the canticle of Moses and of the Hallel on the Canon, the parallel ideas of the Apocalypse have already been compared. In the present chapter the association of the Sanctus remains to be considered, which transforms the song of thanksgiving into a heavenly hymn, the liturgy on earth into a liturgy with heavenly character.

The union of praise between angels and priests is expressed with the mutual exchange of Sanctus and Eucharistic thanksgiving. First the angels intone the Sanctus. The priests, the twenty-four ancients, intone the Eucharistic thanksgiving. Now the Sanctus is replaced by terms from the Eucharistic thanksgiving, and the act of adoration by the twenty-four ancients is replaced by the terms equivalent with the thrice holy.

The cherubim intone the Sanctus (Apoc. 4:8): "And the four living creatures had each of them six wings: and round about and within they are full of eyes. And they rested not day and night saying: Holy, holy, holy, Lord God Almighty, who was and who is and who is to come." In the following verse the Sanctus is replaced by three terms, the third of which is "benediction" (*eulogia*): "And when those living creatures gave glory and honor and benediction to Him that sitteth on the throne." In 5:11 f. many angels round about the throne join in the praise of the lamb with a sevenfold praise, the three last members of which are again the three terms: honor, glory, benediction: "Saying with a loud voice: the Lamb that was slain is worthy to receive power and divinity and wisdom and strength and honor and glory and benediction." In 7:12 all the angels break forth in a sevenfold praise in which occur the Eucharistic terms "benediction" and "thanks-giving" (*eucharistia*): "And they fell down before the throne upon their faces, and adored God, saying: Amen. Benediction and glory and wisdom and thanksgiving, honor and power and strength to our God forever and ever. Amen."

The twenty-four ancients intone the Eucharistic thanks-giving (11:17): "We give Thee thanks, O Lord God almighty, who art and who wast and who art to come: because Thou hast taken to Thee Thy great power, and Thou hast reigned." After the Sanctus intoned by the cherubim, the twenty-four ancients join in the Sanctus, because their praise is described with three terms equivalent to the three terms with which the Sanctus of the angels was designated (Apoc. 4:9–11): "And when those living creatures gave glory and honor and benediction to Him that sitteth on the throne, who liveth forever and ever; the four and twenty ancients fell down before Him that sitteth on the throne, and adored Him that liveth forever and ever, and cast their crowns before the throne saying: Thou art worthy, O Lord our God, to receive glory and honor and power: because Thou hast created all things; and for Thy will they were, and have been created."

In the great triumphant song over the victory of the Lamb, sung together by the cherubim, all the angels, the twenty-four ancients with all those who adore God on earth, Alleluja is replaced by three terms equivalent to the three terms with which the Sanctus was described (Apoc. 19:1–8): "After these things, I heard as it were the voice of much people in heaven, saying: Alleluja. Salvation and glory and power.

. . . And again they said: Alleluja. And the four and twenty ancients and the four living creatures fell down and adored God that sitteth upon the throne, saying: Amen; Alleluja. And a voice came out from the throne, saying: Give praise to our God, all ye His servants (cf. Ps. 112) and you that fear Him, little and great (cf. Ps. 113:13). And I heard as it were the voice of a great multitude, and as the voice of many waters, and as the voice of great thunders, saying: Alleluja. . . . Let us be glad and rejoice and give glory to Him" (cf. Ps. 117:24).

Concelebration

The union of Sanctus, Eucharistic hymn, and Alleluia implies that the heavenly liturgy is a concelebration of angels, priests, and saints, of the Church triumphant with the Church on earth.

The cherubim open the adoration of God with the singing of the Sanctus. The twenty-four ancients follow (4:9-11): "And when those living creatures gave glory and honor and benediction . . . the four and twenty ancients fell down before Him that sitteth on the throne and adored Him . . . saying: "Thou art worthy, O Lord our God, to receive glory and honor and power."

After the opening of the book by the Lamb, the cherubim and the twenty-four ancients adore with a common canticle (5:8 f.): "And when He had opened the book, the four living creatures and the four and twenty ancients fell down before the Lamb, having every one of them harps and golden vials full of odors, which are the prayers of saints. And they sung a new canticle, saying: Thou art worthy, O Lord, to take the book . . . because Thou wast slain and hast redeemed us." In the same song many angels join round about the throne and the living creatures and the ancients (5:11 f.):

"And the number of them was thousands of thousands, saying with a loud voice: The Lamb that was slain is worthy to receive power and divinity and wisdom and strength and honor and glory and benediction." In the next verse the song of glory is extended in the same melody through heaven and earth (5:13): "And every creature which is in heaven and on the earth and under the earth, and such as are in the sea, and all that are in them, I heard all saying: To Him that sitteth on the throne and to the Lamb, benediction and honor and glory and power forever and ever." In heaven resounds the echo (v. 14), "Amen" ("So be it").

In the singing of Alleluja which celebrates Christ's victory, there are joined the multitudes of angels, the twenty-four ancients, the four cherubim, and all the just and faithful on earth. Apoc. 19:1–8: "I heard as it were the voice of much people [angels and saints] in heaven, saying: Alleluja. . . . And the four and twenty ancients and the four living creatures fell down and adored God that sitteth upon the throne, saying: Amen; Alleluja. And a voice came out from the throne [Christ speaking as man], saying: Give praise to our God, all ye His servants, and you that fear Him, little and great. and I heard as it were the voice of a great multitude [universal Church], and as the voice of many waters, and as the voice of great thunders, saying: Alleluja."

THE LITURGY OF THE APOCALYPSE AS THEOPHANY

The Eastern liturgies explicitly unfold the sacred Eucharistic drama as a theophany. The same idea is expressed in the Roman liturgy with the Sanctus. The common, primary source and model of these ideas is the liturgy of the Apocalypse.

The entire vision of the Apocalypse is a theophany given to St. John. This theophany combines the features of the

great theophanies of the Old Testament: to Moses in the
burning bush, on Mount Sinai, to Isaias, to Ezechiel, to Daniel.
Just as the visions of the great prophets were revealed in
the colors and figures of the Temple worship, so is the theophany of the Apocalypse revealed with the surroundings,
terms, and ideas of the liturgy of the Temple. The last reason
is to be seen in the revelation given by God to Moses about
the Temple worship. The vision of St. John proclaims the second coming of Christ and the glory of the beatific vision. All
these associations show that there is one, continuous line run-
ning from God's first revelation and institution of the original
worship up to the last revelation and ultimate unfolding
manifestation of the divine glory.

The vision of the Apostle opens in analogy to God's manifestation to Moses on Mount Sinai. As on Sinai (Exod.
19:16–20) thunders were heard, lightnings were seen, and
a voice like a trumpet called Moses to come up to the top of
the mount, so the Apostle saw lightnings, heard thunders,
and a voice (Apoc. 4:1) "of a trumpet speaking to me, said:
Come up hither." The theophany in the burning bush is reflected in the names of God added to the Sanctus of the Apocalypse (4:8): "Holy . . . Lord God Almighty, who was and
who is and who is to come." (Cf. Exod. 3:14.)

The vision of Isaias is represented with the manifestation
of God upon a throne (Apoc. 4:2; cf. Isa. 6:1), with the appearance of the twenty-four ancients upon thrones (Apoc.
4:4; Isa. 24:23), with the seraphim (Apoc. 4:6; Isa. 6:2) singing the Sanctus (Apoc. 4:8; Isa. 6:3).

Ezechiel is represented in the description of God upon the
throne surrounded by a rainbow (Apoc. 4:2; Ezech. 1:27).
Again with fire and lightnings as on Sinai (Apoc. 4:5; Ezech.
1:13); with the "four living creatures" round about the throne

(Apoc. 4:6; Ezech. 10:1), called by Ezechiel cherubim, "round about and within they are full of eyes" (Apoc. 4:8; Ezech. 1:18 and 10:12).

The prophet Daniel is alluded to in his vision of the mystery of the Incarnation with its eschatological marks. His description applies to the second coming of Christ as High Priest at the beginning of the Apocalypse (1:13), and at the end appearing as King of kings and Lord of lords (19:11–16; cf. Dan. 7:13 f.), surrounded by an indefinite number of angels (Apoc. 5:11; Dan. 7:10).

PARALLEL TEXTS

Exod. 3:14	Apoc. 4:8
God said to Moses: I am who am.	Holy . . . Lord God Almighty, who was and who is and who is to come.

Exod. 19:16–20	Apoc. 4:1, 4
And behold thunders began to be heard, and lightning to flash, and a very thick cloud to cover the mount. And the noise of the trumpet sounded exceeding loud. . . . And the Lord came down upon Mount Sinai, in the very top of the mount; and He called Moses unto the top thereof.	And behold a door was opened in heaven. And the first voice which I heard, as it were, of a trumpet speaking with me, said: Come up hither. . . . And from the throne proceeded lightnings and voices and thunders.

Isa. 6:1	Apoc. 4:2
I saw the Lord sitting upon a throne high and elevated.	And behold, there was a throne set in heaven, and upon the throne one sitting.

Isa. 24:23

When the Lord of hosts . . . shall be glorified in the sight of His ancients.

Isa. 6:1 f.

And His train filled the temple. Upon it stood the seraphim.

Isa. 6:3

And they cried one to another and said: Holy, holy, holy, the Lord God of hosts.

Apoc. 4:4

And round about the throne were four and twenty seats; and upon the seats four and twenty ancients sitting.

Apoc. 4:6

And in the sight of the throne was, as it were, a sea of glass like to crystal; and in the midst of the throne, and round about the throne, were four living creatures.

Apoc. 4:8

And they rested not day and night, saying: Holy, holy, holy, Lord God Almighty.

Ezech. 1:27 f.

I saw as it were the resemblance . . . of fire shining round about; as the appearance of the rainbow when it is in a cloud on a rainy day: this was the appearance of the brightness round about.

Ezech. 10:1,4

And I saw, and behold in the firmament that was over the heads of the cherubim there appeared over them as it

Apoc. 4:2 f.

And behold there was a throne set in heaven, and upon the throne one sitting. And he that sat was to the sight like the jasper and the sardine stone. And there was a rainbow round about the throne, in sight like unto an emerald.

Apoc. 4:5 f.

And from the throne proceeded lightnings . . . and in the midst of the throne were four living creatures.

were the sapphire stone, as the appearance of the likeness of a throne. . . . And the glory of God was lifted.

Ezech. 1:18

And the whole body was full of eyes round about all the four.

Ezech. 10:12

And their whole body and their necks and their hands and their wings . . . were full of eyes.

Dan. 7:10

A swift stream of fire issued forth from before him; thousands of thousands ministered to him, and ten thousand times a hundred thousand stood before him.

Dan. 7:13 f.

I beheld therefore in the vision of the night, and lo, one like the son of man came with the clouds of heaven. And he came even to the Ancient of days, and they presented him before him. And he gave him power and glory and a kingdom. . . . His power is an everlasting power

Apoc. 4:8

And the four living creatures had each of them six wings. And round about and within they are full of eyes.

Apoc. 5:11

And I beheld, and I heard the voice of many angels round about the throne and the living creatures and the ancients; and the number of them was thousands of thousands.

Apoc. 14:14

And I saw; and behold a white cloud, and upon the cloud one sitting like to the son of man.

that shall not be taken away,
and his kingdom that shall
not be destroyed.

THE LITURGY OF THE TEMPLE

The vision of the Apocalypse has this in common with the great Old Testament theophanies, that it is expressed in figures and terms of the liturgy of the Temple as that liturgy was revealed and ordained and promised by God to Moses.

The liturgy of the Temple in Jerusalem was climaxed by the entrance of the high priest once a year into the holy of holies, with his appearance "in the sight of God," who was present in the Shekinah, in the fiery cloud, called "the glory of God" and "the majesty of the Lord," hovering over the propitiatory throne in the midst of the adoring cherubim.

This liturgy was revealed, ordained, and promised by God to Moses. Exod. 25:1–37: "And the Lord spoke to Moses, saying: Speak to the children of Israel. . . . And they shall make Me a sanctuary, and I will dwell in the midst of them. According to all the likeness of the tabernacle which I will show thee, and of all the vessels for the service thereof; and thus you shall make it. Frame an ark of setim wood. . . . And thou shalt overlay it with the purest gold within and without. . . . Thou shalt make also a propitiatory of the purest gold. . . . Thou shalt make also two cherubim of beaten gold, on the two sides of the oracle. . . . Thence will I give orders and will speak to thee over the propitiatory, and from the midst of the two cherubim. . . . Thou shalt make also a candlestick of beaten work of the finest gold. . . . Thou shalt make also seven lamps and shalt set them upon the candlestick."

Exod. 26:31–34; 30:1–6: "Thou shalt make also a veil. . . . And the veils shall be hanged on with rings; and within it thou shalt put the ark of the testimony. And the sanctuary and the holy of holies shall be divided with it. And thou shalt set the propitiatory upon the ark of the testimony in the holy of holies. . . . Thou shalt make also an altar of setim wood. . . . Thou shalt overlay it with the purest gold and thou shalt set the altar over against the veil that hangeth before the ark of the testimony before the propitiatory."

Exod. 40:31–33: "After all these things were perfected, the cloud covered the tabernacle of the testimony, and the glory of the Lord filled it. Neither could Moses go into the tabernacle of the covenant, the cloud covering all things and the majesty of the Lord shining, for the cloud had covered all." (Cf. Lev. 8:2; III Kings 8:10.)

The theophany on Mount Sinai and those to Isaias, Ezechiel, and Daniel were revealed in the symbolism of the worship ordained by God.

Exod. 24:10 f., 16 f.: "And they saw the God of Israel; and under His feet as it were a work of sapphire stone, and as the heaven, when clear. . . . And they saw God, and they did eat and drink. . . . And the glory of the Lord dwelt upon Sinai, covering it with a cloud six days; and the seventh He called him out of the midst of the cloud. And the sight of the glory of the Lord was like a burning fire upon the top of the mount, in the eyes of the children of Israel."

In the vision of Isaias, in which the lips of the prophet were cleansed, we find allusions to the temple, to the propitiatory throne of the holy of holies, to the cherubim, to the altar of incense, and to "the glory of the Lord."

Isa. 6:1, 4: "I saw the Lord sitting upon a throne high and elevated; and His train filled the temple. Upon it stood the seraphim. . . . And the house was filled with smoke. . . And one of the seraphim flew to me; and in his hand was a live coal, which he had taken with the tongs off the altar." In the vision of Isaias the cherubim are replaced by seraphim.

In Ezechiel's vision is seen the temple, the propitiatory throne, the cherubim, and "the glory of God." King Solomon had added to the original two cherubim two more (cf. III Kings 6:23, 28: "And he made in the oracle two cherubim. . . . And he overlaid the cherubim with gold"). It is therefore the temple of Solomon to which the vision of Ezechiel alludes.

Ezech. 1:4 f., 26; 10:4: "And behold a whirlwind came out of the north, and a great cloud, and a fire infolding it. . . . And in the midst thereof the likeness of four living creatures. And above the firmament that was over their heads was the likeness of a throne, as the appearance of the sapphire stone. And the glory of the Lord was lifted up from above the cherub to the threshold of the house. And the house was filled with the cloud, and the court was filled with the brightness of the glory of the Lord."

Ezech. 10:18: "And the glory of the Lord went forth from the threshold of the temple and stood over the cherubim."

In the vision of Daniel, which is very like that of Ezechiel, the distinction between the "Ancient of days" upon the throne (heavenly Father) and the "one like the son of man" (the incarnate Word) foreshadowing the mystery of the Incarnation, is more distinct, and the second coming to the Last Judgment is more emphasized.

Dan. 7:9–14: "I beheld till thrones were placed and the Ancient of days set . . . his throne like flames of fire: the wheels of it like a burning fire. A swift stream of fire issued forth from before him: thousands of thousands ministered to him, and ten thousand times a hundred thousand stood before him. I beheld therefore in the vision of the night, and lo, one like the son of man came with the clouds of heaven. And he came even to the Ancient of days and they presented him before him. And he gave him power and glory and a kingdom; and his kingdom that shall not be destroyed."

The Apocalypse presents a complete picture of the temple in Jerusalem: the courts, the interior, the holies with the golden candlestick and with the golden altar of incense; the holy of holies with the ark, with the propitiatory throne, the cherubim, with Christ as High Priest, with the sacrifice of light and incense, with the perpetual sacrifice of the lamb.

Apoc. 1:12: "And being turned, I saw . . . in the midst of the golden candlesticks, one like the Son of man, clothed with a garment down to the feet . . . girt with a golden girdle." Christ appears in the vestments of high priest in the sanctuary of the temple, offering the sacrifice of light. (Cf. Zach. 3:4; Ezech. 9:2.)

In the second vision, beginning with the second chapter, the holy of holies is opened; we see the propitiatory throne, the cherubim, the representatives of the holy priesthood.

Apoc. 4:2: "And immediately I was in the spirit . . . and behold there was a throne set in heaven, and upon the throne one sitting . . . and round about the throne were four and twenty seats and upon the seats four and twenty ancients sitting." King David (cf. I Par. 24:4) had distributed the duties of the temple to the sixteen sons of Eleazar and the eight sons of Ithamar.

In the appearance of the Lamb in the midst of the heavenly hierarchy and in the act of ascending upon the throne, we may understand the perpetual daily sacrifice of the lamb as well as the great sacrifice on the day of propitiation, when the blood of the victim was poured out about the propitiatory throne in the holy of holies.

Apoc. 5:6: "And I saw; and behold in the midst of the throne and of the four living creatures, and in the midst of the ancients, a Lamb standing, as it were slain." (Cf. Exod. 29:39.) "And he came and took the book out of the right hand of him that sat upon the throne." This act contains the significance of the sprinkling of the blood of the victim upon the propitiatory throne, which means the ratification and acceptance of the sacrifice by God.

The idea of the altar of holocausts and of the altar of incense appears in the following passages.

Apoc. 6:9: "I saw under the altar the souls of them that were slain for the word of God."

Apoc. 8:3: "And another angel came and stood before the altar which is before the throne of God having a golden censer; and there was given to him much incense, that he should offer of the prayers of all saints upon the golden altar which is before the throne of God."

A scene like that of the dedication of the temple (Exod. 40:32 f.; Lev. 8:2; Num. 7:1; III Kings 8:10) is described (Apoc. 18:8): "And the temple was filled with smoke from the majesty of God and from His power." Lastly the paradise is called "the holy city of Jerusalem" (Apoc. 21:3): "And he took me up in spirit to a great and high mountain; and he showed me the holy city of Jerusalem, coming down out of heaven from God, having the glory of God."

CELEBRATION OF THE EUCHARIST AS THEOPHANY

The Sanctus of the ancient liturgies and of the Roman Canon is introduced after the manner of the liturgy of the

Apocalypse, combining the features of the theophanies of the Old Testament.

The Eastern liturgies conceive the liturgical action, on the one hand, as the entering into heaven with Christ as High Priest. On the other hand, from the aspect of the approach of God toward men, consecration and communion are interpreted as the manifestation of the glory of God, as a theophany, implying the entire mystery of the incarnate Word in its different stages in nativity, resurrection, with special emphasis on the second coming.

The liturgy of the *Apostolic Constitutions* (8) unites with the seraphim of Isaias, the cherubim of Ezechiel, the angelic choirs of St. Paul, and the vision of the Apocalypse: "For all these things, glory be to Thee O Lord Almighty. Thee do the innumerable hosts of angels, thrones, dominations, principalities, authorities, and powers (Col. 1:16), Thine everlasting armies, adore. The cherubim (Ezech., chap. 10) and the six-winged seraphim (Isa., chap. 6) . . . together with thousand thousands of archangels, and ten thousand times ten thousand of angels (Dan. 7:10) incessantly, and with constant and loud voices (Apoc. 4:8), and let all the people say it with them, Holy," etc.

In the fragment of Deir-Balizeh and in the anaphora of Serapion the manifestation of the glory of God over the propitiatory throne is put into parallel with consecration (containing an allusion to the sacerdotal prayer of Christ).

Deir-Balizeh: "Fill us also with Thy glory which is with Thee."

Serapion: "Thee assist thousands of thousands and ten thousands of ten thousands of angels (Dan. 7:10), archangels, thrones, dominations, principalities, powers (Col. 1:16); Thee assist two most honored seraphim with six wings

(Isa., chap. 6). . . . Heaven and earth are full of Thy glory. Full is heaven, full is the earth with Thy magnificent glory, Lord of glories. Full likewise this sacrifice with Thy glory and Thy communication."

The liturgy of St. James prays (at the prayer of incense): "Sovereign almighty King of glory, manifest Thyself," an invocation analogous to the request of Moses (Exod. 33:18); "Lord, show me Thy glory." In the same liturgy the Eucharistic celebration is called the "dreadful and awful approach"; "His holy and glorious appearing." The cherubikon sounds: "Let all mortal flesh be silent, and stand with fear and trembling, and meditate nothing earthly within itself: for the King of kings and Lord of lords, Christ our God, comes forward to be sacrificed and to be given for food to the faithful; and the bands of angels go before Him (Luke 2:13) with every power and dominion (Col. 1:16) the many-eyed cherubim (Ezech. 10:12) and the six-winged seraphim (Isa. 6:2) . . . crying aloud (Apoc. 19:5) the hymn Alleluja, alleluja, alleluja."

The liturgy of St. Mark: "Round Thee stand ten thousand times (Dan. 7:10) . . . and Thy most honored creatures, the many-eyed cherubim (Ezech. 10:12) and the six-winged seraphim (Isa. 6:2), singing aloud (Apoc. 19:5) the triumphal and thrice holy hymn to Thy great glory, Holy," etc. In the prayer of incense is asked, "Let Thy glory encircle us"; in the offering prayer, "We pray and beseech Thee, O Lord in Thy mercy, to let Thy presence rest upon this bread and this chalice . . . while angels, archangels, and Thy holy priests stand round and minister for Thy glory."

The liturgy of the Copts introduces the angels with the twenty-four ancients: "Through the supplications of Thy mighty luminous heavenly spirits, Michael, Gabriel, Raphael, and of the four incorporeal living creatures and of the four and twenty elders and of all the choirs of angels and heavenly hosts."

The Byzantine liturgy unites in the cherubikon at the great entrance the theophany of Ezechiel, Isaias, and the Apocalypse, and explicitly applies them to the Eucharistic coming of God: "We who mystically represent the cherubim and join with them in singing the thrice holy hymn to the life-giving Trinity, let us lay aside all the cares of this life . . . for we are now to receive the King of all, who comes escorted by unseen hosts of angels. Alleluja, alleluja, alleluja."

The introduction of the Sanctus in the Roman Preface is according to the spirit of the Apocalypse, a combining of the theophanies of the Old Testament, of Isaias, Ezechiel, and Daniel.

There are four different kinds of prefaces according to the groups of angels enumerated. The preface of the Nativity, Epiphany, Easter, Ascension, Sacred Heart, Christ the King, the Apostles, and of the dead have this formula: "Therefore, with the angels and archangels, with the thrones and dominations, with the entire army of heavenly hosts, do we sing the hymn of Thy glory, saying without end." "Therefore" establishes the connection with the motive of thanksgiving. Thrones and dominations are supplied by St. Paul (Col. 1:16); "the entire army of heavenly hosts" is derived from Luke 2:13 (with the association of Dan. 7:13): "And suddenly there was with the angel a multitude of the heavenly army, praising God." The conclusion: "do we sing, saying without end," associates Isa. 6:3, "cried one to another, and said," and the angels of Bethlehem "praising God and saying," further the Apocalypse 4:8, "and they rested not day and night saying," with the Sanctus of the Roman Preface.

The second group comprises the prefaces of Lent, the Holy Cross, the Blessed Virgin, St. Joseph, and common preface: "Through whom Thy majesty the angels praise, the dominations adore, the powers tremble. The heavens and heavenly virtues, also the blessed seraphim, concelebrate in common exultation. We pray that Thou wouldst deign to admit our voices with them, saying in suppliant confession." "Through whom" establishes the connection with the mediation of Christ. St. Paul is represented with "dominations and powers" from the Epistle to the Colossians 1:16, with "virtues" from Eph. 1:21, joined to the seraphim of Isaias. "Heavens" may refer to Apoc. 19:1: "the voice of much people in heaven."

The Preface of Pentecost has this formula: "Therefore rejoices the whole world upon earth with unbounded joy. But likewise the heavenly virtues, and the angelic powers sing together a hymn of Thy glory, saying without end." It is the concelebration of heaven and earth expressed. There is no special group of angels mentioned in this Preface.

The Preface of the Blessed Trinity is the only one in which the cherubim are mentioned. "Which (Thy glory) the angels praise and archangels, the cherubim and seraphim, who do not cease to cry daily (continually) saying." The praise of the angels is immediately connected with the mystery of the feast: "What we believe about Thy glory upon Thy revelation." The term "with one voice" alludes to Apoc. 5:11: "And I heard the voice of many angels . . . saying with a loud voice."

The immediate object of the praise in all prefaces is either the glory of God, or the majesty of God: in the first group we say: "We sing the hymn of Thy glory," likewise on Pentecost. In the Trinity Preface it is "Thy glory," on the feast of

Pentecost it is again the "hymn of glory." In the second group of prefaces (Lent, the Holy Cross, the Blessed Virgin, St. Joseph, and the common preface) it is "Thy majesty." In these two terms all the theophanies and the presence of God in the holy of holies are alluded to: the pillar of fire, the fiery cloud. The Shekinah, as it was called, means: "Glory of God," "Majesty of the Lord." Exod. 24:16: "And the glory of the Lord dwelt upon Sinai." Lev. 16:2: "For I will appear in a cloud over the oracle." III Kings 8:10–11: "And it came to pass (at the dedication of the Temple of Solomon), when the priests were come out of the sanctuary, that a cloud filled the house of the Lord. And the priests could not stand to minister because of the cloud; for the *glory of the Lord* had filled the house of the Lord." Isa. 6:1: "And His train filled the temple . . . and the house was filled with smoke." Ezech. 10:4: "And the *glory of the Lord* was lifted up from above the cherub to the threshold of the house; and the house was filled with the cloud and the court was filled with the brightness of the *glory of the Lord.*" Apoc. 15:8: "And the temple was filled with smoke from the *majesty of God* and from his power."

ANALYSIS OF THE TEXT

"Holy, holy, holy, Lord God of hosts!
Heaven and earth are filled with Thy glory"

St. Thomas summarizes the ideas of the Sanctus of Isaias with these words: "They praise three things: the Trinity of persons, the unity of majesty, the generosity of providence (because the communication of His goodness extends down to the last creatures understood with the term earth)." [2] The

[2] *In Is.*, c. 6, n. 1.

thrice holy refers to the Trinity of persons; "Lord God of hosts" to the unity of nature, "the earth is filled with Thy glory" refers to the manifestation of the glory of God in creation.

The liturgical Sanctus has added "heaven" in the manifestation of the glory of God. This addition appears already in the fragment of Deir-Balizeh, and in the anaphora of Serapion. It was known to Didymus [3] and to St. Cyril of Alexandria.[4]

About the liturgical Sanctus, St. Thomas has this interpretation: "About the consecration to be accomplished with supernatural power, the faithful are inspired with devotion in the preface; therefore they are admonished to lift up their hearts to the Lord, and therefore at the end of the preface the faithful praise the divinity of Christ together with the angels saying: Sanctus, etc." [5]

The basis for St. Thomas' interpretation is the unity and contiguity of the Eucharistic prayer directed toward the consecration and its object. Because of the connection with the "Benedictus," St. Thomas says that with the Sanctus the divinity of Christ is to be adored, while with the Benedictus His humanity is the object of praise.

Some authors understand the association of our thanksgiving with the song of the angels merely as an exhortation to imitation of the angels, who do not cease day and night to adore God, who tremble before His majesty, who glorify Him with exultant joy, with most profound devotion, with highest enthusiasm.[6]

[3] *De Trinitate. PG*, 39, 364.
[4] *De fide ad Theodosium. PG*, 76, 1133.
[5] *Summa theol.*, IIIa, q. 83, a. 4.
[6] Cf. B. Botte, *op. cit.;* Maur Gregoire, *op. cit.*, pp. 161–75.

INTENTION OF THE CHURCH

As a summary of the chapters on the Sanctus of the Mass, we add these conclusions.

1. The liturgical Sanctus is a confession of faith that the Eucharistic thanksgiving is the highest worship of the Blessed Trinity. The verbs "to sing, to praise, to glorify, to say Sanctus," which introduce the Sanctus, are equivalent to "give thanks" in the unity and contiguity of the Eucharistic prayer, they explain and specify the giving thanks. The thrice holy is therefore a threefold thanks to God, to the Blessed Trinity, just as it is in the context of Isaias.

2. It is a confession of faith in the celebration of the Holy Eucharist as a theophany, as a fulfillment of what was fore-told in the figures and symbols of the theophanies of the Old Testament. It is a confession of faith that the Holy Eucharist is a sacramental anticipation of the second coming of our Lord, of the ultimate theophany. It is a confession of faith in the dogma of the Real Presence of the glory of God. It is a confession of faith in the Holy Eucharist as the great sacrifice which was prefigured on Sinai and in the Temple of Jerusalem. It is a confession of faith in the glory of God which appeared in the Incarnate Word as fulfillment of the prophetic manifestations of God in the Old Testament, made present in the Holy Eucharist as continuation and extension of that glory in the Church. What was figure and type in the "Glory of God" and in the "Majesty of the Lord" in the holy of holies, what was limited in space and time to the Temple of Jerusalem, glory is now spread in spirit and in truth throughout heaven and earth. Christ glorified present in heaven and Christ glorified present upon the Eucharistic altar in the Eucharistic tabernacle, this we confess with the Sanctus.

3. The Sanctus is a confession of faith in the ministry of the angels at the Eucharistic sacrifice, in the concelebration of heaven and earth. In the revelation and in the precepts given by God to Moses about the cult of the Temple, there was contained the symbol of the adoration and ministry of the angels in the cult. Just as the symbolic presence of God was replaced by the Real Presence in the Eucharist, so likewise the prophetic symbol of the adoring angels. The argument from the Old Testament as type and figure is supplemented by the traditional doctrine of the Fathers, that the angels are present at the sacramental re-enactment of Nativity, Passion, and Resurrection, as they were present and ministered at the historical Nativity, Passion, and Resurrection of our Savior. This idea is expressed in the Sanctus of the Nativity Preface (and the prefaces belonging to the same group) with the angels from Luke 2:13.

4. The liturgical Sanctus, continuing, explaining, and specifying the idea of "let us give thanks," contains its import. It is therefore an invocation of God's blessing and the anticipated giving thanks for it. It is the prayer that the Blessed Trinity may send forth its glory in the Eucharist as extension and continuation of the mystery of the Incarnation. The Sanctus asks for the manifestation of the glory of God, that heaven and earth may be filled with the glory of God in the building up of the mystical Christ through the glory and fire of the live coal, through the Eucharistic Christ.

CHAPTER XIV

The Benedictus

ON the feast of the Tabernacles the Hallel was sung with special solemnity. The feast of Tabernacles, one of the three great feasts of the Jewish liturgy, was celebrated primarily in commemoration of their forefathers' dwelling in tents in the wilderness (Lev. 23:43), and in thanksgiving for the permanent abode given them in the Promised Land and, after the erection of the Temple, in thanksgiving for a permanent place of worship. On the last day of the feast a procession went round the altar of holocausts seven times, the people carrying branches of palms and myrrh. At the words of Ps. 117:25–26, "O Lord, save me (Hosanna); O Lord give good success. Blessed be He that cometh in the name of the Lord. We have blessed you out of the house of the Lord," the Israelites danced and waved the lulab (boughs) with great enthusiasm, shouting "Hosanna, Hosanna."

When our Lord entered Jerusalem in triumph, a great multitude (Matt. 21:9) "spread their garments in the way: and others cut boughs from the trees, and strewed them in the way: and the multitudes that went before and that followed, cried, saying: Hosanna to the son of David: Blessed is He that cometh in the name of the Lord. Hosanna in the highest" (cf. Mark 1:9; Luke 19:38). In the form recorded by St. Luke resounds the song of the angels in Bethlehem: "Blessed be the King who cometh in the name of the Lord, peace in heaven and glory on high."

INTRODUCTION TO THE CANON

Parts of the Benedictus with eschatological meaning are found at the end of the thanksgiving prayer of the *Didache* (X, 6): "Let grace come and let this world pass away. Hosanna to the God (Son) of David. If anyone is holy, let him come; if anyone is not so, let him repent. Maranatha. Amen."

In the Eucharistic prayer of the liturgy of the *Apostolic Constitutions* (8) these acclamations are found as preparation for Holy Communion. The priest announced: "Holy things for holy persons." The people answered: "There is one holy; there is one Lord, one Jesus Christ; blessed forever, to the glory of God the Father. Amen. Glory to God in the highest, and on earth peace to men of good will. Hosanna to the Son of David. Blessed be He that cometh in the name of the Lord, being the Lord God who appeared to us. Hosanna in the highest."

In the liturgy of St. James, the Benedictus is already connected with the Sanctus in the form: "Hosanna in the highest; blessed is He that cometh in the name of the Lord. Hosanna in the highest." It was probably the liturgy of Jerusalem which first added these verses to the Sanctus. In the sixth century it is found in the Byzantine liturgy, whence it was transmitted to the Roman liturgy.

INTERPRETATION

The original meaning of these verses within the Hallel is Messianic. Hosanna, or Hosianna, means: "Save, we beseech." It is an expression of joy and gratitude. "Hosanna to the Son of David" were grateful and joyful words, addressed to God, beseeching Him to save and to bless His royal Son, the Messiah, whose coming had been so long expected. "Hosanna in the highest" means: from the highest heaven, save and protect this royal heir.

It is the meaning of these acclamations at the entrance in Jerusalem, that this prophecy is fulfilled in Christ. Our Lord gave to these words an eschatological meaning, testifying at the same time that He came into this world by nativity as the expected Messiah (Matt. 23:39): "For I say to you, you shall not see Me henceforth till you say: Blessed is He that cometh in the name of the Lord."

In the liturgy of the *Apostolic Constitutions* the Benedictus applies to the coming of Christ by Holy Communion. In the connection with the Sanctus the idea of coming to the sacrifice is clearly emphasized.

There is expressed also the relation of the mystery of the Blessed Trinity to that of the Incarnation on the one hand, and of both to the mystery of the Holy Eucharist. The words "Full is heaven and earth of Thy glory" establish the connection between the mystery of the Trinity with the mystery of the Incarnation: the Incarnation is the manifestation of the glory of God, in the Son of God proceeding *ad extra*. After the ascension of our Lord His glory is in heaven. By the Holy Eucharist, the same glory returns to the earth.

These acclamations apply historically to the nativity of the Messiah, to His entry for His sacrifice in Jerusalem, to His second coming. These significations are implied also in the Benedictus of the Canon: it means the re-enactment of the Nativity, His entry to the sacrifice, the anticipation of His glorious second coming.

CHAPTER XV

The Preconsecratory Invocations [1]

A MAIN problem in the history of the Roman Canon is the interpretation of the various prayers of invocation (before consecration: *Te igitur, Hanc igitur, Quam oblationem;* after consecration: *Supra quae, Supplices te rogamus*). In the present chapter we limit our discussion to the preconsecratory invocations, and prescind from the question whether they are derived from a postconsecratory invocation or vice versa.

The *Traditio opostolica* of St. Hippolytus [2] did not contain any preconsecratory invocation. This Canon is no more than a paraphrase of the "giving thanks" as found in the historical narrative of the institution of the Eucharist. With the invocations a new element, different in tone and color, was introduced. The contrast between the old form of the Canon with its latreutic-Eucharistic character and its triumphant jubilant tone on the one hand, and the humble, imploring supplication of the added prayers on the other, is evident. Moreover, the new element (the invocations) grew in importance so as to constitute finally, together with the interspersed interces-

---

[1] Cf. *Orate Fratres*, XIX (1945), 440–51, 481–92.
[2] R. H. Connolly, *The So-called Egyptian Church Order and Derived Documents*, in *Texts and Studies*, contributions to biblical and patristic literature; ed. by J. Armitage Robinson, Vol. VIII, Cambridge, 1916.

sory prayers, the main body of the Canon. The original anaphora, at present exstant as preface and final doxology, was reduced to a kind of framework of the Canon.

In this chapter we intend to show that the primary motive for the introduction of an invocation before consecration, and the common idea of all three invocations, is the "blessed" of the historical narrative of the institution of the Eucharist which begins with the words: "Who the day before He suffered, etc." We can prove that the intention of the Church in introducing these prayers was to execute the command of our Lord, "Do this for a commemoration of Me," inasmuch as the Church understood the command to extend likewise to the blessing contained in the thanksgiving prayer of our Lord before He consecrated.

PRESENT STATE OF THE PROBLEM

Reviewing the different opinions about the intention of the Church in introducing the preconsecratory invocations, we are caught in the labyrinth of conjectures and combinations of theories. To give a sketch of the present state of the question we select those authors who either contribute positive elements to an adequate interpretation, or illustrate the uncertainty and historical obscurity.

Most of the various interpretations refer to the third preconsecratory invocation: "Do thou, O God, deign to bless what we offer" (*Quam oblationem*). But what they have to say about the third invocation applies equally to all three. Many authors understand them simply as amplifications of one and the same idea. Even if, with Cardinal Schuster,[3] we maintain that the second invocation, *Hanc igitur*, is the *oratio post nomina*, its impetratory idea it has nevertheless

[3] *The Sacramentary* (London, 1924), I, 283.

in common with both the others, except that it is joined to
an intercession. The present Canon indicates clearly enough
in its grammatical structure the connection of all three invocations. The first, *Te igitur*, extends as far as *"haec sancta
sacrificia illibata."* After the interruption caused by the insertion of the intercessory prayer, the original idea is taken
up by the second invocation by means of a particle (*igitur*):
"Hanc igitur." The connection between the second and the
third invocation is established by the relative pronoun in the
Quam oblationem. . . .

St. Thomas [4] in his interpretation of the *Quam oblationem*,
without inquiring into its origin and history, and considering
merely the text of the prayer, understands it as a petition for
the effect of consecration: "Then he (the priest) proceeds
to the consecration itself, wherefore he asks first for the effect of consecration, saying, '*Quam oblationem*, etc.' " St.
Thomas adds further (in the ad 7 of the same article) that
this invocation serves to make actual the intention of the
priest, which, if missing, would impede the efficacy of the
words of consecration.

Many commentators simply follow the interpretation of
St. Thomas without taking notice of the comparison he adds,
saying: "It is not unfitting that we ask from God what most
certainly we know He will accomplish, just as Christ (John
17) asked for His glorification." This comparison of the invocation of the Canon with the petition for glorification in
the sacerdotal prayer suggests that St. Thomas saw in the
former an element of the sacerdotal prayer. St. Thomas does
not state expressly that the invocation of the Canon has its
type in the sacerdotal prayer, but his quotation and comparison suggests that this is his thought.

[4] *Summa theol.* IIIa, q. 83, a. 4 c.

R. Buchwald [5] finds in the invocation an element of the paschal supper, of the Jewish ritual: Christ gave thanks with a customary Jewish blessing, which in form was a prayer of thanksgiving, but implicitly an invocation for divine blessing. The first Christian generation, who knew perfectly the technical significance of such a thanksgiving, kept the traditional form of a pure thanksgiving anaphora. A later generation, no longer Jewish, forgot the technical meaning of the "thanksgiving," i.e., the implicit invocation of the divine blessing, and added what seemed wanting, namely, the invocation that God would consecrate. In this way Buchwald explains the introduction of all invocations of the Canon, and particularly the much discussed epiklesis. His too arbitrary reconstruction of the original invocation cannot be accepted. But his fundamental idea has very much impressed Salaville,[6] A Fortescue,[7] and others.

P. Cagin, O.S.B.,[8] derives the preconsecratory invocations from a petition for fruitful Communion found in the ancient anaphora of the *Traditio apostolica* of St. Hippolytus. Cagin, who in his excellent analysis of that anaphora has shown its "quasi Pauline origin," discovered in the invocations a further influence of the spirit and words of St. Paul. He understands the preconsecratory invocations as petitions for acceptance of the Eucharistic sacrifice, evidently with reference to the terms "acceptable," "accept" (cf. Rom. 15:16,31; Phil. 4:18; Titus 2:14). His interpretation is followed by M. de la Taille.[9]

[5] *Die Epiklese in der roemischen Messe;* in *Weidenauer Studien,* 1906, pp. 21–56.

[6] "Epiklese eucharistique," *Dict. théol. cath.*

[7] *The Mass* (London, 1922), p. 404.

[8] *L'Eucharistia, Canon primitif de la Messe,* Paris, 1912. Cf. A. Baumstark, "Das Problem des roem. Messkanons," *Eph. lit.,* LIII (1939), 204–43.

[9] *Mysterium fidei* (Paris, 1129), pp. 319–24.

Cardinal Schuster, accepting the preconsecratory invocation as original (he considers the postconsecratory epiklesis as a derivation from the preconsecratory invocation), and calling it an epiklesis, has this to say: "The 'Quam oblationem' begs almighty God to grant consecratory efficacy to the words of eucharistic institution, an efficacy which is invoked in all Liturgies, and especially in the Roman rite, in which the Gospel account of the Last Supper proceeds from its bare historical significance, to assume the character of a sacramental formula precisely by virtue of the intention proclaimed by the sacred minister in uttering the words of the epiklesis—ut nobis fiat corpus et sanguis dilectissimi Filii tui." [10]

W. J. Lallou declares: "Considered historically, the original raison d'être for the inclusion of this prayer into the Canon might have been that of a consecratory invocation." [11] Later he continues (p. 78): "We grant that historically the 'Quam oblationem' could not owe its introduction into the Canon as a declaration of the intention of the celebrant to carry out the divine mandate, to repeat what had been effected at the Last Supper. We know that there is no historical ground for supposing such a prayer morally possible in an age when even the precise moment of consecration was only hazily defined." "Though not a scientific conclusion . . . the 'Quam oblationem' may indeed well be a vestige . . . of the unpreserved expressions used by our Lord Himself, when He gave thanks and blessed the bread and the wine, before the first of all transubstantiation" (79).

[10] Op. cit., I, 282.
[11] The "Quam oblationem" of the Roman Canon (Washington, 1943), p. 74.

Thanksgiving and Blessing in the New Testament

The phrase "giving thanks He blessed" of the Canon is not found in Scripture. In the three Gospels and in I Cor. we find in the introduction to the consecration of each species only one term, either "giving thanks" or "blessing," but never both. That these two terms are synonymous in the New Testament language is generally admitted, since they are substituted for each other, not only in the texts of the institution of the Eucharist, but also on other occasions. For an illustration, we quote the four Eucharistic texts and add other examples.

Matt. 26:26: Jesus took break and blessed and broke it.

Matt. 26:27: And taking the chalice, He gave thanks and gave to them.

Mark 14:22: Jesus took bread; and blessing, broke.

Mark 14:23: And having taken the chalice, giving thanks.

Luke 22:19: And taking bread, He gave thanks.

I Cor. 11:24: And giving thanks, broke.

I Cor. 11:25: In like manner also the chalice.

Matt. 14:19: He took the five loaves . . . and looking up to heaven, He blessed.

Matt. 15:36: And taking the seven loaves . . . and giving thanks.

I Cor. 10:16: The chalice of benediction which we bless.

As in other details, so also in the use of the terms "giving thanks" and "blessing" the reports of the sacred authors can be distinguished into two groups. St. Matthew and St. Mark use the verb "bless" before the consecration of the bread; before the consecration of the chalice they use the expression "give thanks." St. Luke and St. Paul use "give thanks" for the bread, and simply the term "likewise" before the consecration of the chalice. But in I Cor. 10:16, St. Paul uses "bless" in reference to the consecrated chalice. Again St. Matthew in the related incident of the first multiplication of loaves uses the verb "bless," for the second multiplication he uses the verb "give thanks" (Matt. 14:19; 15:36).

The text of our Lord's prayer of thanksgiving is not recorded in Holy Scripture. In all probability both these synonymous terms refer to the Jewish form of blessing called *Berakah*, a formula which was in wording a thanksgiving, but implicitly contained an invocation of the divine blessing. Some authors refer to the ritual of the Sabbath meal, when bread is blessed with the words: "Blessed art Thou, O Lord our God, King of the universe, who bringest forth bread from the earth," and wine with the words: "Blessed art Thou, O Lord our God, King of the universe, who hast created the fruit of the vine." Others refer to the special blessing of the paschal supper. That the terms "give thanks" and "bless" refer to some ritual form of blessing can be gathered from the fact that the words of the prayer are not recorded. We have a similar instance, where Holy Scripture refers to a ritual prayer without giving the text, in the hymn mentioned by Matthew 26:30, and by Mark 14:26. Neither of the two Evangelists has recorded the text of the hymn for the simple reason that it was the ritual hymn of the Passover, the great Hallel (Ps. 112–117), known to every Jew. Analogously, the sacred authors did not record the words of the blessing, since everyone knew them.

Even apart from a knowledge of the Jewish ritual, a comparison of Christ's thanksgiving before the institution of the Eucharist with His thanksgiving before the miracle of the awakening of Lazarus shows the import of Christ's thanksgiving prayer (John 11:41–43): "And Jesus lifting up His eyes, said: Father, I give Thee thanks that Thou hast heard Me. . . . And when He had said these things, He cried with a loud voice: Lazarus, come forth." Two points should be noted. 1. The thanksgiving implied or supposed an impetratory invocation. The object of the invocation is the miracle itself. Explicitly the prayer is an anticipated thanksgiving for the fulfillment of the petition. 2. The prayer itself is not the exercise of the divine power of working the miracle, but is previous to the miracle; it is the implicit impetration of it and the explicit thanksgiving for it.

Whether Christ used the words of a Jewish blessing or some other expression of thanksgiving and impetration in pronouncing the unrecorded words over bread and wine before the first transubstantiation, it is certain that He imparted to these words a very profound and entirely new significance. It was in His intention not the empty Jewish blessing, but an impetration and thanksgiving for the divine blessing that bread and wine were to receive by transubstantiation and that their species were to contain.

HISTORICAL DEVELOPMENT OF THE PHRASE, "GIVING THANKS HE BLESSED"

The history of the term "to give thanks" and the history of the phrase of the Canon "giving thanks He blessed," are as it were two beautiful poems in different meters, both radiant with the enthusiasm of early Christianity. The one ("to give thanks") contains the outlines of the theological treatise of the Holy Eucharist, the other portrays as in a crystallized nucleus the whole Canon. To determine exactly the specific significance of the phrase "giving thanks He blessed" as intended by the Church, we shall first sketch the history of the terms "to give thanks" and "to bless," and then cite the texts which show the historical development of the phrase "giving thanks He blessed."

On the basis of the profound meaning, the terms "to give thanks" and "to bless" received their meaning from Christ at the Last Supper through the institution of the Blessed Sacrament, when they were made to reflect the glory of the wondrous object of impetration and thanksgiving. Christian antiquity gave them a new technical meaning: "to give thanks" and "to bless" became the equivalent of "to consecrate" and "to celebrate the New Testament sacrifice." This development began in apostolic times and was completed at the time of St. Justin (martyred about 167). St. Paul (I Cor. 10:16) already speaks of the consecrated chalice as the "chalice of benediction which we bless." He uses this expression to remind his hearers of the significance of the Old Testament Passover cup as a type of the sublime chalice of the New Testament, but applies the terms "blessing" and "we bless" equally to the prayer of invocation and to the consecration. It is the process known in logic as the analogy of attribution: the terms are transferred from the prayer with the implicit petition to the object of the prayer, namely, first to the action which produces this object, and then to the effect itself. As an analogical term, the verb "to give thanks" or "to bless" signifies the thanksgiving prayer (petition and thanksgiving), then the consecration which is asked for and for which thanks are rendered, and in the third instance it signifies the whole Eucharistic rite, prayer and consecration together. Only by taking account of this analogy of attribution in the terms "to give thanks" and "to bless" will our interpretation of the Eucharistic texts of the postapostolic time be safeguarded from errors (cf. *Didache*, 9, 10, 14; St. Ignatius M., *ad Eph.*, 13:1; *ad Philad.*, 4; *Ad Smyrn.*, 7, 8). Although the verbs "to give thanks" and "to bless" were often used indifferently with the analogical significance as explained, the verb "to give thanks" (in Greek, *eucharistein*) was used with a certain preference in the meaning of "to consecrate." The substantive, however, *eucharistia*, was reserved exclusively for the Blessed Sacrament, while the substantive *eulogia* (from the verb "to bless") became the exclusive technical term for the unconsecrated bread which after Communion was distributed among clergy and laity.

We must distinguish, furthermore, between the history of the terms "to give thanks" and "to bless" and their varied analogical significances, and the history of the phrase of the Canon "giving thanks He blessed" and of the terms "to give thanks" and "to bless" within the Canon. By a gradual development the Church has added the term "He blessed" to the scriptural term "giving thanks," thus forming the phrase "giving thanks He blessed." We have first to verify this statement and then to inquire into the Church's motive for introducing the phrase and its exact significance.

The venerable anaphora of the *Traditio apostolica* of St. Hippolytus is a pure "thanksgiving" Canon. The *Traditio* itself is from the beginning of the third century, but the liturgy recorded goes back to apostolic times, as the title indicates and the author himself testifies several times in the course of his work. This form of the Canon is one continuous song of thanksgiving. The historical narrative of the institution in this Canon reads as follows: "Who, when He was delivered to the voluntary passion . . . , taking bread, giving thanks to Thee, said: Take and eat. . . ." In close adherence to the scriptural text of the Eucharistic institution, only the one term, "giving thanks," is used.

In the anaphora of the fragment of Deir-Balizeh, deriving

from the third century or perhaps the beginning of the fourth century, both terms already appear: "In that night in which He was betrayed He took bread and blessing it and giving thanks He broke and gave it to His disciples and apostles saying. . . ." The two terms are introduced as present participles and connected by "and," i.e., coordinated. "This coordination gives to the phrase a form of transition. Furthermore the order of the terms is to be noted. It is apparently the logical order intended: first He asks for the blessing, and then He gives thanks for it, "blessing it and giving thanks." But the coordination of the two terms could likewise suggest the distanct acts following each other.

In the Canon of the *De sacramentis* of St. Ambrose (most probably), both terms are connected as in the present Roman Canon. The historical narrative of the institution reads as follows: "Who on the day before He suffered took bread in His holy hands, looked up to heaven to Thee, holy almighty Father, eternal God, giving thanks, blessed, broke. . . . Likewise also the chalice, when they had supped, the day before He suffered, He took it, looked up to heaven to Thee, holy almighty Father, giving thanks, blessed. . . ." Twice in the text of the *De sacramentis* there occurs the phrase: "giving thanks, (He) blessed": before the consecration of the host as well as before the consecration of the chalice.

The text of the Roman Canon reads more easily and more fluently because of the elimination of the somewhat heavy repetitions. In the introduction to the consecration of the chalice the phrase "who on the day before He suffered" is omitted. But the phrase "giving thanks He blessed" appears both times, before the consecration of the host as well as that of the chalice.

The significance of the terms "to give thanks" and "to

bless" within the Canon is definite and univocal. Since the meaning of these terms throughout the preconsecratory Canon is dependent on their meaning within the historical narrative of the institution, we can limit our investigation to their significance within the historical narrative, "Who on the day before, etc." Because of its character as a historical report of the institution of the Holy Eucharist, no change of meaning in these terms could take place within this narrative, for otherwise the historical truth of the report would be affected. That is to say, the analogical significance outlined above could not be extended into the historical report of the Canon. Within the Canon both terms retained the univocal significance of the Gospel narrative, or, in other words, the meaning Christ had given them, "When on the day before He suffered (He) took bread, etc."

If finally we inquire into the reason why the Church accepted the phrase "giving thanks He blessed" although she was conscious of the historical character of the narrative of the institution, we can find two reasons which complement each other. With scrupulous accuracy the Church wished to preserve and to transmit every word she knew either by tradition or from Holy Scripture about the institution, in order to comply with the command to do what our Lord had said and done "on the day before He suffered." The conjunction of both terms "to give thanks" and "to bless" within the Canon is therefore a combining of the different versions of the scriptural reports of the institution, inspired by the desire not to omit anything that might be of importance in the execution of the command of Christ. The change from the coordinate form "blessing and giving thanks" to the final phrase "giving thanks He blessed" is proof of this explanation. To correspond most closely to the historical fact that it was one act, one prayer, with which our Lord invoked the blessing and gave thanks for it, the phrase "giving thanks He blessed" was obviously the more suitable. This formula does not leave any doubt that it was a thanksgiving prayer which implied, or contained and supposed, a blessing.

Another reason for the addition of the term "to bless" can be seen in the progress and development of an implicit truth to its explicit expression. Although the Church was inspired by the intention not to omit any word of the historical report, this does not mean that the Church added the term "to bless" merely to multiply synonymous expressions, but to point out explicitly what was implicitly contained in the one term "giving thanks." "Giving thanks" signifies directly the act of thanksgiving, indirectly the act of invocation of a blessing. Vice versa, the term "to bless" signifies directly the invocation of the blessing. In the phrase "giving thanks He blessed" both ideas are explicitly pointed out. That we have here in fact the process and development from an implicit truth to its explicit formulation is confirmed by another addition within the same narrative of the Canon, namely, "lifting up His eyes to heaven." No scriptural text contains this phrase within the narrative of the institution of the Eucharist. With these words the Canon testifies a second time that our Lord's thanksgiving prayer contained an invocation and impetration of the divine blessing.

Such is the history of the phrase "giving thanks He blessed" within the historical narrative of the institution of the Holy Eucharist as contained in the Canon, and it reveals the motive and intention of the Church in this development.

CHAPTER XVI

Development of the Invocations Parallel to the "Giving Thanks He Blessed"

IT is not an arbitrary hypothesis but a historical fact that the introduction of the first preconsecratory invocation and its development are parallel to the introduction of the term "blessed" in the historical narrative of the Eucharistic institution and to the development of the whole phrase "giving thanks He blessed." The oldest forms of the Canon, which employed only one term in the historical narrative, namely, "giving thanks," do not have any preconsecratory invocation. With the addition of the term "blessed" appears simultaneously also the preconsecratory invocation. But not only is the introduction of the first invocation dependent on the introduction of the term "blessed" in the historical narrative, but the whole development of the preconsecratory Canon and its final structure reflect the development of the narrative.

The anaphora of the *Traditio apostolica* of St. Hippolytus, which uses only "giving thanks" in the story of the institution, has only the Preface (to describe it in terms of the present Roman Canon), which is followed immediately by the historical narrative: "We give Thee thanks, O God, through

Thy beloved Son Jesus Christ . . . (the history of the life of Christ from Nativity to Passion follows) . . . who, when He was delivered to the voluntary Passion . . . (reason of Passion follows) . . . taking bread, giving thanks to Thee, said: Take ye and eat. . . ."

In the Canon of the papyrus of Deir-Balizeh both terms appear in the historical narrative, i.e., "blessing and giving thanks," and at the same time the first preconsecratory invocation between "Sanctus" and the narrative: "Fill us also with Thy glory, which is with Thee and deign to send Thy Spirit upon these creatures and make the bread the body of the Lord and Savior Jesus Christ, the chalice however the blood of the New Testament; because our Lord Jesus Christ in that night in which He was betrayed took bread and blessing it and giving thanks He gave it to the disciples saying. . . ."

The Canon of St. Ambrose' *De sacramentis* has an invocation that shows very close affinity with the *Quam oblationem* invocation of the present Roman Canon, and its narrative has the phrase "giving thanks He blessed" as well as the mute invocation contained in the external visible gesture "He looked up to heaven to Thee, holy almighty Father, eternal God." The text reads: "Make for us, he says (i.e., the priest), this offering ascribed, ratified, reasonable, acceptable, which is the figure of the body and the blood of Jesus Christ. Who on the day before He suffered, took bread in His holy hands, looked up to heaven to Thee, holy, almighty, eternal God, giving thanks He blessed, broke, and gave what was broken to His apostles and His disciples saying: Take ye and eat ye all of it. For this is My body which shall be broken for many. Likewise He took the chalice, after they had supped, looked up to heaven to Thee, holy, almighty Father, eternal God, giving thanks He blessed, gave it to His apostles. . . ."

The Roman Canon presents the climax and the end of the parallel development between the invocations and the historical narrative. Comparing the invocations of the Roman Canon with those of the *De sacramentis,* we notice two additions: 1. the gesture of raising the eyes toward heaven and the invoking of the name of God as an introduction to the first invocation; 2. the addition of the term "blessing" in the first invocation, and the addition of the phrase "deign to bless" in the third preconsecratory invocation. Both additions testify to the identity of the idea of "blessing" and of invocation and perfect the parallelism in structure between the invocations and the historical narrative. The rubric of the Roman Canon: "The priest extending, raising somewhat and joining his hands, raising also his eyes to heaven," corresponds to the "looked up to heaven" of the narrative. "Therefore most gracious Father" of the first invocation corresponds to the narrative "unto Thee, O God, His almighty Father." Further evidence that the idea of the invocations is the "blessing," that the Church understands the invocations as her blessing corresponding to the blessing of Christ within the historical narrative, is furnished by the addition of the term "blessing" in the first invocation, and the addition of "deign to bless" in the third. For a final confirmation of our thesis that the preconsecratory Canon, i.e., the preconsecratory invocations, has the "blessing" as its fundamental idea, we refer to a quotation of St. Augustine. In his Commentary on I Tim. 2:1 ("I desire, therefore, first of all, that supplications, prayers, intercessions, and thanksgivings be made for all men"), he adapts this text to the different parts of the liturgy: "By supplications we understand the prayers which we say in the celebration of the sacraments before that which is upon the table of the Lord is begun to be blessed. By prayers (we understand) that which we say when it is blessed (Canon before consecration) and sanctified (consecration) and broken for distribution (Communion)."

Conclusions from This Parallel Development

Two conclusions can be deduced from the parallel development of the invocations and the "giving thanks He blessed." 1. The preconsecratory invocations are the authentic interpretation of the impetratory idea implicitly contained in the "giving thanks" and explicitly enunciated in the "He blessed." 2. The invocations are the execution of the command of our Lord to "Do this for a commemoration of Me" inasmuch as the Church understands this command to extend also to the blessing which Christ invoked before He consecrated. With these two conclusions we have defined the main motive of the Church in introducing the preconsecratory invocations. We can now add some explanations.

We said, first of all, that the invocations give us the Church's interpretation of the invocation of Christ contained in His thanksgiving prayer and expressed in His blessing. The invocations interpret the "He blessed" by a process of development analogous to the development of any dogmatic truth *ab implicito ad explicitum*. Buchwald, we will recall, held that the Church wished the invocations inserted for the sake of those Christians (non-Jewish) who did not know the technical meaning of the term "thanksgiving," i.e., who did not know that it connoted a blessing or an invocation of the divine blessing. For an adequate criticism of his theory we must distinguish between the idea of the preconsecratory invocations and their actual insertion in the Canon. It is correct to say that the "giving thanks" of the narrative of the institution implicitly contains an invocation, just as the ritual

Jewish thanksgiving contained an invocation for divine blessing. So far as the actual insertion of the preconsecratory invocations is concerned, however, it does not seem necessary
to suppose that the technical meaning of the "thanksgiving"
was unknown to the Christians of the Hellenist and Roman
world. The actual insertion is sufficiently explained by the
Church's intention to point out explicitly in these invocations what was implicitly contained in the "giving thanks"
together with her desire to carry out Christ's command, as
explained below.

We said, secondly, that the invocations are the execution
of the command of our Lord "Do this for a commemoration of
Me," so far as the Church understands this command to include the invoking of the divine blessing contained in Christ's
"giving thanks." Many authors, Scholastics and modern interpreters, have to a certain extent anticipated this conclusion.
St. Thomas, for instance, says concerning the *Quam oblationem* that with this prayer the priest asks for the effect of
the consecration, that it is a petition which actualizes his
intention to consecrate. The very same idea is proposed by
Cardinal Schuster. According to him the invocation purposes
the begging for the sacramental grace of the transubstantiation, of asking God to grant consecratory efficacy to the
words of the Eucharistic institution. Cardinal Schuster has
sensed the parallelism between the invocation and the "He
blessed" of the historical narrative. A similar explanation is
given by W. J. Lallou, who says: "We conclude simply that
the *Quam oblationem* is an expressive prayer by which the
intention of the celebrating priest is made actual at the very
moment that he proceeds to fulfill at Mass the mandate of
Jesus Christ to His first priests at the Last Supper, 'Do this
in commemoration of Me.'"

None of the authors referred to, however, pretends to have given a complete interpretation on the basis of historical research. They propose merely an analysis of the text of the invocations itself. This traditional interpretation of the text appears, in the light of the two conclusions set forth above, as a correct, but only partial and implicit, statement of the content of the invocations. It is true that the invocations contain the petition for the effect of the consecration, ask for the consecratory efficacy of the words pronounced in the person of Christ, and make actual the intention of the celebrating priest. But such interpretations do not express the specific intention of the Church in introducing the invocations. Moreover, there existed a prayer in the Canon before the insertion of any of these invocations, one of apostolic origin, which already contained the petition for the effect of the consecration. It asked for the consecratory efficacy of the words pronounced in Christ's person, and made actual the intention of the celebrating priest: namely, the thanksgiving prayer before consecration, the "Eucharistic" anaphora, or what we now call the Preface. For that is the import of its introductory words: "Let us give thanks to the Lord our God." This intention is then specified in the course of the Preface by the phrase "through Christ our Lord," and grammatically and ideologically connected with the historical narrative by means of the relative pronoun, "who on the day before He suffered," etc. In this way the ancient Church interpreted and executed the command of our Lord "Do this in commemoration of Me" so far as it extended to the thanksgiving prayer of Christ and the invocation of the divine blessing contained in it. The thanksgiving prayer of the ancient anaphora is one continuous phrase, whereby the "thanksgiving" of the priest is identified with the thanksgiving of Christ; the

intention of the priest and of the Church is brought into conformity with the intention of Christ, who—when and how
and so far as He—on the day before He suffered . . . gave
thanks and said, etc. This unity and continuity is the characteristic feature of all the ancient forms of the Canon, for
instance, of the anaphora in the *Traditio apostolica* of St.
Hippolytus: "Gratias tibi referimus, Deus, per delictum
puerum tuum Jesum Christum . . . qui, cumque traderetur
voluntariae passioni . . . accipiens panem, gratias tibi agens
dixit. . . ." The purpose of the grammatical connection is to
conform, to identify, the "gratias tibi referimus" of the priest
and of the Church with the "gratias tibi agens" of Christ. Nor
is the case otherwise in the later forms of the Canon, and it
is still the same in our present Roman Canon, notwithstanding all the insertions and interpolations that occurred from
the second century until about the time of St. Gregory I.

The Church, therefore, did not insert the invocations in
order that they might serve as the first and exclusive prayer
to make actual the intention to consecrate, or to ask for the
sacramental grace of the transubstantiation; for this had
been done since apostolic times by the preconsecratory anaphora. What is new and what the Church intended by the
addition of the invocations is: to say and to do a second time
with explicit words what was implicitly said and done by
the "Let us give thanks to the Lord our God" and the anaphora
and the present Preface. The invocations are just as much an
unfolding of the thanksgiving of the Eucharistic anaphora
and of the content of the Preface, as the addition of the "He
blessed" is an unfolding of the "giving thanks" of the historical narrative of the institution.

The intention of the Church in introducing the invocations
is therefore not accurately specified by saying that they were

meant to petition for the effect of the consecration, to beg
consecratory efficacy for the words of institution, to make
actual the intention to consecrate, although the invocations
do contain these ideas. The intention of the Church is much
more comprehensive, concise, exact, beautiful, and perfect;
the Church intends to conform her intention and her action
with the intention and action of Christ, to conform her blessing with the blessing of Christ. The thanksgiving of Christ
included the petition for the divine blessing, for the veiled
glory of the Eucharistic mystery, for ratification, for adscrip-
tion, for acceptance of His sacrifice. The words of the invocation of Christ, of His blessing, are not recorded. It is not
necessary to know them in order to fulfill His command to
"Do this. . . ." It suffices if we conform exactly with His
intention, with what He had in mind when He commanded
us to do what He did, when, on the day before His passion,
He took bread and "gave thanks." By the invocations we ask
no other blessing than that which Christ asked on the day
before His passion when He took bread and "giving thanks
blessed."

For a confirmation of our interpretation we call attention
to a detail in the historical narrative which shows once more
the eagerness of the Church to assimilate and exactly to
conform her intention and the intention of the priest with
the intention of Christ. In the invocation of Christ within the
narrative "Who on the day before He suffered," the pronouns
"Thee" and "His" are most carefully set off and expressed:
"Who . . . having raised His eyes to heaven, unto Thee,
O God, His Father almighty, giving thanks to Thee, blessed,"
etc. Mind and heart, will and intention of the Church and of
the priest are united with the mind and heart and intention
of Christ; the intentions of both flow together into one.

The Significance of the "Therefore" in the First Invocation

It is a strange phenomenon that a simple little word like "therefore" in the first invocation of the Canon (*Te igitur*) should give so much trouble to liturgists. As a matter of fact, historians of the liturgy confess not to know the function of the "therefore" in the present Canon; they do not know with what other prayer exactly it is supposed to connect the first invocation. For an explanation most of the authors refer to the recasting of the Canon. When the Canon was rearranged, they say, the *Te igitur*, formerly preceded by another prayer, became the first prayer of the Canon, and in this way the "therefore" lost its function even though it was not removed from its context. Its presence in the Canon has no other significance, according to these same authors, than that of a forgotten relic. Some interpreters, like Cardinal Schuster, believe it has the function of sustaining, in some degree, the traditional continuity of the Canon, but find also that it forms a rather arbitrary connection with something preceding, like the "vere Sanctus" of the Gallican rite.

Although certainly there was a rearrangement of the Canon in the time between Pope Gelasius I (492–96) and Pope Gregory I (590–604), we can hardly imagine that the recasting of so venerable an object as the sacred Canon should have been so very violent. The popes of the sixth century, for instance, considered the Canon as of apostolic origin. Pope Vigilius, writing to Bishop Profuturus of Braga (538), remarked: "Ordinem precum in celebritate Missarum nullo nos tempore, nulla festivitate significamus habere diversum, sed semper eodem tenore oblata Deo munera consecrare. . . . Quapropter et ipsius canonicae precis textum direximus subter adjectum quem, Deo propitio, ex apostolica traditione suscepimus." It is true that this "apostolic tradition" has to be understood in a wider sense, so as to permit, for instance, of the work of the "Scholasticus" [1] of whom St. Gregory speaks. But this apostolic tradition refers certainly to the main ideas of the Canon, to the fundamental intention of the prayers and their development. We can therefore not imagine that the Pope who rearranged the Canon should not have proceeded with due respect and reverence for these principles.

The relation and connection between preface and invocations of the preconsecratory Canon can give the basis for a satisfactory explanation of the "therefore" in question, without forcing one to see in it a meaningless relic. Considered as the connecting link between Preface and Canon, the "therefore" of the first invocation not only has a meaning, but has the important function of establishing the beautiful ideological unity of the whole preconsecratory Canon. The "therefore" connects the two parts of the preconsecratory Canon, the Preface and the invocations, the Eucharistic and the impetratory part, the thanksgiving with the blessing, in order to give a complete interpretation of the words "giving thanks He blessed." The close grammatical connection which exists between the two terms "giving thanks" and "He blessed" in the phrase "giving thanks He blessed" is reflected in the prayer of thanksgiving and blessing of the Church and of the priest. The "therefore" connects the thanksgiving of the Church with the blessing of the Church, the Preface with the invocation, in a unity similar to that now obtaining in the phrase "giving thanks He blessed."

This function of the "therefore" becomes evident when we

[1] Cf. St. Jerome, *De viris illustribus*, c. 99; *PL*, 23, 737.

consider the immediate terms which are affected by it. The particle is inserted into an invocation of God: "Thee, therefore, most gracious Father." Hence the other terminus of the established relation has likewise to be some invocation of God. This we find in the invocation at the beginning of the Preface: "to Thee, holy Lord, Father almighty, eternal God." The reason that the parallelism and connection of these two invocations established by the "therefore" was overlooked, may have been the change in adjectives: "clementissime Pater" we say at the beginning of the invocations, "Sancte Pater omnipotens aeterne Deus" at the beginning of the Preface. Responsible for this change is most probably the supplicatory character of the invocations.

To show in schematic outline the twofold parallelism between Preface and invocations on the one hand, and between the whole preconsecratory Canon (Preface and invocations) and the historical narrative of the institution on the other, we here list the corresponding elements of all three parts, of Preface, of invocations, and of the narrative.

Preface:	1. Lift up your hearts. . . . We have them lifted up to the Lord.
	2. To thee, holy Lord, Father almighty, eternal God.
	3. Let us give thanks to the Lord our God.
Invocations:	1. Rubric: The priest extending and raising somewhat his hands . . . and raising his eyes to heaven.
	2. Thee, therefore, most gracious Father
	3. We humbly beg of Thee and entreat Thee to . . . bless.
Historical narrative:	1. Having raised His eyes to heaven.
	2. Unto Thee, O God, His Father almighty.
	3. Giving thanks He blessed.

CANON OF THE *Apostolic Tradition*
OF ST. HIPPOLYTUS

Let the deacons bring him (the bishop) the offering and, laying hands upon it together with all the priests, he shall say giving thanks: The Lord be with you; and all say: And with thy spirit. Lift up your hearts! We have them (lifted) unto the Lord. Let us give thanks to the Lord. It is meet and just. And forthwith he shall continue thus:

We render thanks unto Thee, O God, through Thy beloved Son Jesus Christ, whom in these last times Thou didst send to us as Savior and Redeemer and the Angel of Thy will; who is Thy inseparable Word, through whom Thou didst make all things and in whom Thou wast well pleased; whom Thou didst send from heaven into the Virgin's womb, and who, conceived within the womb, was made flesh and was demonstrated to be Thy Son being born of the Holy Spirit and a Virgin; who fulfilling Thy will and preparing for Thee a holy people stretched forth His hands as He suffered that He might release from suffering those who have believed in Thee; who when He was delivered to the voluntary passion, that He might abolish death and rend the bonds of the devil and tread down hell and enlighten the just and establish the ordinance and demonstrate the resurrection, taking bread, giving thanks to Thee, said: Take ye and eat: This is My body which is broken for you. Likewise also the chalice, saying: This is My blood, which is shed for you; when you do this, do it unto My commemoration. Mindful therefore of His death and resurrection we offer Thee bread and the chalice thanking Thee because Thou hast found us worthy to stand before Thee and minister unto Thee. And we beg that Thou send Thy Holy Spirit upon the oblation of holy Church, gathering into one all the saints who partake that they may be filled with the Holy Spirit unto the strengthening of their faith in truth, that we may praise and glorify Thee through Thy Son Jesus Christ, through whom glory and honor be unto Thee, to the Father and the Son with the Holy Spirit in Thy holy Church now and world without end. Amen.

CHAPTER XVII

The Individual Preconsecratory Invocation Te igitur clementissime Pater

"WE, therefore, humbly pray and beseech Thee, most merciful Father, through Jesus Christ Thy Son, our Lord, that Thou wouldst accept and bless these gifts, these presents, these holy unspotted sacrifices."

This invocation is parallel to the phrase of the Preface, "We give thanks to Thee, O holy Lord, Father almighty, eternal God, through Christ our Lord." The term "Father almighty" of the Preface is replaced with "most merciful Father" because of the suppliant character of the invocation. St. Cyril of Jerusalem uses this term speaking about the Eucharistic invocations: "After we have sanctified ourselves by these spiritual praises, we ask the most merciful God, that He may send the Holy Spirit upon the gifts proposed." [1] The Holy Eucharist is the manifestation of the omnipotence of God and the manifestation of the mercy of God. As sacrifice of propitiation and petition, an idea expressed primarily in the invocations, it is an appeal to the mercy of God (Dan. 9:9): "O Lord, to us belongeth confusion of face. But to Thee, the Lord our God, mercy and forgiveness." II Cor. 1:3:

[1] *Cat. myst.*, 5, 4; *PG*, 33, 1072.

"Blessed be the God and Father of our Lord Jesus Christ, the Father of mercies and the God of all comfort." God is addressed with the superlative "most merciful" because He "spared not even His own Son, but delivered Him up for us all," an act to be renewed in the Eucharistic sacrifice. There occur two superlatives in the course of the preconsecratory invocations: at the beginning of the first invocation "most merciful Father," and at the end of the last "Thy most beloved Son," which like a frame mark the unity of this part of the Canon as an invocation to the "most merciful Father" to give us again in sacrifice the body and blood of "His most beloved Son." There resounds in this superlative also the appeal of Christ to His heavenly Father in the sacerdotal prayer (John 17), where He appealed to His Father with all affection of heart and tenderness of feelings, repeating five times the term "Father."

It means another intensification of the power of supplication that the mediation of Christ is introduced with the words "through Jesus Christ, Thy Son, our Lord," while in the Preface the mediation of Christ is simply referred to with "through Christ our Lord."

"We humbly pray, and beseech Thee": these two verbs are synonymous. The duplication of terms, a characteristic mark of Hebrew literary style, expresses the intensity of the prayer, signified visibly with the profound inclination. Some parallelism could be seen between the two terms "pray and beseech" and "bless and accept," i.e., the object prayed for; and again some correspondence to the terms "gifts, presents, sacrifices."

"That Thou wouldst bless and accept." The terms "bless" and "accept" occur four times each in the course of the invocations, a sign of their importance. "To bless" is found in the first invocation, the second time in the *Quam oblationem* immediately before consecration; its idea is contained in the *Supra quae*, finally in the petition for fruitful Communion in the second part of the *Supplices te rogamus:* "We may be filled with all heavenly blessing." The term "accept" occurs in the first invocation, then in the *Hanc igitur* with "graciously to accept"; further in the *Quam oblationem* with "vouchsafe to make in all things acceptable," finally in the postconsecratory invocation *Supra quae* with "acept them."

These two terms can be distinguished from each other as generic (the term "to bless") from the specific ("to accept"). The first "to bless" refers to sacrifice and sacrament, whereas the term "to accept" refers specifically to the sacrifice, and means the acceptance on the side of God, which is the external complement of the sacrifice, making it efficacious.

There is another little detail like the "therefore," connecting the "giving thanks" of the Preface with the invocations, namely, "supplices." This term concludes the Preface in the phrase "supplici confessione dicentes" (of the Prefaces of Lent, the Holy Cross, the Blessed Virgin, St. Joseph, Common Preface), and continues with "suppliantly we pray and beseech Thee."

The terms "these gifts, these offerings, these holy and unblemished sacrifices" suppose consecration accomplished, because only Christ Himself is the holy and unblemished sacrifice. This is again an instance of the dramatic concept in the Canon. The accumulation of three terms, referring to one and the same oblation of the body and the blood of Christ, expresses the supreme value of this oblation.

In the terms "holy and unblemished" resounds the great prophecy of Malachias (Mal. 1:11), which is alluded to throughout the Canon: in the Offertory "this immaculate host"; in the *Quam oblationem* with "legitimate oblation"; in the prosphora immediately after consecration with "the pure host, the holy host, the immaculate host"; in the *Supra quae* with "the holy sacrifice, the immaculate host."

In the prophecy of Malachias, God reproaches the priests that they despise Him, offering oblations which are not according to the law (Lev. 23:12): "a lamb without blemish of the first year shall be killed for a holocaust of the Lord." The carelessness and negligence, the unworthiness and corruption of the priests is reproached (Mal. 1:7): "To you, O priests, that despise My name. . . . You offer polluted bread (term for sacrifice) upon My altar . . . in that you say: the table of the Lord is contemptible. If you offer the blind for sacrifice, is it not evil? And if you offer the lame and the sick, is it not evil? And now beseech ye the face of God that He may have mercy on you. . . . I have no pleasure in you, saith the Lord of hosts: and I will not receive a gift of your hand. For from the rising of the sun even to the going down, My name is great among the Gentiles: and in every place there is sacrifice and there is offered to My name a clean oblation."

The Old Testament sacrifices were not acceptable and valid *ex opere operato*, they were dependent on the disposition and dignity of the priest. This great difference is emphasized in the first place with the contrast between the "polluted bread" and the "clean oblation." Secondly, it is the difference between the objects of sacrifice: in the Old Testament they were irrational animals; in the New Testament "the spiritual, reasonable sacrifice."

In the prophecy of Malachias God exhorts to humble and suppliant prayer (Mal. 1:9): "And now beseech ye the face of God, that He may have mercy on you." Inspired by this exhortation, the priest bows profundly and prays: "humbly we pray and beseech thee." In the prophecy God refuses the unworthy gift of an unworthy priest (Mal. 1:10): "I have no pleasure in you, saith the Lord of hosts: and I will not receive a gift of your hand." The priest of the New Testament entreats God "to bless and to accept," to "look down with favorable and gracious countenance," not to refuse the sacrifice because of the defects and sins of priest and people, but to accept it because of its intrinsic purity, holiness, and infinite goodness: the immaculate host, the holy and unspotted sacrifice, the pure host, the holy host, the holy bread of life eternal and the chalice of everlasting salvation.

It is the host of which St. Peter (alluding to Lev. 23:12 and to Mal. 1) says (I Pet. 1:18 f.): "You were not redeemed . . . but with the precious blood of Christ, as of a lamb unspotted and undefiled."

Hanc igitur oblationem

"This oblation, therefore, of our service, and that of Thy whole family, we beseech Thee, O Lord, graciously to accept and to dispose our days in Thy peace, and to command us to be delivered from eternal damnation, and to be numbered in the flock of Thine elect. Through Christ our Lord. Amen."

Origin

The prayer is originally a variable invocation and intercessory prayer for some special intention on special occasions, for instance, consecration of a bishop, anniversary of the consecration, nuptial Mass, requiem. There are six *Hanc igitur* variants in the Leonine Sacramentary, thirty-eight in the Gelasian, four in the present missal (Maunday Thursday, Easter, Pentecost, consecration of a bishop). St. Gregory changed it from an exceptional insertion to a permanent prayer and added: "dispose our days in Thy peace."

INTERPRETATION

No agreement exists among the liturgists about the meaning of this prayer. A. Baumstark [2] regards it as an extension of the following invocation *Quam oblationem*. The wording, the grammatical connection with the relative pronoun in the following prayer, the Canon of the *De sacramentis,* which has only one prayer instead of two, seem to confirm his idea. Cardinal Schuster [3] holds that it would not formerly have constituted one prayer with the *Quam oblationem.* According to him it is the *Oratio post nomina.* At the time when the diptychs were read by the deacon, the celebrant continued with the *Communicantes.* When the deacon had finished the reading of the names with the clause "we offer . . . this sacrifice of praise," the celebrant took up the idea of oblation and continued "Hanc igitur oblationem."

For an adequate interpretation we have to consider two thoughts expressed in the prayer, the one noted in the opinion of Baumstark, the other in the sentence of Cardinal Schuster. There is no doubt that the external form of the prayer is analogous to the following invocation "Quam oblationem." It is the intention of the composer to establish the continuation and connection of the invocations, to emphasize the unity of the Eucharistic prayer. On the other hand there appears a new idea of the special intention for which the sacrifice is offered as a sacrifice of petition and propitiation. Whereas the following invocation asks generally for the acceptance of the Eucharistic oblation, in the *Hanc igitur* the

[2] *Liturgia Romana a liturgia dell' Escarcato.* Rome, 1904.
[3] *Op. cit.,* I, 279.

special intention is expressed. This special intention connects the prayer likewise with the previous intercession (and its secondary intentions).

According to this proposed solution, the word "therefore" in this prayer connects the *Hanc igitur* on the one hand with the first invocation "Te igitur clementissime Pater," and on the other hand with the phrase "which we offer to Thee" of the intercession for the Church, further with the "for which we offer" of the Memento for the living.

The words "of our service and that of Thy whole family" distinguish the body of the clergy from the body of the faithful in the same manner as the *unde et memores* says "we Thy servants, and likewise Thy holy people."

"Graciously to accept" continues obviously the idea of the first invocation with its "that Thou wouldst accept."

"To dispose our days in Thy peace" is the special intention imposed permanently by St. Gregory I as a kind of perpetual *oratio imperata*. It is taken from the special *Hanc igitur* of the anniversary Mass of the consecration of a bishop (*Leonine Sacramentary*, missa in natale Episcoporum, September 28): [4] "This oblation, therefore, which I Thy servant and priest offer to Thee that Thou without any merit of mine but in the largess of Thy ineffable mercy hast bestowed upon me the priestly office, accept placated and confirm in Thy piety what Thou hast worked in us, and dispose my days in most merciful guidance."

For two reasons St. Gregory I inserted this invocation: the celebration of the anniversary of his accession to the throne of Peter was discontinued because of his humility; he ordained that the bishop should rather come to visit Rome for

[4] V. L. Kennedy, "The Pre-Gregorian Hanc igitur," *Eph. lit.*, L (1936), 349–58. Cf. Thomas Michels, in *Jb. L.W.*, XIII (1933), 188–90.

the Natalitia Sti. Petri and called the celebration of his own feast a *vana superfluitas;* secondly, the sad condition of his time, Italy being ravaged by pestilence, famine, and war, demanded a special prayer for peace.

The words *ut placatus accipias* specify the sacrifice as a sacrifice of propitiation. St. Gregory knows that war and pestilence are punishments for sin and asks acceptance of the sacrifice in order to finish temporal punishment and to avert eternal damnation. Fittingly he adds his petition to the petition for acceptance of the sacrifice as propitiation.

The rubric that the priest has to hold his hands outstretched over the offerings while saying this prayer, is another expression of the propitiatory idea contained. This gesture occurs first in a French missal of the fourteenth century and was prescribed universally by Pope Pius V. Formerly the prayer was said with a profound inclination (still observed by the Dominicans and Carmelites). Cardinal Schuster found the substance of this rubric already in the Canons of St. Hippolytus, and refers to a representation of the Eucharist of the third century in the cemetery of Callistus.

The rubric is certainly inspired by an Old Testament rite (Lev. 1:4; 16:20 f.; Ps. 50:19) which expresses the vicarious atonement: Lev. 1:3 f.: ". . . to make the Lord favorable to him, and he shall put his hand upon the head of the victim: and it shall be acceptable, and help to its expiation." Lev. 16:21: "And putting both hands upon his head, let him confess all the iniquities of the children of Israel, and all their offenses and sins."

Quam oblationem

"Which oblation do Thou, O God, we beseech Thee, vouchsafe to make in all things blessed, legitimate, ratified, reason-

able, and acceptable: that it may become for us the body
and blood of Thy most beloved Son, our Lord Jesus Christ."

Origin

This prayer is the original preconsecratory invocation. If
the Canon of the *Traditio apostolica* by St. Hippolytus is
the original Roman Canon, then the *Quam oblationem* is derived from the postconsecratory invocation: "And we beg
that Thou send Thy Holy Spirit upon the oblation of holy
Church." With regard to what has been said about the interpretation of the epiklesis, there would be no difficulty of a
dogmatic nature in admitting such a development. In the
Traditio apostolica it is addressed exclusively to the Holy
Spirit. As preconsecratory invocation it is addressed to the
Father. We could find it quite reasonable that the insertion
of a preconsecratory invocation should express that it is
an invocation for consecration, not merely, as a postconsecratory invocation would appear, for fruitful Communion
and for the effect of sacrifice and sacrament. The association
with the "blessed" of the narrative of the institution of the
Eucharist, further with the sacerdotal prayer of our Lord,
show sufficiently its fundamental idea.

Interpretation

The relative pronoun in "Which oblation" resumes and
continues the invocation of the preceding prayer *Hanc igitur*
as well as of the first invocation *Te igitur clementissime Pater*.

"In all things" means thoroughly, perfectly, in every respect. We can hear in these words the eagerness to please
God perfectly, but also the confidence that this sacrifice will
meet with all requirements of the divine will. The same
idea is stressed with the five terms: "blessed, legitimate, rati-

fied, reasonable, aceptable." These terms are to a certain extent synonymous and express the intensity of the invocation and the perfection of the Eucharistic sacrifice.

Several times the attempt has been made to interpret these five terms as the members of one systematic division. Many theologians have accepted with St. Thomas the interpretation of Paschasius Radbertus.[5] St. Thomas refers to it (*Summa theol.*, III a, q. 83, a. 4 ad 7) under the name of St. Augustine. The fundamental thought of this interpretation is that the prayer refers to the mystical sacrifice of the faithful; that it is an invocation that the sacrifice may become fruitful for us. (Note: St. Thomas says merely "it seems"; in his reference to the sacerdotal prayer of Christ he considers the *Quam oblationem* a petition for consecration, a renewal of the intention to consecrate.) In this opinion "blessed" would signify the blessing of grace bestowed upon us by the Holy Eucharist; "ascribed" would mean our enrollment in heaven; "ratified" would mean our intimate incorporation into Christ; "reasonable," i.e., a means to deliver us from any bestial sense. This interpretation is based on the one hand on the words of the prayer "that it may become for us"; on the other hand it is based on the significance the terms "acceptable" and "reasonable" have in some passages of the Epistles of St. Paul. Speaking of the oblation of the Gentiles, St. Paul says (Rom. 15:16): "that the oblation of the Gentiles may be made acceptable and sanctified in the Holy Ghost"; speaking of his personal sacrifice (Rom. 15:31): "That the oblation of my service may be acceptable in Jerusalem"; about all personal sacrifices (Rom. 12, 1): "present your bodies a living sacrifice, holy, pleasing unto God, your reasonable service"; Titus 2:14: "a people acceptable, a pursuer of good works." We

[5] *De corpore et sanguine Domini*, Vol. II, chap. 12.

have to admit the derivation of the terms from St. Paul. With regard to the place of the prayer, as preconsecratory invocation, and also on account of the wording, we have to say that it is primarily a prayer for consecration and secondarily by the way of connotation a prayer for the effect of sacrifice and sacrament.

Abbot Ildefonse Herwegen [6] sought a systematic interpretation of the five terms from the vocabulary of the Roman law: "ascribed" would mean given over to the possession of another; "ratified," acceptance of the gift offered; "acceptable," that all requirements of the law have been complied with. It is correct to say that the oblation from the side of the giver and the acceptance of the gift by God complete the sacrifice as an act of religion, of justice toward God. These ideas certainly are expressed in these terms.

Another systematic interpretation of all five terms was attempted by J. B. Reus, S.J.[7] This author finds in the prayer the idea of the prophecy of Malachias (Mal. 1:6–14). He refers to the ancient liturgies which contain this prophecy (*Didache*, c. 14; St. Justin, *Dialogue with Trypho*; Liturgy of St. Mark; Liturgy of St. James); further to the fact that the Old Testament types (Abel, Abraham, Melchisedech) are in the Roman Canon, so that the absence of the prophecy of Malachias would be a strange phenomenon. According to his opinion the term "blessed" should then refer to the opposite of Mal. 1:6 f.: "You offer polluted bread upon My altar . . . in that you say: the table of the Lord is contemptible"; "ascribed" should refer to vv. 8–9: "If you offer the blind for sacrifice, is it not evil? And if you offer the lame and the sick,

[6] *Theol. Quartalschrift* (Tuebingen, 1917), pp. 438 f.
[7] "De natura orationis canonis: Quam oblationem," *Eph. lit.*, LVIII (1944), 23–41.

is it not evil?"; "ratified" should refer to v. 10: "I have no pleasure in you, saith the Lord of hosts: and I will not receive a gift of your hand"; "acceptable" should refer to vv. 12–14: "that the table of the Lord is defiled; and that which is laid thereupon is contemptible with the fire that devoureth it."

It is justifiable to look for the great prophecy of Malachias within the Canon. It may have had some influence in some of the five terms. There is, however, a reference to the prophecy of Malachias much more distinctly recognizable in other prayers of the Canon, e.g., "these holy unspotted sacrifices" of the first invocation; further "the pure host, the holy host, the immaculate host," of the prosphora after consecration; finally also in the "holy sacrifice, immaculate host." To see in each term of the *Quam oblationem* represented the one or other verse of the prophecy of Malachias, seems too far-fetched, particularly for the reason that these five terms are not of common origin. The *De sacramentis* does not have the term "blessed"; it was added at the time of the rearrangement of the Canon and emphasizes the idea of the "blessed" of the *Qui pridie* as we have shown above.

The rest of the terms which are of earlier origin express the idea of a legitimate, valid, acceptable sacrifice: "ascribed" is derived from Apoc. 21:27: "There shall not enter into it anything defiled . . . but they that are written in the book of life of the Lamb." Here is the opposition to "defiled" as in the prophecy of Malachias. "Ratified" may be understood as legitimate (cf. St. Ignatius, *Ad Smyrn.*, *PG*, 5, 713: *Una illa Eucharistia legitima est, quae fit sub episcopo*). "Reasonable" is of Pauline origin and was understood in the ancient liturgies as the opposite of "bloody" sacrifice: *Sacrificium incruentum.* With this meaning it is found already in St. Justin. In *De sacramentis* are recorded both terms: *Hostia rationabilis* and

208 CANON OF THE MASS

hostia incruenta. "Acceptable" is again of Pauline terminology (Titus 2:14: "that He might cleanse to Himself a people acceptable"), but applies in the Canon to the acceptance of the Eucharistic sacrifice.[8]

The words "that it may become" contain a twofold beautiful allusion to Gen. 1:3 and to Luke 1:38. It is first the allusion to the "Fiat" of the creation with the meaning, that it is by divine creative power that transubstantiation is accomplished. Secondly there is allusion to the beautiful analogy between the consecration and the Incarnation with the same words found in Luke 1:38: "Be it done unto me according to thy word." [9]

"Of Thy most beloved Son, our Lord Jesus Christ": this is the only text of the Canon which gives to our Lord the epithet "most beloved Son" with an allusion to the testimony of the heavenly Father at the baptism in the Jordan and a similar testimony on Mount Tabor (Matt. 3:17; 17:5): "This is My beloved Son, in whom I am well pleased." The superlative intensifies the invocation and forms a beautiful symmetrical conclusion of the preconsecratory Canon, which began with the invocation of the "most merciful Father" and concludes with the object of the invocations, "that it may become for us the body and blood of Thy most beloved Son, our Lord Jesus Christ." [10]

[8] O. Casel, "Oblatio rationabilis," *Tuebingen theol. Quartalschrift,* XC (1917–1918), 429–38. *Jb. L.W.,* IV (1924), 37: "Die logike Thysis der antiken Mystik in christlicher Umdeutung."

[9] J. Brinktrine, "Die transformatio (transfiguratio) corporis et sanguinis Christi in den abendlaendischen Liturgies," *Theologie und Glaube,* VIII (1916), 311–18.

[10] M. E. Petersen, "Dona, munera, sacrificia," *Eph. lit.,* XLVI (1932), 75–77; J. Brinktrine, *Die heilige Messe* (Paderborn, 1931), p. 155.

CHAPTER XVIII

The Intercessory Prayers

THIS third group of prayers of the Canon (prayers of praise and thanksgiving; invocations; intercessory prayers) is found before the consecration: (a) prayer for the Church (second part of the first Canon-prayer beginning with "in primis quae tibi offerimus"); (b) the commemoration of the living; (c) the *Communicantes*. After the consecration: the commemoration of the dead and the *Nobis quoque peccatoribus*. (The *Hanc igitur* before the consecration is partly an invocation, partly an intercessory prayer, as we have explained above.)

The historical development of the intercessory prayers is in close connection with the development of the invocations and is obscure. Since, however, the historical point of view is of minor importance for an understanding of their meaning, we limit our study of the historical development to the most important steps and refer for the particulars to the monographs on the history of the liturgy.

HISTORICAL DEVELOPMENT

The most ancient liturgical text with an intercessory prayer is the Eucharistic prayer of the *Didache*. It has a double intercessory prayer for the Church: one immediately after the blessing over the wine and bread (9, 4): "Even as this broken bread was scattered over the hills, and was gathered together

209

and became one, so let Thy Church be gathered together from the ends of the earth into Thy kingdom"; another at the end of the thanksgiving for Holy Communion (10, 5): "Remember, O Lord, Thy Church, to deliver it from all evil and to make it perfect in Thy love, and gather it from the four winds, sanctified for Thy kingdom which Thou hast prepared for it."

In these intercessory prayers appears the eschatological spirit of the *Didache* with the implicit quotation from Matt. 24:31: "And He shall send His angels with a trumpet and a great voice: and they shall gather together His elect from the four winds, from the farthest parts of the heavens to the utmost bounds of them." There is heard in it also the influence of Christ's sacerdotal prayer in the three petitions:
"deliver it from all evil"; John 17:15: "that Thou shouldst keep them from evil";
"make it perfect in Thy love"; John 17:26: "that the love wherewith Thou hast loved Me may be in them";
"sanctified for Thy kingdom"; John 17:19: "that they also may be sanctified."

In the thanksgiving prayer of the first Epistle of St. Clement to the Corinthians we find an intercession for all kinds of men, for kings and governors, for the conversion of pagans and sinners, for the Christians themselves, for peace and grace.

St. Justin Martyr speaks of an intercessory prayer (I Apol. 65, 1): "that we, after we have thus cleansed him who believes and is joined to us, lead him to those who are called brethren, where they are gathered together, in order to say common prayers intently for ourselves, for him who has been enlightened, and for all others everywhere." These common prayers were said after the readings and the homily. They were a series of petitions for all sorts and conditions of men.

In the *Traditio apostolica* of St. Hippolytus the common prayers were said before the presentation of the offerings. There is, however, at the end of the anaphora a prayer for the Church very like to the one of the *Didache:* "And we beg that Thou send Thy Holy Spirit upon the oblation of holy Church, gathering into one all the saints . . . unto the strengthening of their faith in truth."

In the prayer book of Serapion the common prayers are found after the homily with the usual intentions for the catechumens, the sick, the fruits of the earth, the Church, bishops, priests, and all those "whose names are written in the book of life." At the end of the anaphora is an intercession for the departed with the recital of certain names containing allusions to the sacerdotal prayer: "We pray also for all the departed whom we commemorate (the names follow). Sanctify these souls (John 17:19), because Thou knowest all; sanctify all the departed in the Lord and let them join all Thy holy angels and give them a place and home in Thy kingdom" (John 17:24).

In the *Catecheses* of St. Cyril of Jerusalem the saint continues after description of the epiklesis: "When the spiritual sacrifice, or the unbloody cult, is accomplished, we then implore God for the common peace of the churches, for the right state of the world, for the emperors, soldiers, and confreres, for the sick, for the afflicted, and generally for all who need help. . . . Afterwards we remember those who died, first the patriarchs, prophets, apostles, martyrs, that God may accept our prayer upon their prayers and intercessions. Then also for the departed holy Fathers and bishops, and generally for all who died from among us." In this intercession the distinct influence of a passage from St. Paul (I Tim. 2:1 f.) is felt, and a group of saints is already introduced, who are remembered as patrons and intercessors supporting the prayers of men.

The *Apostolic Constitutions* contains a twofold intercession, one before the anaphora, the common prayers, with such intentions as: for peace and settlement of the world, for the holy Church, for every bishop, for brethren newly enlightened, for the sick, the afflicted. In the concluding prayer of the priest again an association of the sacerdotal prayer is contained: "O Lord almighty . . . who hast given us by Christ the preaching of knowledge to the acknowledgment of Thy glory and Thy name, which He has made known to us, for our comprehension, do Thou now also look down through Him upon this Thy flock, and deliver it from all ignorance and grant . . . that we may have due reverence of Thy glory, sanctify them by thy Truth . . . vouchsafe them the everlasting life." The second intercession at the end of the anaphora says: "We further pray unto Thee, O Lord, for Thy holy Church spread from one end of the world to another . . . that Thou wilt preserve it unshaken and free from disturbance until the end of the world. . . . We further pray to Thee for me . . . for the king and all in authority . . . also for all those holy persons who have pleased Thee from the beginning of the world . . . patriarchs, prophets, apostles, martyrs," etc.

The liturgy of St. James and that of St. Chrysostom follow the same lines. An organic development is constituted when certain names of living persons were read from diptychs, and the name of the pope with the names of bishops was mentioned. In certain Churches along with the diptychs of the living or of the dead a certain number of saints was mentioned. The place of the intercession is, as a rule, after the consecration, either before or after the epiklesis. In the liturgy of St. Mark it is placed before the consecration, but within the anaphora.

It is a singular fact of the Roman Canon, that the intercession is divided into two groups of prayers, one before the consecration, the second after it. We refer to the most important documents which give the outlines of the development of the intercessory prayers in the Roman Canon.

In the *De sacramentis* (IV, 4) is contained the following passage: "Prayers are said for the people, for the kings, for the rest; when it has come to the accomplishment of the venerable sacrament, the priest does not use any more his own words, but the words of Christ."

The next most disputed document is a letter of Pope Innocent I (402–17) [1] to Decentius, bishop of Gubbio, who asked about the recital of the names of those who made offerings. He received this reply: "The offerings are first to be commended, and the names of those whose offerings they are, are to be read; and this is to be done within the sacred mysteries (i.e., within the Canon) and not in the course of these other things which we place before, that we may open the way for the prayers with the mysteries themselves (or: for the coming mysteries themselves by our prayers). Abbot Cabrol [2] and Dom Cagin [3] maintain that the original place of the intercessory prayers in the Roman Mass was at the offertory. Therefore the passage from the letter of Pope Innocent I would have the meaning, that from then on the intercession is to be made in the Canon instead of before it. Drews, Baumstark, and others maintain the contrary: according to

[1] *Ep.* 24; *PL*, 20, 551–61.
[2] *Les origines liturgiques*, Paris, 1906; cf. M. Maranget, "La grande prière d'intercession," in *Cours et conférences*, etc., pp. 177–91.
[3] *Paléographie musicale*, V.

them the meaning of the passage is that the intercession has to follow the consecration (as in the Antiochian rite). Dom Conally considered absurd such a translation, that we may open with the mysteries the way for the prayers. He says: We do not prepare for certain prayers by the Canon, but we prepare for the Canon by certain prayers. Kennedy explains the obscurity of the text with the literary style of the papal chancery with the result: we may open the way for the mysteries themselves by our prayer.

After all these disputes, it does not seem contradictory to maintain that the passage ordains that the intercession should be made within the Canon, and not before in order to support the intercession with the power of the Canon prayers, a power they would not have if they were said outside the Canon.

The next document of interest is a letter of Pope Boniface (418–22) [4] to Emperor Honorius in which he states that prayers are said for the emperor within the Canon "inter ipsa mysteria, inter preces suas."

Leo I [5] in a reply to Bishop Anatolius of Constantinople refers to the practice of reciting the names of bishops in communion with Rome. The *Leonine Sacramentary* testifies also to the reading of the names of those who had just received baptism.

The best theory about the probable author and about the course of the development of the intercession of the Roman Canon is proposed by V. L. Kennedy, C.S.B. [6] We summarize the main points of his theory.

[4] *PL*, 20, 767.
[5] *Ep.* 80; *PL*, 54, 914.
[6] V. L. Kennedy, C.S.B., *The Saints of the Canon of the Mass.* Citta del Vaticano, 1938.

The author of the decisive and historically mysterious rearrangement of the Roman Canon seems to have been Pope Gelasius I (492–96) for the following reasons. (a) The author of the *Liber pontificalis* (500–525) tells about Gelasius that he composed prefaces and orations: "fecit et sacramentorum praefationes et orationes cauto sermone"; (b) it was this Pope who introduced the Kyrie into the Mass. (c) The common prayers disappear exactly at that time, because they were replaced on the one hand by the Kyrie, on the other hand by the intercession within the Canon. The last trace of the common prayers is found in an instruction of Pope Felix II (483–92) who forbade that mention should be made, within the common prayers, of those who let themselves be rebaptized.

The reform of Pope Gelasius seems to have been in this way. (a) Its definite form was given to the commemoration of the living, which was already in existence for about a century (with petitions for the Church, the pope, the emperor, etc.; prayers for offerers with recital of their names; names of certain other persons, especially of bishops in communion with Rome, possibly already certain saints). The *Communicantes*, however, contained the names of only a small number of saints. (b) The commemoration of the dead was placed at the end of the Canon with some names of saints, but was restricted to Masses for the dead and private Masses only.

This reform was in close adherence to the Eastern liturgies. There are parallels for the *Communicantes* in the liturgy of Jerusalem, Antioch, Constantinople; for the *Nobis quoque peccatoribus* and its list of saints, in the Alexandrian liturgy. Pope Gelasius did not give the final form to these prayers.

The complete list of saints in the *Communicantes* and in the *Nobis quoque peccatoribus* did not exist until Gregory I. It developed in the course of the sixth century and received its final systematic hierarchical order from Pope Gregory I. The names, placed in these prayers at the time of Pope Gelasius (probably seven in each prayer), were: (in the *Communicantes*) the Blessed Virgin, Peter, Paul, Xystus, Laurentius, Cornelius, Cyprianus; (in the *Nobis quoque peccatoribus*) Joannes, Stephanus, Marcellinus, Petrus, Agnes, Caecilia, Felicitas.

In the course of the sixth century the additions made were probably these: (a) the names of apostles at the occasion of the dedication of the Apostoleion between 555 and 574; (b) Cosmas and Damian at the occasion of the dedication of their church by Pope Felix IV about 530; (c) Clement, added probably by Pope John II; (d) John and Paul added by Pope Agapitus (535–36); (e) Chrysogonus, added about middle of the sixth century.

The last additions (substantially) were made by Pope Gregory I. He is usually credited with the decisive rearrangement of the Canon. But, in the consideration of this chapter, the reform work of St. Gregory is limited to a very few minor points. The whole Canon in its present structure was already in existence before Gregory I. His additions are: "diesque nostras in tua pace disponas" inserted in the *Hanc igitur* which he ordained as a regular prayer; addition of Matthias, Barnabas, Agatha, Lucia; and the rearrangement in hierarchical order.

As a result of this chapter we may conclude that Pope Gelasius deserves the credit given him by the Stowe Missal, wherein the Canon is headed: "Canon dominicus papae Gilasi."

Scriptural Background

The texts from Scripture which have contributed to the intercessory prayers of the Canon are chiefly: the canticle of Moses, the Hallel; the words of St. Paul (I Tim. 2:1 f.); the sacerdotal prayer with ideas and structure; the intercessory prayer of Christ on the cross; the liturgy of heaven described in the Apocalypse.

The intercessory prayers of the Canon ask for the Church, for the people of God, protection, guidance, redemption, and eternal salvation. These petitions are prefigured in the prophetic words of the canticle (Exod. 16:11): "In Thy mercy Thou hast been a leader to the people which Thou hast redeemed" (in the prophetic vision the future events are seen as accomplished facts). Again (Exod. 16:17): "Thou shalt bring them in, and plant them in the mountain of Thy inheritance, in Thy most firm habitation which Thou hast made, O Lord: Thy sanctuary, O Lord, which Thy hands have established."

Psalm 114 of the Hallel prays (v. 3): "The sorrows of death have compassed me: and the perils of hell have found me. I met with trouble and sorrow; and I called upon the name of the Lord. O Lord, deliver my soul." Psalm 116:17 f. continues: "I will sacrifice to Thee the sacrifice of praise. I will pay my vows to the Lord." Likewise the intercessory prayers of the Canon ask in the prayer for the living "for the redemption of their souls, for the hope of salvation and their preservation." In the *Hanc igitur* is prayed for peace and preservation from eternal damnation. The words of the commemoration for the living, "who offer to Thee, the eternal God, their vows," are taken from ps. 116:18 f.: "I will pay my vows to the Lord in the sight of all His people; in the courts of the house of the Lord, in the midst of thee, Jerusalem." These words prefigure likewise the petitions: "let us be counted among the elect" in the *Hanc igitur;* further the passage of the *Nobis quoque peccatoribus:* "admit us in Thy largess into their society (saints)."

The first and immediate scriptural model of the intercessory prayers is the text from St. Paul, I Tim. 2:1 f.: "I desire therefore, first of all that supplications, prayers, intercessions, and thanksgivings be made for all men: for kings and for all that are in high station; that we may lead a quiet and a peaceable life in all piety and chastity." The influence of this text, visible throughout the history of the Canon, is represented in the present Canon in the petition for the peace of the Church: "for thy holy Catholic Church, that Thou wouldst deign to give her peace in the whole world." The commentator of the Epistles of St. Paul of the fourth century (*Commentaria in XIII epistolas Beati Pauli,* Rome, 370–75) testifies explicitly to the influence of this passage upon the Canon. Likewise St. Augustine in his commentary upon this passage (*Epist. 149 ad Paulinum*).

The influence of the sacerdotal prayer upon the development of the intercessory prayers was referred to already several times. We list here merely the main ideas of the sacerdotal prayer which have inspired the intercessions.

Our Lord prayed for His disciples, for the followers of the disciples; He prayed for their unity, protection, sanctification, and final glory. "Not for them only do I pray, but for them also who through their word shall believe in Me . . . that they may be one, as We also are one." These words have their parallel in the petitions of the Canon: "In the first instance for thy holy catholic Church . . . that thou wouldst "deign to protect, to unite and guide her." The same ideas are found in the *Nobis quoque peccatoribus:* "into whose company (saints) we implore Thee to admit us." The same disposition is required in the Canon, "the faith of whom is known to Thee," as from the disciples: "Because the words which Thou gavest Me, I have given to them. And they have received them and have known in very deed that I came out from Thee: and they have believed that Thou didst send Me." The tender expression of v. 9 "because they are Thine" as a reason why the Father should hear the intercession, is reflected in the Canon; "for Thy Church," "together with Thy servant our Pope"; "Thy servants."

The arrangements of the intercessory prayers into two groups, one before, another after consecration, this symmetrical distribution, has likewise its exemplar in the sacerdotal prayer of Christ. He prayed first for His disciples (v. 9), and then, after the consecration of Himself for His bloody sacrifice, He prayed for the followers of the disciples (v. 20).

While the communion of saints is testified throughout Scripture, the communion of heaven and earth in the Eucharistic liturgy is especially revealed in the Apocalypse. As there is communion in the thanksgiving (Apoc. 11:17), "We give Thee thanks, O Lord God almighty," so is expressed the communion in the invocations and intercessions (Apoc. 5:8; cf. 8:3): "And when He had opened the book, the four living creatures and the four and twenty ancients fell down before the Lamb, having every one of them harps and golden vials full of odors, which are the prayers of the saints."

The intercession of Christ upon the cross reproduced in the Canon unites the Canon of the bloody sacrifice with that of the unbloody sacrifice. The thief on the right asked from the cross (Luke 23:42 f.): "And he said to Jesus: Lord, remember me when Thou shalt come into Thy kingdom. And

Jesus said to him: Amen I say to thee, this day thou shalt be with Me in paradise." The Byzantine liturgy gives evidence that this prayer has influenced the wording of the Memento of the intercessory prayers. In the prayer said during the procession of the great entrance, priest and deacon alternate: "May the Lord God remember us all in His kingdom. . . . May the Lord God remember thy priesthood in His kingdom." Particularly before Communion the choir sings: "Make me this day a sharer in Thy mystical supper, O Son of God. For I will not reveal Thy mysteries to Thine enemies, nor kiss Thee with the kiss of Judas, but as the thief says: Remember me, O Lord, in Thy kingdom. Alleluja, alleluja, alleluja." In the same way we remind our Lord Jesus Christ in the prayer for the living, "Remember, O Lord," and in the prayer for the departed, "Remember also," and with the same affection we pray, "To us sinners also . . . not weighing our merits but freely granting pardon."

BASIC IDEAS OF THE INTERCESSORY PRAYERS

The Eucharistic sacrifice is, according to the Council of Trent,[7] not only a sacrifice of praise and thanksgiving, but likewise a sacrifice of propitiation and petition: "The holy synod teaches that it (the Eucharistic sacrifice) is truly propitiatory; . . . by its oblation God is placated, grants grace and the gift of penance, forgives crimes and sins, even very grave ones. It is, namely, one and the same victim, the same who offers now by the ministry of the priests, who offered Himself once upon the cross, with the only difference in the mode of oblation. . . . It is not only for the sins, punishments, satisfactions, and other needs of the living, but also for those who died in Christ, and are not yet completely purified, cor-

[7] Sess. 22, c. 2 and can. 3; *DB*, nos. 940, 950.

rectly offered, according to the tradition of the Apostles." Can. 3: "If anyone should say, that the sacrifice of the Mass is merely a sacrifice of praise and thanksgiving, or a mere and empty commemoration of the sacrifice accomplished upon the cross, but not of propitiation; or only to the benefit of those who communicate in it, and is not to be offered for the living and for the departed, for the remission of sins, their punishments, for satisfactions and other needs: A. s." This is the primary basis of the intercessory prayers. It is merely a specifying of this idea, if the subject who offers intercession, and the object for which it is offered, is distinguished with several prayers.

The second, basic idea contained in the intercessory prayers is the proper causality of the Eucharistic sacrifice. For an adequate appreciation of this idea we must distinguish the different subjects who offer the sacrifice: (a) Christ, the principal offering priest; (b) the ministering priest; (c) the Church offering through the ministry of the priest; (d) the faithful who in one way or other take part actively in the oblation. As far as Christ is concerned, the Eucharistic sacrifice produces its effect *ex opere operato* (Trid., Sess. 22, c. 1: "This is the clean oblation which cannot be contaminated by the unworthiness or malice of those who offer it." As far as the Church is offering, it produces its effect *ex opere operantis ecclesiae*, again independently from the worthiness of the offering priest. Now there is a third group of fruits *ex opere operantis* dependent on the disposition of the priest and of the faithful, on their grace, piety, and devotion. It is only fitting that we should ask with prayers for the fruits which result from the sacrifice *ex opere operato*, just as we ask for the consecration, although we know that God will accomplish it. The intercessory prayers, however, have a very

special reason concerning the fruits which depend upon
the disposition of priest and faithful, so that according to
the degree of piety and devotion the fruits of the sacrifice
can be increased, accidentally and in subordination to the
fruits *ex opere operato.*

Notwithstanding these facts, the causality of the Eucharistic sacrifice is different from the causality of the sacraments.
It is the primary and direct end of the sacraments to communicate grace to men, whereas it is the primary end of the
sacrifice to offer to God the due worship of praise and
thanksgiving, to placate Him and to ask for His gifts. Therefore are the sacraments instruments of grace and produce
grace immediately, directly. Now, the sacrifice has, according
to the will of God, likewise as its purpose to convey to us
the fruits of redemption, and is in this sense also a means
of grace; it is, however, not an instrument of immediate communication of grace, but causes grace rather mediately, indirectly, by placating God (as propitiation), by moving
God (as petition) to dispense His grace and benefits of all
kinds. As the sacrifice upon the cross was the meritorious
cause of all graces of redemption, so is the Eucharistic sacrifice the moral cause of their distribution. As such it applies
the propitiatory and impetratory effects *per modum im-
petrationis,* and each time in a measure depending on the
decree of God. Consequently, although the causality is one
ex opere operato, grave sins are forgiven through the Eucharistic sacrifice mediately and indirectly, imparting the grace
of contrition or the grace of other virtues. The same applies
proportionately to venial sins. But it produces immediately
and directly the remission of satisfactions due for sins after
their remission, and also immediately and directly are forgiven punishments to be suffered in purgatory.

CHAPTER XIX

The Individual Intercessory Prayers, In primis . . . pro Ecclesia sancta catholica

"IN the first place which (sacrifices) we offer Thee for Thy holy Catholic Church, which mayest Thou vouchsafe to pacify, guard, unite, and govern throughout the world; together with Thy servant our Pope, and our Bishop, as also all orthodox promoters of the Catholic, Apostolic faith."

This is the most ancient of the intercessory prayers. In the interpretation of this prayer we may distinguish the object (persons) for whom intercession is made, the object which is petitioned. A particular question is the addition of the names of the Pope, of bishops, and of rulers.

The prayer is offered for the universal Church. The priest, in offering the sacrifice, represents first of all the Church. The Church it is, therefore, for which the sacrifice is offered in the first place. The sacrificial fruit which falls to the share of the entire Church is called the general fruit. In the Eucharistic sacrifice Christ offers Himself for the Church; the Church offers herself through the priest for her own welfare. It is for the benefit of the Church that the daily sacrifice was instituted, and for this end it is offered. In the sacrifice the stream of blessings is poured out throughout the Church and unto all her children, who receive their share each single member *according to their disposition* and according to their *position* within the mystical body, according to their *contribution to the common welfare* of the Church.

The pronoun "Thy" which repeatedly occurs in the intercessory prayers (Thy Church, Thy servant our Pope, Thy servants and handmaids, Thy sinful servants) recalls the expression of the sacerdotal prayer (John 17:9): "I pray for them. I pray not for the world, but for them whom Thou hast given Me: because they are Thine."

Four special blessings are particularly mentioned as the object of impetration: "which mayest Thou vouchsafe to pacify, guard, unite, and govern throughout the world." This formula is the last remnant of the former common prayer. (Good Friday is now the only day on which it is said in its entirety as it used to be said at every Mass before the reform of Pope Gelasius.) A letter of Pope Vigilius (538–55) to Emperor Justinian speaks of an "ancient tradition" and mentions the three terms: *adunare, regere, custodire* (in the Oratio on Good Friday the term *gubernare* is missing). The idea of these terms and the whole phrase is inspired by St. Paul (I Tim. 2:1 f.): "I desire therefore, first of all that . . . intercessions . . . be made . . . that we may lead a quiet and a peaceable life in all piety and chastity." There resound in this phrase also the loving words of our Lord about peace (John 14:27): "Peace I leave with you: My peace I give unto you. Not as the world giveth, do I give unto you. Let not your heart be troubled nor let it be afraid" (cf. the parallel in the prayer before Holy Communion: "O Lord Jesus Christ, who saidst to Thine apostles: Peace I leave you, My peace I give you . . . vouchsafe to give that peace and unity which is agreeable to Thy will"). The terms "guard" and "unite" are taken from the sacerdotal prayer (John 17:11): "Holy Father, keep them in Thy name . . . that they may be one, as We also are."

The words "throughout the world" associate a beautiful idea from the Old Testament (Wisd. 18:24): "For in the priestly robe which he wore was the whole world," as a symbol of the universal intercessory power of the high priest of the Old Testament. The high priest represented the whole earth as mediator between God and mankind. God ordained that in the vestments be visible the symbols of all the elements of the earth (on the two onyx stones and on the twelve gems of the rational before his breast were the symbols of the twelve tribes): Exod. 28:9 f.: "And thou shalt take two onyx stones: and shalt grave on them the names of the children of Israel. Six names on one stone and six on the other, according to the order of their birth"; v. 12: "And Aaron shall bear their names before the Lord upon both shoulders, for a remembrance"; v. 29: "And Aaron shall bear the names of the children of Israel in the rational of judgment upon his breast, when he shall enter into the sanctuary: a memorial before the Lord forever."

In the *Didache* the intercession for the Church has associated an eschatological color (*Didache*, IX, 4): "Let Thy Church be gathered together from the ends of the earth into Thy kingdom" and (X, 5): "gather it from the four winds," with an allusion to Matt. 24:31: "And He shall send His angels with a trumpet and a great voice: and they shall gather together His elect from the four winds, from the farthest parts of the heavens to the utmost bounds of them."

The unity prayed for is specified with the addition of the names of the Pope and the Bishop, as the principle of that unity. This is a homage to the visible head of the Church, and at the same time a prayer for the Holy Father and for the Bishop, who together with the other principal members of the mystical body receive their particular large share from the universal sacrificial fruit. They contribute chiefly to the common welfare of the Church, they promote principally her glory and holiness, they stand in great need of light and strength to persevere in the care for the flock entrusted to them, for unity and freedom, for faith and grace.

The word "pope"[1] was originally used in a wider sense; in the Eastern Church it is still equivalent to "priest." It was restricted in the Roman Church to signify at first bishops only, and then in the fourth century exclusively the Supreme Pontiff. Pope Siricius (d. 398) probably was the first to use it in this sense. Gregory VII (1073–85) prescribed it as the title of the successors of St. Peter.

The addition of the name of the Bishop and of other bishops was in the course of the fifth century a question of their orthodoxy, just as the reciting of the names of Pope and Bishop was a sign of the celebrant's orthodoxy. To this practice Pope Leo I alludes in his reply to Bishop Anatolius of Constantinople.[2] The Council of Vaison ordained: "And we found it right, that the name of the Lord Pope, whoever occupies the apostolic throne, shall be recited in our churches"

---

[1] P. de Labriolle, "Une esquisse de l'histoire du mot Papa," *Bulletin d'ancienne littérature et d'archéologie chrétienne* (Paris, 1911), pp. 215–20.

[2] The commemoration of the Pope in the Mass is mentioned in the Acts of the Roman Council under Pope Symmachus (498–514). Ennodius put the question before the fathers of the Council. Cf. Labbe, *Con. nova collectio* (Venice, 1767), VIII, 282: "Deinde pro quaestionum tormentis venerabilem Laurentium (Milan.) et Petrum (Ravennat.) episcopos a communione Papae se suspendisse replicatis. . . . Ullone ergo tempore, dum celebrarentur ab his sacra Missarum a nominis eius commemoratione cessatum est? Unquam pro desideriis vestris sine ritu catholico et cano more, semiplenas nominatim antistites hostias obtulerunt?"

(can 4). Pope Pelagius I (556–61),[3] writing to the Bishop of Toscana, complains: "How can you believe that you are not separated from communion with the universal Church if you do not mention my name within the sacred mysteries, as the custom is?"

"As all orthodox promoters of the Catholic faith." The term "orthodox" is very seldom used in the West to designate Catholics. It may indicate that this phrase is from the Antiochian rite. The "promoters of the Catholic faith" means such persons as have a special merit about faith.[4] St. Cyprian (Epistle to Bishop Felix of Saragossa) qualifies a bishop as *fidei cultor ac defensor veritatis*. On the entrance to the Church of SS. John and Paul the term refers to the founder of the church: "Quis tantas Christo venerandas condidit aedes? Si quaeris: cultor Pammachius fidei" ("Who has built such a splendid temple for Christ? Thou shalt know it was Pammachius promoter of faith").

In the Middle Ages the name of the Emperor of the Holy Roman Empire was added, following the advice of St. Paul (I Tim. 2:2): "For kings and for all that are in high station." St. Clement refers to such a prayer, and the *Apostolic Constitutions* has it: "We further pray to Thee for the king and all in authority." Pope Boniface (418–22) in a letter to Honorius [5] states that prayers are said for him "within the mysteries themselves, within their prayers" (abolished in 1570 by Pope Pius V).

It was also a custom of the Middle Ages to add a prayer for the celebrant himself (likewise found in the *Apostolic*

[3] *Ep*, 5; *PL*, 69, 398: "Quomodo vos ab universi orbis communione separatos esse non creditis, si mei inter sacra mysteria, secundum consuetudinem, nominis memoriam reticetis?"

[4] Cf. M. Maranget, *op. cit.*; A. Daniels, "Devotio," *Jb. L.W.*, I (1921), 40–60.

[5] *PL*, 20, 767.

Constitutions): "Be merciful also to me, Thy most unworthy servant, and cleanse me from offenses of sins."

COMMEMORATION OF THE LIVING

"Remember, O Lord, Thy servants and handmaids, and all here present, whose faith and devotion are known to Thee; for whom we offer, or who offer up to Thee this sacrifice of praise for themselves and all pertaining to them, for the redemption of their souls, for the hope of their salvation and safety, and who pay their vows unto Thee, the eternal God, living and true."

St. Jerome (d. 420), in his Commentary on Ezechiel, made the remark: "The deacon reads publicly in the churches the names of those who offer." These names, together with those of others, principally ecclesiastical and secular dignitaries, persons of merit and distinction, of living and departed, were listed on diptychs. The Gelasian and Gregorian Sacramentaries do not mark names to be mentioned. On the third Sunday of Lent, however, the Gelasian has the rubric that the names of the neophytes are to be mentioned at the Memento within the action: "Within the action, where is said Memento . . . of Thy servants and handmaids, who . . . and there are to be recited the names of men and women who receive the infants for baptism."

It is a historical problem at what place these diptychs were read before the rearrangement by Pope Gelasius. The phrase "who offer up to Thee" would suggest the Offertory. There is, however, in the Antiochian rite the same phrase, although the prayer was certainly not said at the Offertory.

"For whom we offer": these words are missing in all early Sacramentaries. This addition may have been inserted at a time when the Offertory procession was discontinued (cf.

Micrologus, c. 13); or at the time when the Mass foundations were multiplied, so that to such Masses the formula should apply "for whom we offer," whereas for the traditional practice the form "who offer up to Thee."

"Sacrifice of praise" and the words "who pay their vows" are an allusion to the Hallel psalm 115:17–19: "I will sacrifice to Thee the sacrifice of praise . . . I will pay my vows to the Lord." The words "sacrifice of praise" together with "for the redemption of their souls, for the hope of their salvation and safety" express beautifully the threefold idea of the Eucharistic sacrifice: praise, propitiation, petition.

The *Communicantes*

"In communion with and honoring the memory especially of the glorious ever Virgin Mary, Mother of God, and our Lord Jesus Christ; as also of Thy blessed apostles and martyrs Peter and Paul, Andrew, James, John, Thomas, James, Philip, Bartholomew, Matthew, Simon and Thaddaeus, Linus, Cletus, Clement, Xystus, Cornelius, Cyprian, Lawrence, Chrysogonus, John and Paul, Cosmas and Damian, and all Thy saints; by whose merits and prayers grant that we may in all things be made secure by the aid of Thy protection. Through the same Christ our Lord. Amen."

The origin and development of this intercessory prayer depends on the origin and development of the cult of the saints. The cult of the saints in its turn had its origin in the ancient funeral liturgy, in the celebration of the birthday of the deceased. The Christians changed the earthly birthday into the heavenly, celebrating the anniversary of the death as Natalitia sanctorum. The practice of public cult began toward the middle of the third century. It received a new impulse with the peace of Constantine.

The saints of the Roman Canon have all the happy associations of the history of the Roman Church of the time of the martyrs. This list itself is a memorial of the interior life of the early Church, a testimony of her piety, of the fervor of devotion, of the flowering of her liturgy. These saints of the Roman Canon are like lilies and roses adorning the majestic structure of the Roman Church and of the Roman Canon, their own property. They breathe into it the atmosphere of the local history of Rome, of the Roman Church, of her faith and fidelity, of her heroism and immortal glory.

About the insertion of saints into the intercessory prayers we have the testimony of St. Cyril of Jerusalem (in *Cat. Myst.*), who enumerates the three groups of intercessory prayers: (a) for peace of the Church, for rulers, etc.; (b) the memory of the saints; (c) the departed. In the *Apostolic Constitutions* the intercession at the end of the anaphora is distinguished into three groups: (a) for the Church, celebrant, king, and all in authority; (b) the saints; (c) for the people and all sorts of men. The commemoration of the saints reads: "We further offer to Thee also through all those holy persons who have pleased Thee from the beginning of the world— patriarchs, prophets, righteous men, apostles, martyrs, confessors, bishops, presbyters, deacons, subdeacons . . . with all whose names Thou knowest." St. Augustine [6] refers in several passages to the commemoration of the saints and distinguishes it from the commemoration of the departed: "Therefore at the table of the Lord we do not commemorate in the same way the martyrs as the rest who departed in peace, so that we would pray for them; but rather in this sense that they may pray for us, so that we may follow their examples." Again in *De virginitate*: "The faithful know in what

[6] *Serm.* 84 *in Jo.; PL*, 35, 1847.

place the names of the martyrs and at what place the names of the departed religious persons are to be mentioned at the altar." [7]

St. Augustine indicates as the reason why we should commemorate the saints, especially the martyrs, at the Eucharistic sacrifice, that their death resembles the death of our Lord.

Cardinal Schuster [8] finds the starting point for the *Communicantes* in the "episcopal diptychs" added to the name of the Pope and refers to the passage of St. Leo I [9] and St. Gregory I.[10] He admits, however, also another reason: "Nor should this double litany of saints (*Communicantes* and *Nobis quoque peccatoribus*) appear strange to anyone; it is a purely literary device in order to give honor to the two tables of the diptychs accompanying each list of names to be presented before God with the powerful advocacy of their heavenly patrons."

Batiffol thought that the list of the saints was inserted in the fifth century and completed by Pope Symmachus (d. 514). L. V. Kennedy, however, ascribes its introduction to Pope Gelasius, but admits that it existed theretofore in simpler form. The final arrangement in hierarchical order is the work of St. Gregory I.

STRUCTURE

The present order of the names of the saints in both the *Communicantes* and in the *Nobis quoque peccatoribus* is

---

[7] *PL*, 40, 423.

[8] *Op. cit.*, I, 274.

[9] *Ep.* 80; *PL*, 54, 914: "De nominibus autem Dioscori, Juvenalis et Eustathii ad sacrum altare recitandis . . . iniquum nimis est atque incongruum eos . . . sanctorum nominibus sine discretione misceri."

[10] *Ep.* 39; *PL*, 77, 714: "Quod autem . . . fratrem et coepiscopum nostrum Joannem Ravennatis Ecclesiae inter missarum solemnia nominetis, requirenda vobis consuetudo antiqua est."

(a) as to the apostles not found in Scripture, (b) as to the martyrs not the historical order of the development or intensity of their cult, but as the result of a deliberate arrangement, or rearrangement in hierarchical order.

The list of apostles in Matthew has the closest similarity to the list of the Canon (Matt. 10:2; Mark 3:16; Luke 6:14; Acts 1:13).

Matt. 10-2	Canon
Simon Petrus	Petrus
Andreas	Paulus
Jacobus Zebedaei	Andreas
Joannes	Jacobus
Philippus	Joannes
Bartholomaeus	Thomas
Thomas	Jacobus
Matthaeus	Philippus
Jacobus Alphaei	Bartholomaeus
Thaddaeus	Matthaeus
Simon	Simon
	Thaddaeus

The differences between the scriptural list and the list of the Canon may be explained as follows: the insertion of Paulus after Petrus is on account of their common cult; the insertion of Thomas after Joannes may be in connection with the dedication of a chapel in the basilica of St. Peter under Pope Symmachus (498–514). The association of Jacobus and Philippus and their insertion after Thomas may be in connection with the dedication of the basilica of the Apostles, built under Popes Pelagius and John III.

The list of the saints is not in the historical order of the development and intensity of their cult: Linus and Cletus did not have any cult in the first six centuries; there exists no document about their martyrdom. It is obvious that the names were inserted and added after Peter in order to show the apostolic succession from Peter to Clement (who is found in the list of Milan, which is closer to the original chronological order, if not the actual historical order). St. Lawrence, the most honored saint of Rome after the princes of the apostles must originally have been placed higher, as the list of Milan shows (second after the apostles).

There was probably, even before the rearrangement by Pope Gelasius, some list of saints in the Canon. The result of the reform of Pope Gelasius was probably: seven saints in the *Communicantes,* and seven in the *Nobis quoque peccatoribus:*

Communicantes	Nobis quoque peccatoribus
Blessed Virgin	Joannes (Baptista)
Peter	Stephanus
Paul	Marcellinus
Xystus	Petrus
Lawrence	Agnes
Cornelius	Caecilia
Cyprianus	Felicitas

At the time of the dedication of the church of the Apostles (555–74) the list of the apostles was supplemented. Clement may have been added by Pope John II (533–35), who was formerly priest of the title of St. Clement. Joannes and Paulus were probably added by Pope Agapitus (535–36) who was formerly "clericus ad Sanctos Joannem et Paulum"; Chrysogonus may have been added in the middle of the sixth century under the influence of Ravenna.

The last additions were made by Pope Gregory I. He added Linus and Cletus to complete the list of the early Roman Pontiffs, further Matthias and Barnabas to fill the list of the apostles, Ignatius because of his relations with Rome (his letter to Rome, his martyrdom in Rome), finally the women saints Agatha and Lucia (Perpetua was probably inserted close to the time of St. Gregory; Anastasia through the influence of Constantinople in the first half of the sixth century). St. Gregory intended on the one hand to give an equal number of saints in order to balance the twelve apostles and to assimilate the list to the twenty-four ancients of the Apocalypse. He inserted Linus and Cletus to fill the list of the early Roman Pontiffs. He balanced the list of saints of the *Nobis quoque peccatoribus* with an equal number of men and women saints (seven each), in symmetry to the two choirs of saints in the *Communicantes*.

Communicantes

Blessed Virgin
12 Apostles
12 saints martyrs: 5 popes: Linus
                           Cletus
                           Clemens
                           Xystus
                           Cornelius
              1 bishop: Cyprianus
              2 clerics: Laurentius
                         Chrysogonus
              4 laymen: Joannes et Paulus
                        Cosmas et Damianus

Nobis quoque peccatoribus

seven men	seven women
	Joannes (Baptista)	
Stephanus	Felicitas
Matthias	Perpetua
Barnabas	Agatha
Ignatius	Lucia
Alexander	Agnes
Marcellinus	Caecilia
Petrus	Anastasia

PARTICULAR INTERPRETATION

The title of this prayer *Infra actionem,* i.e., "within the action," originated in connection with the special clauses inserted for certain feasts. These special *Communicantes* in their augmented form were printed among the prefaces with the superscription *Infra actionem,* i.e., to be said within the Canon at the place of the *Communicantes.* In the course of time this superscription of the special *Communicantes* was looked upon as the regular title of this prayer and given also as heading to the *Communicantes* in the normal place.

"Communicating and celebrating the memory" is a difficult phrase, with two participles without a definite verb. A. Fortescue [11] says they have to be taken as equivalent to *Communicamus et memoriam celebramus* and he refers to a similar instance in the Epistle to the Romans. Others connect the phrase with the preceding prayer: "They offer up to Thee, O Lord, their vows and do so as belonging to the communion of saints, and they fulfill this communion toward the saints of heaven by venerating their memory." Cardinal Schuster [12]

[11] *The Mass,* p. 332.
[12] *Op. cit.,* I, 274.

connects it with the first intercession, joining it to the names of the Pope and the Bishop. The insertion on special feasts, he says, separates these two participles from each other. They do not refer to the same object. Further, at the time of the insertion of this intercession the idea of being in communion with the Pope and Bishop was considered as very important.

There is however against this theory the fact that the *Communicantes* would connect with some prayer from which it is separated through the Memento of the living. At least in the present arrangement it seems more probable that the *Communicantes* would refer to the communion of saints, the more so since the insertions which separate the two participles from each other are only exceptions. Finally, the term "memoriam venerantes" can be understood as specifying the term "Communicantes."

"Memoria" signified originally the tomb and relics of the saints. Later it received the meaning of efficacious remembrance of the saints, equivalent to petition for their intercession.

"In the first place of the glorious ever Virgin Mary, Mother of God and our Lord Jesus Christ." The phrase "in the first place" assimilates this prayer with the intercession for the Church and reveals their common origin. And the insertion of the name of the Mother of God is the result and memorial of the Council of Ephesus. The title "gloriosae semper virginis Genetricis Dei et Domini nostri Jesu Christi" is in itself a proof of this statement. The title "semper virginis" occurs frequently after the year 350. The title "Genetricis Dei et Domini nostri Jesu Christi" is a combination of the "Theotokos" of the Greek and of the customary title of the West: "mater Domini nostri Jesu Christi."

There is no doubt that the names of the apostles Peter and Paul were the first to be inserted in any prayer of intercession. The names of Linus and Cletus are missing in the Milan Canon. No cult of them existed in the first six centuries. There is no record of their martyrdom. This gives proof that their names were inserted with the intention of establishing the apostolic succession from Peter to Clement. St. Clement enjoyed universal veneration throughout the first four centuries because of his letter to the Corinthians. He was once identified with Clement the companion of St. Paul and also with the Consul Clement Flavius who suffered martyrdom under Domitian. His name became connected with the church of the "titulus Clementis," probably named so after its founder, but dedicated to St. Clement at the end of the fourth century. At that time he was already thought of as a martyr, surrounded by many legends: they tell that he was exiled, worked wonders in the region of the Black Sea, suffered martyrdom, and was cast into the sea. At the prayers of the faithful the sea receded and the body was found in a beautiful marble palace. Pope Sixtus II (257–58) was a victim of the persecution of Valerian, who forbade gatherings in the cemeteries. The saint was seized there and immediately executed and buried in the most impressive papal crypt of Callistus. He was honored by the Romans along with Peter and Paul and Lawrence. His name was certainly in the original list of the Canon. Pope Cornelius (251–53) was sent into exile by Emperor Gallus and probably died a natural death; but because of the sufferings he endured for the faith he is venerated as a martyr (Cyprianus, *Epist.* 67, 6: "Cyprianus Collega noster sacerdos pacificus ac justus et martyrii dignatione Domini honoratus"). Very probably the depositio took place at Rome on September 14, the day on which the *dies natalis* of St. Cyprian was celebrated. The commemoration of both is found in the liturgical books on the same day. St. Jerome (*De viris illustribus,* c. 62) testifies that Cyprian suffered martyrdom under Valerian and Gallienus on the same day as Cornelius, but not the same year. This is the reason why they are mentioned together, probably already in the original Canon list. St. Lawrence, the patron of the city of Rome, is the most celebrated saint after SS. Peter and Paul. He was honored with a church by Constantine and his name is surrounded with many legends. The *Liber pontificalis,* after recording the death of Pope Xystus with the six deacons, continues that, on the third day after the death of St. Xystus, his deacon Lawrence suffered martyrdom. For this reason his name is found in the Canon together with Pope Xystus. St. Chrysogonus entered the Canon at the time of the political flourishing of the exarchate of Ravenna and is the result of a fusion of the memory of the founder of the *titulus Chrysogoni* of the third century, who at the beginning of the sixth century was identified with St. Chrysogonus, bishop and martyr of Aquileia, in the third century. The latter was held in high honor at Ravenna at the end of the fifth century, whence his cult passed to Rome sometime before the middle of the sixth century.

"Joannes et Paulus" represents another instance where the glory of a founder of a titulus (in the third century "titulus Byzantii," at the end of the fourth century "titulus Pammachii") was merged with the names of saints (from relics preserved in that church, two of whom were John and Paul) and adorned with legends. The cult of Cosmas and Damian developed in Constantinople in the first half of the fifth century, spread to Ravenna and at the beginning of the sixth century to Rome. Their names were inserted in the Roman Canon probably at the time of the dedication of their church on the Forum by Pope Felix IV (483–92). This edifice was formerly the temple of Romulus and Urbis Romae.

"And of all Thy saints." Pope Vigilius, speaking of the insertion to be made in the *Communicantes* on certain days, says that the names of the saints, whose feasts were celebrated, were to be mentioned "commemorationem . . . eorum facimus, quorum natalitia celebramus." Under Pope Gregory III (731–41) another addition was made as a result of the erection of a chapel in the Vatican basilic dedicated to all saints. A decree of the Roman Council of 732 had the passage: "and of all saints, but also celebratifg the natalitia of Thy holy martyrs and perfect just confessors, whose solemnity we celebrate today in Thy sight." The addition of the names of the saints of the feast disappeared in 1570.

The clause "by whose merits and prayers grant that in all things we may be guarded by Thy protecting help" declares the intention in commemorating the saints as stated by St. Augustine: "Therefore it is ordained by the discipline of the Church, that the martyrs are remembered at the altar of God in a place where prayer is not offered for them. For the rest of the departed who are commemorated prayer is offered. It would be an injustice to pray for a martyr, by whose prayer rather we have to be recommended." [13] *Serm.* 84: "Therefore at the table of the Lord we do not commemorate the martyrs in the same way as we do the others who rest in peace, by praying for them; but rather that they may pray for us, so that we may follow their steps." [14]

[13] *Serm.* 84 *in Jo.; PL*, 35, 1847: "Ideo ad mensam Domini non sic martyres commemoramus, quemadmodum alios, qui in pace requiescunt, ut etiam pro eis oremus; sed magis ut ipsi orent pro nobis, ut eorum vestigiis adhaereamus."
[14] E. Hosp, *Die Heiligen in Canon Missae*, Graz, 1926; R van Doren, "Les saints du canon de la messe," *Questions liturgiques et paroissiales*, XVI (1931), 57–70; A. Baumstark, "Das Communicantes und seine Heiligenliste," *Jb. L. W.*, I (1921), 5–33.

CHAPTER XX

Introduction to the Consecration

THE words of the historical narrative of the institution of the Holy Eucharist, which introduce the consecration of the host and of the chalice, are not exactly the words recorded in Scripture. Just as the words of consecration themselves, so the words which introduce them were originally transmitted by oral tradition. St. Matthew and St. Luke did not intend to give a complete description of all incidents at the Last Supper and to reproduce all the words spoken by Christ. They wished to mention that important event as the ultimate proof given by Christ of His love. They record only the essential elements of the realization of the Pasch of the New Testament. They record primarily the fact; they omit for instance the command, "Do this," etc., and suppose the particulars to be well known by oral teaching and through the liturgy. The narrative of St. Luke is likewise of such a sort that we can see he did not consider himself obliged to mention every detail. St. Paul refers explicitly to oral tradition (I Cor. 11:23): "For I have received of the Lord that which also I delivered unto you,"etc., and records the institution chiefly in order to correct abuses in Corinth which occurred in connection with the love-feasts; he recalls the fact and the purpose of the institution of the Holy Eucharist in order to show what disposition and what preparation are required of those who partake of this greatest of all sacraments.

Comparing the Canon text with the scriptural reports and with the earlier liturgies, we find a certain development from an older tradition which is in close adherence to the text of St. Paul (I Cor. 11) to a more developed form. The modifications and additions follow two principles: combining the different Scripture texts in the text of the Canon; explaining what is implicitly contained in the words transmitted.

"Who, the day before He suffered, took bread into His holy and venerable hands, and with eyes lifted up toward heaven, unto Thee, O God, His almighty Father, giving thanks to Thee, did bless, break, and give unto His disciples, saying: Take, and eat ye all of this."

There is no indication of time in the Gospels. St. Paul is the only one who has made such an indication (I Cor. 11:23): "The same night in which he was betrayed," etc. Most of the Eastern liturgies have the Pauline formula, "In the night in which He was betrayed." The formula, "Who the day before He suffered," etc., is characteristic of the Roman and all the Western liturgies. The change from the Pauline formula to the Roman formula which replaces the mention of the betrayal with the commemoration of the Passion, is ascribed by the *Liber pontificalis* [1] to Pope Alexander I (105–15): "Hic passionem Domini miscuit in praedicatione sacerdotum, quando missae celebrantur." But the historical authority of this document in its records about the second century is not without doubt, nor is there evidence that these words refer to this insertion before the consecration. Cardinal Schuster,[2] supposing these words refer to this place, thinks that the commemoration of the Passion at this place originally must have been much longer, as, for instance, in the *Traditio*

[1] *Liber pont.*, p. 127.
[2] *Op. cit.*, I, 291.

apostolica: "who . . . stretched forth His hands as He suffered that He might release from suffering those who have believed in Thee; who when He was delivered to the voluntary passion, that He might abolish death and rend the bonds of the devil and tread down hell and enlighten the just and establish the ordinance and demonstrate the resurrection." One reason for the change, "who the day before," was probably to indicate the time more accurately. Another reason may have been to omit the name of Judas for reverence, just as Theodore of Mopsuestia [3] remarks about the omission of Judas (Judas Thaddaeus) in the *Communicantes:* "It is not fitting that an image of malice occur within the symbols of our salvation."

The insertion of reference to the Passion may have been the result of the command of St. Paul (I Cor. 11:26): "For as often as you shall eat this bread and drink the chalice, you shall show the death of the Lord." Although this command is met with in the Anamnesis immediately after the consecration, it could have been likewise a reason for a second commemoration before the consecration, giving the central part of the Canon some symmetrical structure (cf. *Traditio apostolica*). Another reason for the emphasis on the Passion may have been the heresy of Docetism, which denied the reality of our Lord's Passion.

On Holy Thursday the Roman Canon has a modified formula: "Who the day before He suffered for the salvation of us all, that is, today," etc. Dom G. Morin [4] maintains that this was at one time the regular formula of every Mass, introduced probably as a protest against predestinationism of the fifth century (cf. the antiphon of St. Benedict that preserves the

---

[3] *Opuscula et textus; series lit.*, fasc. II (1933), pp. 20–22. Cf. A. Mingana, in *Woodbrooke Studies*, 1922–33.

[4] *Rev. Bened.*, XXVII (1910), 513–15. Cf. *DB*, no. 160a.

formula: "Sanctissime confessor Domini, monachorum Pater et Dux Benedicte, intercede pro nostra omniumque salute").

"In His holy and venerable hands." This phrase is not found in any of the scriptural texts. It is an addition to and amplification of "He took bread" with the intention of emphasizing the most holy priesthood of Christ.

This phrase is found in the *Apostolic Constitutions:* "holy and undefiled hands"; in the liturgy of St. James: "in his holy and pure and immortal hands"; in the liturgy of St. Mark: "in His holy, pure, and immaculate hands." The Canon of the *De sacramentis* has only: "holy hands."

The term "hands" is used frequently in Scripture as a symbol of the divine activity by creation, providence (Heb. 1:10: "The heavens are the works of Thy hands"; Luke 1:66: "The hand of the Lord was with him"; Luke 23:46: "Into Thy hands I commend My spirit"). In the present text this term signifies the consecration as the theandric action of Christ, a causality in which the divine Word applies the humanity as an organic instrument. On account of the substantial consecration of the humanity of Christ by the divinity, the hands of our Lord are consecrated and consecrating, sanctified and sanctifying, venerable and adorable. The priesthood of Christ and His sacerdotal hands are holy and venerable beyond the sanctity of any other priest, who is sanctified accidentally. Christ speaks of the life-giving power of His flesh in connection with the promise of the Holy Eucharist (John 6). The Fathers of the Church emphasize so much the life-giving power of the body of Christ that it seems as if they would only in His flesh find that power, and not in His words. They say, for instance, that He spoke as God when He commanded the waves; but that He used His hands in the awakening of the dead: daughter of Jairus, youth of Naim. The Fathers intended to say, that in the commanding words of Christ the indwelling of the divine power in his humanity did not so much appear as in the touch with the hands.

The words "with His eyes lifted up to heaven" are not found in Scripture within the narrative of the institution of the Eucharist. They occur, however, in the narrative of the first multiplication of loaves (Matt. 14:19; Mark 6:41; Luke 9:16): "He took the five loaves and the two fishes; and looking up to heaven, He blessed and broke and gave the loaves to His disciples." Likewise at the raising of Lazarus we read (John 11:41–43): "And Jesus lifted up His eyes, and said, Father I thank Thee that Thou hast heard Me." The third instance is in the sacerdotal prayer (John 17:1): "And lifting up His eyes to heaven, He said," etc.

The phrase is found in the *Apostolic Constitutions:* "and looking up to Thee His God and Father"; in the liturgy of St. James: "lifting up His eyes to heaven"; in the liturgy of St. Mark: "and lifting up His eyes to His Father." These words, says Benedict XIV, are part of tradition. They are a mute invocation accompanying and emphasizing the act of giving thanks. "Unto Thee, O God, His almighty Father"; this addition is parallel to the invocation at the beginning of the Preface and in the first invocation of the Canon.

"Giving thanks to Thee, He blessed"; the thanksgiving of our Lord is still more explicit with the addition of the words "to Thee." The change in the pronouns "unto Thee, O God, His almighty Father, giving thanks to Thee" express the distinction between Christ's relation as the only-begotten Son to His Father, and the relation of the children of adoption to their Father in heaven (cf. John 20:17: "I ascend to My

Father and to your Father, to My God and to your God").
"Take and eat ye all of this." None of the scriptural texts
have the words "all of this." Matt. 26:26: "Take ye and eat";
Mark 14:22: "Take ye"; St. Luke omits the phrase entirely;
in St. Paul (I Cor. 11:24) the words "Take ye and eat" are an
interpolation from Matthew by a copyist. The "all" is supplied from the words about the chalice (Matt. 26:27): "Drink
ye all of this." St. Mark has the words (14:23): "and they all
drank of it." That the Canon insists on the "all" in the words
referring to the host as well as to the chalice, reveals the idea
of the necessity of the Eucharist proclaimed by our Lord
(John 6:54): "Amen, amen I say unto you: except you eat
the flesh of the Son of man and drink His blood, you shall
not have life in you. He that eateth My flesh and drinketh
My blood hath everlasting life: and I will raise him up in
the last day." In this addition as in others the tendency appears to supply mutually in both formulas of consecration
what is found in the one and in the other.

"In like manner, after supper, taking also this excellent
chalice into His holy and venerable hands: and giving thanks
to Thee, He blessed, and gave to His disciples, saying: Take,
and drink ye all of it."

"In like manner" is taken from the account of St. Paul
(I Cor. 11:25); "after He had supped" occurs identically in
Luke 22:20 and I Cor. 11:25. "This excellent chalice" is an
addition, found in the Gelasian Sacramentary. It is inspired
by Ps. 22:5: "Thou hast prepared a table before me, against
them that afflict me. Thou hast anointed my head with oil;
and my chalice which inebriated me, how excellent (*quam
praeclarus*) it is!" As the words of the psalm prophetically
say, the Lord is the good Pastor, giving all consolation in the
Eucharistic banquet, all joy in the chalice of salvation. The

pronoun "this" is inserted to testify that there exists identity between the chalice consecrated by our Lord at the Last Supper and the consecrated chalice on the altars everywhere. "This" is the chalice, to which applies the expression of the psalm: grand, glorious, magnificent. The insistence on the words of institution as the consecrating form, expressed with this addition, is still more emphasized with another addition —"mysterium fidei." [5]

The Eucharistic chalice is "excellent": in the sense of Ps. 22:5, because it is the type and sacramental anticipation of the beatific joy (*Summa theol.*, IIIa, q. 83, a. 5 ad 9): "With the chalice is signified in one way the passion of Christ . . . in another way the beatific joy, which is also prefigured in this sacrament."

[5] Cf. Fortescue, *op. cit.*, p. 336.; F. Hammen, *Die liturgischen Einsetzungsberichte.* Muenster i. W., 1928.

CHAPTER XXI

The Consecration

T HE Canon is a preparation for the words of consecration, it is an echo, a mirror, an extension of them. The Canon is the theology of the Holy Eucharist, of the power and the effect of the divine words. Under the guidance of the Holy Ghost, the Church has surrounded these divine words with a fragrant wreath, with a glorious halo, whereby nature and grace, art and faith, vie with one another in the effort to express the great hidden truth.

HISTORICAL DEVELOPMENT OF THE WORDS
OF CONSECRATION

The Canon had its history, development, changes, reforms, until it became the "unchangeable rule" of offering the Eucharistic sacrifice. Not so the words of consecration. Our Lord's words remained unchanged within the Eucharistic rite from the time when the first Canon was written, even from the time before any Canon and any Gospel were written, from the Eucharistic celebration of the apostles to our own days. This stability of the words of Christ, around which the prayers of the Canon grew up, were unfolded like rose leaves round a shining diamond, is in itself a most solemn testimony for the perennial faith of the Church, that with the words of Christ, and exclusively through them, transubstantiation is accomplished.

The stability of the words of consecration, however, is only relative, i.e., compared with the rest of the Canon, and with regard to the essential sacramental significance. Notwithstanding the absolute stability of the text as form of the sacrament and Eucharistic sacrifice, the formulas of consecration have their proper history; they underwent a certain development. A comparison of them with the corresponding texts of Scripture on the one hand, and with the variants in ancient, especially Eastern, liturgies on the other hand, gives evidence of this statement. The critical textual study reveals at the same time the principles which caused this development, and its influence upon the development and structure of the entire Canon.

Canon Text and Scripture Texts

The text of the words of consecration in the Canon differs from the corresponding texts of Holy Scripture. A superficial comparison reveals differences of two kinds: (a) there are words found in the Canon which are not found in the Scripture texts; (b) there are words missing or changed in the Canon which are found in the Scripture texts. The consecration of the host, for instance, has in the Canon a short formula with the addition of "enim," and with the omission of the relative proposition found in Scripture (Luke 22:19), "Quod pro vobis datur" (I Cor. 11:24: "Quod pro vobis tradetur"); (b) the consecration of the chalice has in the Canon a long formula with the addition of "aeterni" and "mysterium fidei," and has changed (or combined) the relative clause (Matt. and Mark) "qui pro multis effundetur" (Luke, "qui pro vobis fundetur").

The discrepancy between the text of the Canon and the texts of Holy Scripture was noticed in the course of history by theologians and writers. The question of the origin of the Canon text, however, was not treated thoroughly and systematically until recent times, and the explanations presented vary from a rigid traditionalism, which explains the differences from divino-apostolic tradition, to a liberal traditionalism, which admits a development and changes introduced by the Church. Ratherius, O.S.B., bishop of Verona (890–974) noticed their differences from the texts of Holy Scripture but, out of reverence for the sacred words which according to him are transmitted by divino-apostolic tradition, advised: "De caetero, quaeso, ne solliciteris." [1] Like him, most authors treating this question explain the differences with divino-apostolic tradition from which rather the texts of Scripture deflect, since the sacred authors did not intend to give a word by word report of the sacred rite, well known through oral tradition and the liturgy.

Florus Diaconus (d. 859) explained the addition of "aeterni" and "mysterium fidei" as insertions from Scripture without indicating its author; he refers for "aeterni" to Heb. 10:14 ("Una enim oblatione consummavit in sempiternum sanctificatos"), to Heb. 13:20 ("in sanguine testamenti aeterni"); for "mysterium fidei" he refers to John 6:64 ff. and to I Tim. 3:9 ("habentes mysterium fidei in conscientia pura").[2]

Pachasius Radbertus (d. 865) explains the phrase "pro vobis et multis" as based on divine tradition: "Credendum est, quod Christus utrumque dixerit," and observes that it is a combination of the words found in Matthew and Luke.[3]

[1] Cf. L. d'Achery, *Spicilegium, sive collectio veterum aliquot scriptorum,* Paris, 1733. Ep. 6, *De corpore et sanguine Domini;* I, 376.
[2] *Expositio missae; PL,* 119, 53.
[3] *Liber de corpore et sanguine Domini; PL,* 120, 1321.

Pope Innocent III (d. 1216) speaks of the insertions "elevatis oculis," "aeterni," "mysterium fidei," and alludes to two principles of explanation: (a) to divine tradition: "Quis tantae praesumptionis exstitit et audaciae, ut hoc de corde suo tentaverit interponere. Sane formam istam verborum ab ipso Christo acceperunt apostoli et ab ipsis accepit Ecclesia"; "sane multa tam de verbis quam de factis Dominicis invenimus ab Evangelista omissa, quae Apostoli vel supplevisse verbo vel facto expressisse leguntur" (cf. Acts 20:35; I Cor. 15:6); (b) the Pope refers further to other texts of Scripture which may have caused the differences through their influence on liturgy, without, however, determining the author of such changes: "Ceterum ea, quae adduntur in canone missae, possunt ex aliis locis Evangelii comprobari." He refers for "aeterni" to Heb. 9:15.[4]

St. Thomas follows the same view and refers to apostolic tradition, particularly to St. Peter as the author of the Roman liturgy: "Haec conjunctio 'enim' apponitur in hac forma secundum consuetudinem Romanae Ecclesiae, a B. Petro Apostolo derivatam." About the form for the consecration of the chalice he refers to the different Scripture texts on the one hand, and on the other hand to divino-apostolic tradition (mentioned by St. Paul in I Cor. 11:23) about the terms "aeterni" and "mysterium": "Ex traditione Domini habetur, quae ad Ecclesiam per apostolos pervenit secundum illud I Cor. 11:23." [5]

St. Bonaventure (d. 1274) advocates a strict conservatism: "Romana Ecclesia ab ipsis apostolis Petro et Paulo, quos vivos auctores habuit et defunctos custodit, hunc ritum sac-

---

[4] Innocent III, *Decretale "Cum Marthae"*; PL, 214, 1118.
[5] *Summa theol.*, IIIa, q.78, a.2, 3.

rificii accepit, quam hactenus immobili cultu servavit . . . accipienda est (forma) ab ipsis Apostolis, non ab Evangelistis, quia Apostoli ecclesiam instituerunt secundum quod a Domino acceperunt." [6]

The reformers noted likewise the divergence of the Canon text from the scriptural reports, and acted consequently according to their principle about Scripture as the exclusive source of revelation. Luther wrote in 1520: "Curandum est ante omnia, ut omnibus iis depositis, quae ad institutionem huius sacramenti primitivam et simplicem humanis studiis et fervoribus sunt addita . . . ad ipsam solam et puram Christi institutionem oculos et animum vertamus, nec nobis aliud proponamus quam ipsum verbum Christi . . . verba autem Christi quibus sacramentum hoc instituit, sunt haec" (reference to Matt. 26:26; Luke 22:20; I Cor. 11).[7] Luther introduced therefore in his "Formula missae et communionis" the following text: "Hoc est corpus meum, quod pro vobis datur. Hic calix est novi testamenti in meo sanguine, qui pro vobis et pro multis effundetur in remissionem peccatorum." [8] All the reformers with Luther and after him in Germany, Switzerland, France, and England, followed suit and eliminated the additions and differences of the Roman Canon.

The Council of Trent, in reaction to the ideas of the reformers, made the following statements: "Plura quidem a sacris scripturis colliguntur, quaedam vero in ecclesia ex apostolica traditione conservata sunt. Nam quod dicitur 'Hic est calix' a D. Luca et ab Apostolo scriptum est; quod vero sequitur 'sanguinis mei' vel 'sanguis meus novi testamenti,'

---

[6] *Commentaria in IV libros sent.*, IV, q. 2.
[7] Luther, *De capt. Babyl. ecclesiae prealudium* (Weimar, 1888), VI, 513.
[8] E. H. Litzmann, *Lit. Texte*, IV, 16.

'qui pro vobis et pro multis effundetur in remissionem peccatorum,' partim a D. Luca, partim a D. Mattaeo dictum est.
Verba autem illa 'aeterni' et 'mysterium fidei' sancta traditio,
catholicae veritatis interpres et custos nos docuit." [9]

Although the Council does not specify the kind of tradition
which has transmitted the additions of the text in the Roman
Canon, most of later writers understand it as apostolic tradition, coming down in the Roman Church from St. Peter.
Reverence for the sacred text, they say, prevented any change
or addition, and prohibits consequently any other interpretation.

With the progress of historical and archaeological studies
a mitigated traditionalism was defended by a series of writers
(A. de Waal,[10] S. Salaville,[11] P. Battifol,[12] P. Cagin, O.S.B.[13]).
Dom Cagin has compared systematically the texts of Eastern
and Western liturgies corresponding to the text of the Roman
Canon from "Que pridie" to "Quotiescumque," a study that
resulted in the following conclusions. There are to be distinguished three periods in the development of the narrative
of institution: (a) the purely scriptural period, in which appears the tendency to bring the Canon text into agreement
with one of the two groups (Petrine of Matthew and Mark;
Pauline of Luke and I Cor.) of scriptural texts; (b) the
period of scriptural combinations, a movement resulting at
the same time in the diatessaron; (c) the period of extra-
scriptural additions. Substantially the same conclusions with
new particulars about the development of the symmetri-

---

[9] *Catechismus Concilii Tridentini* (ed. Tauchnitz, 1865), p. 181.
[10] "Archaeologische Eroerterungen zu einigen Stuecken im Kanon der
hl. Messe. Die Worte 'Mysterium fidei,'" *Katholik*, LXXVI (1896), 392.
[11] *Dict. théol. cath.*, art. "Epiclese."
[12] *L'Eucharistie*, Paris, 1913.
[13] *L'Eucharistie. Canon primitive de la messe, ou formulaire essentiel et
premier de toutes les liturgies* (Paris, 1912), p. 248.

cal structure of both consecration formulas and its influence upon the artistic structure of the entire Canon have been presented by K. J. Merk.[14]

The Words of Consecration in Ancient and Eastern Liturgies

The comparison of the first group of ancient liturgies, extant in the *Traditio apostolica* of St. Hippolytus, in the fragment of Deir-Balizeh, in the prayer book of Bishop Serapion, in the *Testamentum Domini*, in the *Apostolic Constitutions*, shows clearly the tendency to conformity, symmetry, parallelism of both formulas of consecration. Words contained in the one and missing in the other are mutually supplied. Besides, there appears the tendency to combine both the Petrine and the Pauline texts in the consecration text of the anaphora. The "quod pro multis frangitur" of the *Apostolic Constitutions* is evidently a combination of "qui pro multis effunditur" of Matthew and "quod pro vobis (datur, frangitur)" of St. Paul. In the anaphora of the *Traditio apostolica* is omitted in the consecration of the chalice "in remissionem peccatorum," for the sake of symmetry between the two consecration formulas. In the anaphora of the fragment of Deir-Balizeh, of Serapion, of the *Testamentum Domini*, and of the *Apostolic Constitutions*, to the consecration of the host is added "in remission peccatorum" for the same purpose.

Traditio apostolica:

Hoc est corpus meum	Hic est sanguis meus
quod pro vobis datur	qui pro vobis effunditur

Fragment of Deir-Balizeh:

Hoc meum est corpus	His meus est sanguis

[14] *Der Konsekrationstext der roem. Messe,* Rottenburg a. N., 1915.

quod pro vobis confringitur
in remissionem peccatorum
Prayer book of Serapion:
Hoc est corpus meum
quod pro vobis frangitur
in remissionem peccatorum

qui pro vobis effunditur
in remissionem peccatorum

Hoc est novum testamentum,
   quod est sanguis meus
qui pro vobis effunditur
   in remissionem peccatorum

Testamentum Domini:
Hoc meum est corpus
quod pro vobis confringitur
in remissionem peccatorum

Hic est sanguis meus
qui pro multis effunditur
in remissionem peccatorum

A series of liturgies of later date, which are based on the liturgy of the *Apostolic Constitutions,* demonstrates a further development under the influence of Scripture. There appear combinations which show the intention to combine all particulars as they are found in Scripture in each of the formulas of the anaphora to a perfect symmetry.

S. Jacobi: [15]
Hoc meum est corpus
quod pro vobis frangitur et
   datur
in remissionem peccatorum
S. Basilii:
Hoc est corpus meum
quod pro vobis frangitur
in remissionem peccatorum

Hic meus est sanguis novi
   testamenti
qui pro vobis et pro multis effunditur et distribuitur
in remissionem peccatorum
Hic meus est sanguis novi
   testamenti
qui pro vobis et pro multis effunditur
in remissionem peccatorum

S. Chrysostomi:
Hoc est corpus meum

His est sanguis meus novi
   testamenti

[15] F. E. Brightman, *Liturgies Eastern and Western,* Oxford, 1896.

quod pro vobis frangitur	qui pro vobis et pro multis
in remissionem peccatorum	effunditur
	in remissionem peccatorum
S. Marci:	His est sanguis meus novi
Hoc enim est corpus meum	testamenti
quod pro vobis frangitur et	qui pro vobis et pro multis
distribuitur	effunditur et distribuitur
in remissionem peccatorum	in remissionem peccatorum
S. Cyrilli:	Hic est sanguis meus novi
Hoc est corpus meum	testamenti
quod pro vobis frangitur et	qui pro vobis effunditur et
pro multis tradetur	pro multis debitur
in remissionem peccatorum	in remissionem peccatorum

In these combinations the consecration formula of the liturgy of St. Cyril deserves special attention. In it are combined not only the words, but even the present and future tense of the verbs "quod pro vobis frangitur et pro multis tradetur."

Local liturgies of the East, based on those mentioned above, have made a further step under the dominant influence of Scripture: they have added other words of Scripture with Eucharistic significance, particularly from the promise of the Eucharist (John 6) and from the Epistle to the Hebrews.

Lit. S. Sixti: [16]

Vere hoc est corpus meum (cf. John 6:55: Caro enim mea vere est cibus, et sanguis meus vere est potus)

Lit. S. Joan. Ev.:

Quod pro vobis et pro omnibus in me credentibus frangitur et dividitur (cf. John 6:35: et qui credit in me, non sitiet

[16] Renaudot, *Collectio orientalium liturgiarum*, Frankfurt, 1848.

unquam . . . ut omnis qui videt filium et credit in eum, habet vitam aeternam . . . qui credit in me, habet vitam aeternam)

Lit. Dioscori Alex.:

Quod pro mundi vita frangitur et dividitur illud suscipientibus (cf. John 6:51: et panis quem ego dabo, caro mea est pro mundi vita)

S. Jacobi, Minor S. Jacobi, Duodecim Apost., S. Marci, S. Ignatii, Marutae:

In remissionem peccatorum et vitam aeternam (cf. John 6:55: Qui manducat meam carnem et bibit meum sanguinem, habet vitam aeternam)

S. Chrysostomi Chald.:

Ad remissionem peccatorum et vitam novam quae est in aeternum (cf. John 6:58: Qui manducat hunc panem, vivet in aeternum)

S. Cyrilli:

Hic est sanguis meus, qui confirmat (obsignat) testamentum mortis meae (cf. Heb. 9:17: Testamentum enim in mortuis confirmatum est)

S. Joan. Ev.:

Hic est calix sanguinis mei, novi testamenti, prodigium admirabile (cf. I Tim. 3:16: manifeste magnum est pietatis mysterium)

S. Gregorii Alex.:

Hic est sanguis meus, potus vitae verus (cf. John 6:55: et sanguis meus, vere est potus)

Finally theological reflections and meditative amplifications were added:

S. Petri Ia, S. Clementis, S. Dionysii:

Ad expiationem delictorum et remissionem peccatorum et vitam aeternam

S. Joan. Ev.:

Ad expiationem delictorum, remissionem peccatorum et vitam futuram in saecula

S. Eustatii:

Quod vos et omnes suscipientes fideles praeparat

Lit. B.V.M.:

Quem pro vobis effundit lancea.

DEVELOPMENT OF CONSECRATION FORMULAS OF THE ROMAN CANON

The consecration formulas of the Roman Canon are not perfectly symmetrical. There are at present, however, still visible some traces of symmetrical structure, of the dominant influence of the Scripture texts, of the combination of the Petrine and the Pauline form, even insertions of other texts of Scripture as a result of theological progress. The "enim" in both formulas testifies to symmetrical structure; the "pro vobis et pro multis" is a combination of Petrine and Pauline formulas, the "mysterium fidei" is very probably the result of the progress of Eucharistic doctrine.

A comparison of the text of the Roman Canon with the texts of the *Traditio apostolica* and with the Canon of the *De sacramentis*, forerunners of the present Roman Canon, gives evidence of this structure and of the development according to the principles stated above.

If the anaphora of the *Traditio apostolica* of St. Hippolytus represents the ancient Roman liturgy, then we have evidence that already about 220 the Roman liturgy had developed both consecration formulas in perfect symmetry:

Hoc est corpus meum   Hic est sanguis meus
quod pro vobis confringitur   qui pro vobis effunditur

We admit that the argumentation from the *Traditio apostolica* does not satisfy completely, since it is not above any doubt, though very probable, that the liturgy described by St. Hippolytus represents really the Roman liturgy of his time. But there is no doubt that the Canon of the *De sacramentis* represents the Roman liturgy previous to the present Canon. The author declares emphatically that it is the form of the Roman Church which his Church follows in everything: "Cuius (sc. ecclesiae) typum in omnibus sequimur et formam." [17] The consecration formulas of the *De sacramentis* exhibits a symmetry and parallelism more explicit and more exact than found in any other liturgy, which has molded particularly the introduction of the consecration to an almost word-by-word symmetry.

Consecration of the host:	*Consecration of the chalice:*
Qui pridie quam pateretur	Similiter etiam calicem post-
in sanctis manibus suis ac-	quam coenatum est
cepit	pridie quam pateretur
panem, respexit in coelum ad	accepit
te	respexit in coelum ad te
sancte pater omnipotens	sancte pater omnipotens
aeterne Deus	aeterne Deus
gratias agens benedixit	gratias agens benedixit
fregit, fractumque apostolis	apostolis suis
suis	et discipulis suis tradidit
et discipulis suis tradidit	dicens:
dicens:	accipite et bibite ex hoc
accipite et manducate ex hoc	omnes
omnes	His est enim sanguis meus
Hoc est enim corpus meum	
quo pro multis confringetur	

[17] *De sacramentis*, III, 5.

THE PRINCIPLE OF SYMMETRY IN THE
STRUCTURE OF THE CANON

In the Canon of the *De sacramentis* the symmetrical structure is not confined to the words of consecration. The principle of symmetry has molded likewise the introductions to both formulas. It has extended its influence beyond the narrative of institution upon the rest of the Canon before and after the consecration. The analysis of the structure and contents together with the explanation by the author of the *De sacramentis* reveals this striking parallelism:

Before the consecration:	*After the consecration:*
dicit sacerdos . . . Fac nobis hanc oblationem adscriptam, ratam, rationabilem, acceptabilem, quod figura est corporis et sanguinis Domini nostri Jesu Christi.	dicit sacerdos: Ergo memores . . . offerimus tibi hanc immaculatam hostiam, rationabilem hostiam, increatam hostiam, hunc panem sanctum et calicem vitae aeternae . . .

Not long after the Canon of the *De sacramentis* was written, the Roman Canon was recast and received its definitive shape with a consequent application of the principle of symmetry. It is this symmetrical structure that is proper to the Roman liturgy, which distinguishes the Roman rite from the rest. Just as there are two oblation prayers symmetrically arranged immediately before consecration and immediately after it, so in the course of time the rest of the Canon prayers became symmetrically arranged. The author of the *De sacramentis* enumerates the parts before the oblation prayer "Fac nobis hanc oblationem," etc.: (a) "laudes Deo deferuntur,"

(b) "oratione petitur pro populo, pro regibus, pro caeteris." When the intercessory prayers after the consecration (the *Nobis quoque peccatoribus* and the Memento for the dead) were inserted, no doubt it was done with regard to the symmetrical structure of the Canon. Just as the final doxology corresponds to the "laudes Deo offeruntur" of the Preface, so should the "cum tuis sanctis Apostolis et martyribus" correspond to the *Communicantes;* and the "Memento etiam" should correspond to the Memento of the living.

The principle of symmetry may have been the reason for the insertion and development of the prayer "Supplices te rogamus, jube haec perferri per manus sancti angeli tui in sublime altare tuum," which seems to be the counterpart of the Sanctus and its introduction "Et ideo cum angelis et archangelis."

When St. Gregory the Great, last pope (at least in major parts) to touch the structure of the Canon, inserted his petition "diesque nostros in tua pace disponas," with the introduction "oblationem servitutis nostrae sed et cunctae familiae tuae," this was done so that after the consecration a similar invocation should correspond with the "nos servi tui, sed et plebs tua sancta."

Principal Motive of Symmetrical Structure

Several motives have influenced the symmetrical structure of the Canon and worked it out gradually to a clear architectonic form and to perfect consciousness: the sacerdotal prayer of Christ, the art of the mosaics, the double consecration, the theological controversy about the moment of consecration. We know how beautifully in the sacerdotal prayer of our Lord the petitions for His own glorification and for the glory of His disciples, His intercession for the apostles and for their followers, are arranged symmetrically around verse 19 as the center of the entire prayer, around the words of consecration unto the bloody sacrifice: "I sanctify Myself." We know further that the art of the mosaics reached its climax just at the time when the Canon received its final shape. We know that the same motives inspired the procession of saints in the Communicantes and in the Nobis quoque peccatoribus, which inspired the ancient mosaics in the apse of Maria Maggiore, of the triumphal arch of St. Paul outside the walls, of St. Apollinare in Ravenna. The composers of the Canon looked up with admiration to the glory of the transcendent art in the apse of Maria Maggiore with the Theotokos holding the divine Infant in the center, adored by saints arranged in equal number symmetrically on both sides. Mosaics and Canon have mutually inspired each other: The shining golden mosaics above have inspired the prayers said beneath; the ideas of the prayers have their reflection in the perennial art of the mosaics which surround altar and priest. There is on the other hand the identical source of ideas for both, for Canon and mosaics: the heavenly liturgy of the Apocalypse.

The chief motive, however, which is at the same time a witness for the faith of the ancient Church, is contained in the formulas of consecration themselves: it is the faith of the Church in the power of the words of Christ, the profound reverence before them, their sacramental efficacy, which as a "spiritual sword," accomplish the "mysteria tremenda." This is the principal motive in the development of the words of consecration and of their influence on the structure of the entire Roman Canon. It is the great care for the sacred words, the anxiety that nothing be omitted that may belong to the integrity of the formulas, that caused the Church to supply words mutually in each formula to a perfect parallelism, to supply words from Scripture from the Petrine as well as from the Pauline formula. To emphasize the importance of both formulas caused the Church to introduce both with identical phrases, to arrange the rest of the prayer, as the setting of the sacred words as an extension and amplification of the double giving of thanks, symmetrically on both sides. This structure reached a certain climax at a time when the epiklesis made its appearance. We know positively that it was the West, the Roman Church, St. Ambrose, St. Augustine, and particularly the author of the *De sacramentis* in the texts quoted above, who insisted forcibly on the sacramental power of the words of Christ: "Ubi venitur, ut conficiatur venerabile sacramentum, utitur sermonibus Christi." It is the special merit and particular glory of the Roman Church and the Latin theology to have formulated the ancient faith of the Church, to have pointed out explicitly and precisely, not only in theological writings, but in the entire structure of the Canon that the words of Christ, all of them, but they alone, accomplish the Eucharist. Thus is the structure of the Roman Canon, proper to the Roman liturgy, in itself a solemn monument to the perennial faith of the Church about the consecratory power of the words of Christ.

Types of the Words of Consecration

Upon the cross our Savior prayed with the words of Psalm 21 ("O God, My God, look upon Me: why hast Thou forsaken Me?") in the intention of proving that now these words are being fulfilled (Luke 24:44), since "all things must needs be fulfilled which are written in the law of Moses and in the prophets and in the Psalms concerning Me."

In the cenacle likewise, when our Lord instituted the Holy Eucharist and revealed the fullness of His love, He used prophetic words of Moses about the Pasch and about the sacrifice on Mount Sinai. The type for the words of consecration of the host, "This is My body," are the words of Moses about the Pasch to the ancients of Israel, when he ordained its annual celebration with the Haggadah, i.e., the proclamation of its meaning by the head of the paschal table (Exod. 12:27): "You shall say to them: It is the victim of the passage of the Lord, when He passed over the houses of the children of Israel in Egypt, striking the Egyptians, and saving our houses." His words refer to the command of God (Exod. 12:11): "And thus you shall eat it . . . for it is the phase (that is the passage) of the Lord." The type for the words of consecration of the chalice are the words of Moses on Mount Sinai (Exod. 24:8): "And he took the blood and sprinkled it upon the people, and he said: This is the blood of the covenant which the Lord hath made with you concerning all these words." St. Paul points out this typical relation (Heb. 9:18): "Whereupon neither was the first indeed dedicated without blood. For when every commandment of the law had been read by Moses to all the people, he took the blood . . . sprinkled both the book itself and all the people, saying: This is the blood of the testament which God hath enjoined unto you." This quotation of St. Paul from Exod. 24:8 differs from the original text in Exodus in two points. St. Paul has in mind the prominence of the antitype (Heb. 9:19): "He took the blood with water"—in Exodus water is not mentioned. Further (Heb. 9:20): "This is the blood of the testament which God hath enjoined unto you" —Exodus reads (Exod. 24:8): "This is the blood of the covenant which the Lord hath made with you concerning all these words" (cf. De la Taille, *op. cit.*, p. 75).

The words added to the consecration of the chalice (Matt.

26:28), "which shall be shed for many unto remission of sins," have their type in the words of God to Moses (Exod. 12:13): "And the blood shall be unto you for a sign (i.e., for you a sign for salvation) in the houses where you shall be: and I shall see the blood, and shall pass over you."

The command of Christ (Luke 22:19), "Do this for a commemoration of Me," has its type in the command of God to Moses (Exod. 12:14): "And this day shall be for a memorial to you: and you shall keep it a feast to the Lord in your generations with an everlasting observance." "And you shall observe the feast of the unleavened bread . . . and you shall keep this day in your generations by a perpetual observance." The gravity of this command appears in the proclamation of it by Moses to the ancients of the people (Exod. 12:24): "Thou shalt keep this thing as a law for thee and thy children forever," and to all the people (Exod. 13:3): "Remember this day in which you came forth out of Egypt . . . that you eat no leavened bread . . . and it shall be as a sign in thy hand, and as a memorial from days to days . . . and it shall be as a sign in thy hand, and as a thing hung between thy eyes, for a remembrance: because the Lord hath brought us forth out of Egypt by a strong hand."

Threefold Significance

The words of consecration have a historical and a sacramental significance. In the latter we may distinguish again (a) so far as the words produce what they signify (practical significance); (b) so far as the words proclaim at the same time the truth of them (logical significance).

The words pronounced in the person of the priest have historical significance and recall what Christ did and said in the cenacle and are to be understood as a quotation within the historical narrative of the Last Supper recited by the priest.

The words pronounced by the priest in the person of Christ have sacramental significance, words which effect what they signify. As such they are the setting forth of the Eucharist as the objective memorial of Christ and His passion.

Finally, the words of consecration have a logical significance; they are a statement declaring a truth. St. Thomas explains what kind of truth the words of consecration contain: "Its difference (consecratory formula) from other statements, which have only significative power and not effective power, is the same as between the conception of the practical intellect, which produces its object, and the conception of our speculative intellect, which is (the conception, knowledge) received from the object. . . . Therefore, just as the conception of the practical intellect does not presuppose the object of its knowledge, but effects it, so the truth of the consecratory statement does not presuppose the object signified by it, but effects it; it is the same relation with which the Word of God (truth and knowledge of God) is referred to the objects produced by it." [18] The truth of the consecratory statements is not a truth received from the object, caused by the object ("veritas logica causata et mensurata a rebus"), but it is a causal truth ("veritas logica causalis"), as the truth of the words of creation (Gen. 1:3): "Be light made," as the truth of a creative power of any artist. The words of consecration are true in this sense in the ultimate instant of pronouncing them.

[18] St. Thomas, *Summa theol.*, IIIa, q. 78, a. 4 c.

EUCHARISTIC SIGNIFICANCE

Interpreting the practical significance of the words of consecration, we call it Eucharistic significance to distinguish it from the practical significance of the rest of the sacraments. We explain analogy and difference between consecration on the one hand, and creation, incarnation, and miraculous causality, on the other; we compare the Eucharistic formulas with the rest of sacramental formulas.

Consecration is the work of God, of Christ the divine high priest through the power of the Holy Ghost. There exists therefore an analogy between consecration on the one hand, and creation and incarnation, the working of miracles, on the other hand. As to creation, there is the statement of *De sacramentis:* "The rest of the prayers (before the words of consecration) are said by the priest as his words: praise is given to God, intercession is made for the people, for the kings, for the rest; when it comes to the consecration of the venerable sacraments, then the priest does not use his own words, but uses the words of Christ. They are therefore the words of Christ which effect the sacrament; what words of Christ? These words by which everything is made. The Lord commanded and heaven and earth were made."

There is this difference between creation and consecration (as St. Thomas [19] explains): in creation the divine word acts effectively only in the efficacy of the command of the practical intellect ("per imperium suae sapientiae"); in consecration, however, the divine word acts effectively and sacramentally through the instrumentality and according to the significance of the spoken words of consecration. Besides, in creation no subject was supposed, as there is in transubstan-

[19] *Ibid.*, a. 4 ad 2.

tiation. Secondly, an analogy and difference exist between consecration and the mystery of the Incarnation: As in the mystery of the Incarnation the divine Word has formed the body of Christ through the power of the Holy Ghost, so is it again that the Word through the power of the Holy Ghost accomplishes transubstantiation. There is, however, this difference: in the Incarnation there was no instrumental causality proceeding from the body of Christ which would have cooperated in subordination to the divine causality in the formation of the body, as is the case in consecration, where Christ the high priest applies His humanity as an organic instrument when bread is changed into His body and wine is changed into His blood. In distinction from creation and incarnation, it is common to consecration with the miracles of Christ that in both cases there is employed the instrumental causality of a created being; just as Christ through the imposition of His hands cured the leper (Matt. 8:3), so in the case of the Eucharist he uses the spoken words to effect transubstantiation.

The difference of the consecratory formulas from the forms of the rest of the sacraments is the following [20]: (a) in the Eucharistic formulas no action is signified, whereas in the forms of the other sacraments an action is expressed: "I baptize"; (b) in the Eucharist the sacramental words are pronounced in the person of Christ, "This is My body"; in the other sacraments the words are pronounced in the person of the one who administers them: "I baptize." This difference in the forms has its reason in the fact that the priest as the ministerial cause has not to cooperate with consecration by any action of his; the priest has only to pronounce the words. The Eucharistic sacrament is accomplished with the consecra-

[20] *Ibid.*, a. 1 c. and ad 3.

tion of the matter, an action that is exclusively an action of God. Since the sacramental formula has to correspond to the nature of the sacrament, therefore in the words of consecration no action is expressed and the words are not pronounced in the person of the priest, but in the person of Christ (St. Thomas: "Forma huius sacramenti profertur quasi ex persona Christi loquentis, ut detur intelligere quod minister in perfectione huius sacramenti nihil agit, nisi quod profert verba Christi").

ANALYSIS OF THE WORDS OF CONSECRATION
"FOR THIS IS MY BODY"

The text of the Canon differs from the scriptural texts in the following points: Matt. 26:26 and Mark 16:22 have the identical formula: "This is My body." The Canon has also the same words, except the word "for," which is added in the Canon. St. Luke (22:19) and St. Paul (I Cor. 11:24) add to these words a phrase expressing the sacrificial character, missing in Matthew and Mark and the Canon. Luke 22:19: "This is My body which is given for you" (the Vulgate renders the participle "given" with the present tense, "is given"). I Cor. 11:24: "This is My body, which shall be delivered for you." Of St. Paul's version there exist two readings: (a) "which for you"; (b) "which broken for you" (the Vulgate substitutes "given" for "broken," and the future tense for the present).

About the addition of the particle "for" in the Canon, St. Thomas refers to the tradition of the Roman Church coming down from St. Peter, to whom tradition generally ascribes the original form of the Roman Canon.[21] The principle of the development of the Canon, to combine the varying scrip-

²¹ *Ibid.*, a. 2 ad 5.

tural texts, may have caused the insertion of this particle in order to assimilate the consecration of the host to the consecration of the chalice. In the consecration of the chalice Scripture shows this particle (Matt. 26:28): "For this is My blood." With this particle on the one hand the continuation with the preceding words ("take and eat") is established, and on the other hand the real presence is emphasized.

With regard to the pronoun "this," we refer to the interpretation of St. Thomas: It does not signify the substance of bread nor the substance of the body of Christ, but substance generically (not specifically) contained under these accidents.[22]

It would seem that for the real meaning instead of the verb "is" there should be substituted rather "is becoming" or the imperative form "be made," which would express the action of transubstantiation in analogy to the words of creation, "light be made," and in analogy to the Incarnation, "be it done unto me according to thy word." St. Thomas' interpretation of the verb "is" is very profound and reveals most clearly the causality of a sacramental form. He mentions two reasons why consecration is not signified in its "becoming" ("in fieri"): (a) the change of bread into the body of Christ is not effected successively, but instantaneously; (b) a sacramental form signifies its effect like an artistic idea, in its ultimate state, as the image of the ultimate effect intended. As in the mind of the artist the idea is primarily the form of the finished building ("in facto esse") and secondarily and consequently only of its becoming, so is it with the words of consecration.

The proper sacramental causality is further the reason why the imperative form "be made" is to be excluded, and re-

22 *Ibid.*, a. 2 c. and ad 1, 2.

placed by the indicative. In the act of creation the Word of God acted effectively only (per imperium suae sapientiae), and not by the means of the instrumental causality of sacraments; hence the words (Gen. 1:3), "Be light made. And light was made." In consecration, however, the word of God acts effectively and through the significance of the sacramental formula, which has to express the effect in its ultimate state, "in facto esse."

"My body": the pronoun "My" expresses sufficiently that the words are pronounced in the person of Christ. A formula which would say "the body of Christ" would be invalid for the reason that the formula would not be pronounced in the person of Christ.

"For This Is the Chalice of My Blood"

"For this is the chalice of My blood, of the new and eternal testament, the mystery of faith: which shall be shed for you, and for many, unto the remission of sins." The words of consecration of the chalice are a combining of the texts from St. Luke and St. Paul, partly also from St. Matthew and St. Mark. The particle "for" is taken from St. Matthew. "This is the chalice" are the identical words of St. Luke and St. Paul. "The new testament in My blood," which is found identical in St. Luke and St. Paul, is modified with reference to St. Matthew: "For this is My blood of the testament," and to St. Mark: "This is My blood of the testament," which makes the phrase of the Canon more fluent, "of My blood of the new and eternal testament." The adjective "eternal" is not found in any of the scriptural reports. It is probably inserted from Heb. 13:20: "And may the God of peace, who brought again from the dead the great pastor of the sheep, our Lord Jesus Christ, in the blood of the everlasting testament, fit

you in all goodness, that you may do His will." The words
"mystery of faith" are likewise an addition to the scriptural
text and will be considered in a special chapter. The words
"which shall be shed for you, and for many, unto the remission of sins" are taken partly from St. Matthew (and St.
Mark) 26:28: "which shall be shed for many [the Greek
text has the present tense] unto remission of sins," and partly
from St. Luke (Luke 22:20): "which shall be shed for you."
The words "unto remission of sins" are proper to St. Matthew.

The particle "for," found only in St. Matthew, continues
the idea of the words "Drink ye all of this" and is at the same
time an insistence on the real presence of the blood of Christ.
"The chalice of My blood" means: the contents of this chalice
is "My blood" (metonymy).

"Of the new and eternal testament," "My blood of the
testament," means that it is the ratification of the New Covenant "through My blood," just as it was the meaning of the
words of Moses about the conclusion of the Old Covenant:
"Behold the blood of the covenant which the Lord hath made
with you," as appears also from the whole procedure described in Exodus 24:8, that Moses, after he had read the
book of the covenant and the people had promised to observe it, sprinkled them with sacrificial blood, saying, "Behold," etc. "New" is the testament, with reference to the one
concluded on Sinai which has ceased to exist, which was
merely a figure and type of the truth and reality of the new
testament. The new testament is eternal, whereas the old
testament was merely preparatory, of limited duration. The
new testament, as the reign of the Messiah, is eternal inasmuch as it is ordained from the beginning, and inasmuch as
it will last forever.

The phrase "which shall be shed for you and for many unto

the remission of sins" expresses forcefully the sacrificial character of the Eucharist. Although in the words of consecration of the host the sacrificial character is also expressed in two texts with special terms (not in the Canon); in St. Luke, "This is My body which is given for you," and I Cor. 11:24, "this is My body for you," the intention to express the sacrificial character appears much more clearly in the words of the consecration of the chalice, both in the Scripture and in the Canon. The reason is obvious: [23] the blood consecrated separate from the body signifies by itself much more expressively the passion of Christ, than does the consecrated body. Therefore the phrase expressing the sacrificial idea is rather added to the consecration of the blood and not to that of the body.

"Which shall be shed." The Greek texts of all three Gospels has the participle with the meaning "which is shed." The Vulgate translates "shall be shed." The Greek text shows that in the Eucharist itself the blood is shed (sacramentally), that it is in itself a sacrifice. The Vulgate expresses with the future tense the relation of the Last Supper to the sacrifice on the cross: the Last Supper was the anticipated representation of the sacrifice on the cross. The Eucharistic sacrifice is essentially "relative." The term "to shed the blood" has in the Bible the meaning "to offer sacrifice to God" (Lev. 1:5): "And he shall immolate the calf before the Lord: and the priests the sons of Aaron shall offer the blood thereof, pouring it round about the altar." Rom. 3:25: "the redemption that is in Jesus Christ whom God hath proposed to be a propitiation, through faith in His blood."

"For you and for many." This distinction can be under-

[23] *Ibid.*, a. 3 ad 2, 7.

stood as referring to: (a) the Jews and the Gentiles; (b) the disciples and priests, who offer the sacrifice and who partake of it in Holy Communion, and the rest of the faithful for whom the sacrifice is offered. "Many" can be taken for (a) all, with a special connotation of the immense multitude of the children of Adam; or (b) with reference to those who actually are saved: many, but not all men cooperate with the grace of Christ.

"Unto the remission of sins." These words, found only in Matthew, express once more the sacrificial character of the Eucharist, particularly as propitiatory sacrifice.

"As often as you do these things, ye shall do them in remembrance of Me." Matthew and Mark omit our Lord's command. St. Luke mentions it only once, after the consecration of the host in the short form (Luke 22:19): "Do this for a commemoration of Me." St. Paul mentions it twice (I Cor. 11:24–26): After the consecration of the host: "This do for the commemoration of Me"; after the consecration of the chalice: "This do ye, as often as you shall drink, for the commemoration of Me." The second time St. Paul adds: "For as often as you shall eat this bread and drink the chalice, you shall show the death of the Lord, until He come."

None of the sacred writers had the intention of giving a complete report about the institution of the Holy Eucharist. They supposed it was known by oral tradition and by liturgical practice. Even St. Paul, although he repeats the command twice and enforces it the second time with a special declaration, does not intend to give with his report an instruction about the celebration of the Eucharist. What he intends is to correct abuses in Corinth which occurred in connection with the agape, the love-feast. He recalls the fact and the purpose of the institution in order to show what preparation is required of those who would partake of it, what behavior is demanded of those who would celebrate it.

The Canon reproduces the command only once, after the consecration of the chalice. Its form closely approximates the one of St. Paul in the second place with some modifications. The command of the Canon has to refer to both consecrations, therefore instead of St. Paul's singular "this" it uses the plural "these things." For the same reason St. Paul's words "as often as you shall drink," are replaced in the Canon by the words "as often as you do." Finally, instead of the words "for the commemoration of Me," the Canon has "in remembrance of Me."

The twofold command with the third repetition added in the report of St. Paul in his own words, impresses us with the importance of the commission given by Christ with these words. When He said "Do them in remembrance of Me" He both instituted the Holy Eucharist and ordained the apostles priests.[24] "As often," words which are used by St. Paul in the command after the consecration of the chalice, and are added again in the repetition, explain the connection between the commission and the action to which it refers. With these words our Lord declared His intention that the Eucharist be the perpetual sacrifice in the Church, to be repeated and continued "until He come."

It is to be a perpetual sacrifice in the Church as the antitype of the perpetual sacrifice of the lamb in the Temple as ordained by God (Exod. 29:38–46): "This is what thou shalt sacrifice upon the altar: two lambs of a year old every day continually. One lamb in the morning and another in the evening. With one lamb a tenth part of flour tempered with

24 Cf. Trent, Sess. 22, can. 1 and 2; DB, nos. 948 f.

beaten oil, of the fourth part of a hin: and wine for liba-
tion of the same measure. And the other lamb thou shalt
offer in the evening, according to the rite of the morning
oblation, and according to what we have said: for a savor of
sweetness. It is a sacrifice to the Lord, by perpetual oblation
unto your generations at the door of the tabernacle of the
testimony before the Lord, where I will appoint to speak
unto thee. And there will I command the children of Israel:
and the altar shall be sanctified by My glory. I will sanctify
also the tabernacle of the testimony with the altar, and Aaron
with his sons, to do the office of priesthood unto Me. And I
will dwell in the midst of the children of Israel, and will be
their God: and they shall know that I am the Lord their God,
who have brought them out of the land of Egypt, that I might
abide among them: I the Lord their God."

It is to be a perpetual sacrifice also in fulfillment of this
prophecy of Malachias (1:11): "For from the rising of the
sun even to the going down, My name is great among the
Gentiles: and in every place there is sacrifice and there is
offered to My name a clean oblation."

In practice the Church has interpreted the perpetuity first
with a continued celebration of the Eucharist once a week,
then (e.g., at the time of St. Gregory I) several times a day,
since the time of Pope Innocent III it is as a rule limited to
one time a day for each priest (except on the Nativity and
since the time of Pope Benedict XV on All Souls Day, when
three Masses are permitted for each priest).

In the prophecy of Daniel (12:11) the typical relation between the perpetual sacrifice of the Temple and the Eucharist
is expressed with these words: "And from the time when the
continual sacrifice shall be taken away and the abomination
unto desolation shall be set up, there shall be a thousand two

hundred ninety days." This prophecy refers (a) to the time of the destruction of Jerusalem by Titus and the abolition of the sacrifice of the Temple; (b) to the time of the Antichrist: the Eucharist shall be celebrated until the end of the world. The Antichrist, however, may succeed in preventing its public celebration in fulfillment of the prophecy of Daniel.

"In commemoration of Me." According to the interpretation of H. J. Heuser,[25] the term "commemoration" (Greek anamnesis) is the equivalent of the Hebrew term "azkarah" with the meaning "meal offering remembrance" (cf. Num. 5:18: the sacrifice of remembrance). Consequently there would be contained in this term another evidence for the sacrificial character of the Eucharist. In connection with this interpretation the author refers to the visions of Catherine Emmerich, who heard the words of our Lord: "Do this as a sacrifice of Me." The object of remembrance as given by our Lord Himself is generally "Me"; St. Paul has specified in his repeated command, "you shall show the death of the Lord." About the import of the term "Me" in the command of Christ, and the meaning of its specification by St. Paul, we treat in the question of the *Unde et memores.*

WORDS OF OUR LORD IN SCRIPTURE AND THE CANON

Canon: Take, and eat ye all of this.
Matt.: Take ye and eat.
Mark: Take ye.
Luke: ———
Paul: (Take ye and eat: supplied from Matt.)

Canon: For this is My body.
Matt.: This is My body.

[25] *Ecclesiastical Review,* CV (1936), 363.

Mark: This is My body.
Luke: This is My body, which is given for you.
Paul: This is My body, which (shall be delivered) for you.

Canon: Take, and drink ye all of it.
Matt.: Drink ye all of this.
Mark: ——
Luke: ——
Paul: ——

Canon: For this is the chalice of My blood, of the new and eternal testament: the mystery of faith: which shall be shed for you, and for many, unto the remission of sins.
Matt.: For this is My blood of the new testament, which shall be shed for many unto remission of sins.
Mark: This is My blood of the new testament, which shall be shed for many.
Luke: This is the chalice, the new testament in My blood which shall be shed for you.
Paul: This chalice is the new testament in My blood.

Canon: As often as you do these things, you shall do them in remembrance of Me.
Luke: Do this for a commemoration of Me.
Paul: This do for the commemoration of Me.
This do ye, as often as you shall drink, for the commemoration of Me. For as often as you shall eat this bread and drink this chalice, you shall show the death of the Lord, until He come.

CHAPTER XXII

Mysterium Fidei

THE words "mysterium fidei" shed at once a brilliant light over the formula of consecration, over the altar, over host and chalice. It is as if at this moment priest and Church became conscious of the effect of the divine words, as if the sacred chalice would begin to glow in the fire of divinity, and heaven and earth, angels and saints, exclaim with the priest: "These are the divine mysteries." These words resound so full of glory as the exclamation of the deacon on Holy Saturday when he proclaims with the Paschale praeconium: "Exultent divina mysteria," "let the divine mysteries rejoice," i.e., joyfully be celebrated. These words radiate that sacred awe which inspired St. Cyril of Alexandria, St. Basil, and St. Chrysostom, to call the Eucharistic liturgy "tremenda mysteria." They are filled with the spirit of St. Paul, they contain the central idea of the theology of St. Paul, the "mystery of Christ."

ORIGIN

The words "mysterium fidei" are not found in the scriptural reports of the institution of the Holy Eucharist. They occur only in the First Epistle of St. Paul to Timothy (I Tim. 3:9): "Holding the mystery of faith in a pure conscience." The same idea returns again (I Tim. 3:16): "And evidently great is the mystery of godliness, which was manifested in the flesh, was justified in the spirit, appeared unto angels, hath been preached unto the Gentiles, is believed in the world, is taken up in glory."

Many theologians maintain that the words "mysterium fidei" within the formula of consecration are a matter of divine apostolic tradition. Pope Leo IX [1] declares that these words are "a tradition transmitted by St. Peter, the author of the Roman liturgy." Pope Innocent III says that these words were added to the words of consecration from apostolic tradition and he refers to I Tim. 3:9.

St. Thomas also holds these words as a matter of tradition, transmitted by the apostles to the Church. He insists, however, on divine tradition and understands that the words of Christ are the common source for these words of the Canon as they are for the text I Tim. 3:9: "Ex traditione Domini habetur." [2] The Roman Catechism teaches that these words come from Catholic tradition, but leaves the question open, whether they are of divine tradition, or interpretation by the Church: "Catholicae veritatis interpres et custos nos docuit."

Modern authors are inclined to see in these words a later insertion, taken from I Tim. 3:9 which found its way into the Roman Canon through Gallican influence.

LITURGICAL TRADITION

The liturgical tradition about these words is not universal, not even so far as the immediate sources of the Roman liturgy are concerned.

A similar phrase is found in the *Apostolic Constitutions*

---

[1] *Ep. ad Michaelem Imp.*, cap. 9; cf. Corn. a Lapide *in Matt.* 26:28.

[2] St. Thomas, *Summa theol.*, IIIa, q. 78, a. 3 ad 9: " 'Mysterium fidei' ex traditione Domini habetur, quae ad ecclesiam per Apostolos pervenit, secundum illud I Cor. 11:23: Ego accepi a Domino, quod et tradidi vobis."

(8, 12) as words of our Lord which introduce the consecration of the host: "He broke it, and gave it to His disciples, saying: This is the mystery of the new Covenant: take of it and eat: this is My body, which is broken for many, for the remission of sins." The liturgy of the Copts (anaphora of St. Basil) shows in the introduction to the narrative of the institution the term "great mystery of godliness," however, not as words uttered by Christ: "And He hath instituted for us this great mystery of godliness and religion. For when He was determined to give Himself to death for the life of the world, He took bread into His holy, spotless and pure, blessed and life-giving hands." In the West we find these words in the Gallican liturgy of St. Germanus (d. 576), a rite with Byzantine features, used in Paris in the sixth century. A review of the documents of the Roman liturgy and its sources shows no universal tradition either: these words are not found in the anaphora of the *Traditio apostolica* of St. Hippolytus, they are not in the formula of consecration in the *De sacramentis*. But they are included in the Canon of the Gelasian and Gregorian Sacramentary, and in the Missal of Bobbio, which is the Gallican Sacramentary with the Roman Canon of the Gelasian book. A series of scholars (A. Salaville,[3] A. de Waal,[4] A. Fortescue, Cardinal Schuster) hold that these words were originally an exclamation of the deacon in the moment of consecration in analogy to the exclamations so frequent in Eastern liturgies. In the Byzantine liturgy, for instance, the deacon calls the attention of the faithful to the hearing of the Epistle and the Gospel with the words: "Wisdom: stand up." So it may have been the

---

[3] Salaville, "Epiclese eucharistique," *Dict. théol. cath.*

[4] A. de Waal, "Archaeologische Eroerterungen zu einigen Stuecken im Canon der heiligen Messe, III: Die Worte Mysterium fidei," *Der Katholik,* 1896, pp. 392–95.

practice in the Gallican liturgy to announce the moment of consecration with the words "mysterium fidei." When with the multiplication of Masses and with the introduction of Low Masses, the deacon was dispensed with, and the diptychs were inserted into the Canon and read by the priest, the words "mysterium fidei" likewise were made a part of the Canon. This theory is confirmed by the fact that in the context of the Epistle to Timothy these words are directed to the deacons as an exhortation for worthy conduct because of the high office they hold, to take care of the "mysterium fidei," probably with an allusion to the distribution of the sacred chalice entrusted to the deacons in ancient times. St. Lawrence says of himself that to him is entrusted the dispensation of the blood of the Lord. A remnant of this office of the deacon is to be seen in the rite of the High Mass when the deacon offers the chalice together with the priest.

If we agree with historians that these words are an insertion from I Tim. 3:9, or if we rather hold the view of St. Thomas and the older interpreters that the words are of divine apostolic tradition, it is in either case important to state the meaning these words have in the context of the Epistle to Timothy, in order to arrive at an adequate interpretation of them as part of the Canon.

I Tim. 3:9, 16

St. Paul's first epistle to Timothy was caused by Judaizing teachers in Ephesus who were "speaking perverse things, to draw away disciples after them" (Acts 20, 29). He wrote this first letter in order to assist his disciple Timothy in combating these false teachers. Timothy, whom St. Paul had appointed bishop of the Church of Ephesus, was the one dearest to his heart, intelligent, innocent, gentle, but timid and naturally fearful, who could not so well fight the wicked opponents as St. Paul. The Apostle knew that he had to encourage him, to remind him of the sublime dignity of his office, of the glory of the treasure entrusted to him. He gives him rules regarding the careful choice of ministers of the Gospel, about the moral and spiritual requirements for bishops, deacons and other officials of the Church. He demands particularly of the deacons (I Tim. 3:9), "Holding the mystery of faith in a pure conscience," and concludes his exhortation with a general appeal to Timothy himself for worthy conduct inclusively of all the other ecclesiastical officials, with the lyrical passage (I Tim. 3:16) about the mystery of godliness, taken from a hymn, sung in the early Church, which unfolds before the eyes of his beloved disciple the glorious content of the "mystery of faith": "These things I write to thee, hoping that I shall come to thee shortly; but if I tarry long, that thou mayest know how thou oughtest to behave thyself in the house of God, which is the Church of the living God, a pillar and ground of the truth. And evidently great is the mystery of godliness: who was manifested in the flesh, was justified in spirit, appeared unto angels, was preached among Gentiles, believed in the world, taken up in glory."

Some commentators (cf. Cornelius a Lapide) understand as the "mystery of faith" to which St. Paul refers in this text, literally the Holy Eucharist for the following reason: in the Greek text "to mysterion," "mystery of faith," has the definite article, indicating a certain mystery, the mystery "katexochen." Further, the term "holding" means to serve, to watch, a term which could fittingly refer to the administration of the chalice entrusted to the deacon. St. Augustine at least accommodates the word "mysterium pietatis" to the Eucharist

(*In Jo.*, tr. 26, n. 13): "O mira pietatis dignatio. O inaestimabilis dilectio caritatis. O sacramentum pietatis. O signum unitatis. O vinculum caritatis." Peter Lombard and St. Thomas interpret "mystery of faith" as dogma of faith, which the deacons have to know, to preserve, to transmit incorrupt from all errors to the faithful. The interpretation as dogma of faith is certainly implied, but it does not seem to be complete. For several reasons we may say that these words signify Christ as object of faith and worship. These reasons are the following. (a) The definite article of both terms of "mysterium fidei" and of "mysterium pietatis" indicates a certain mystery, the mystery "katexochen." (b) Both terms refer to the same object. (c) The primary idea of mystery in the theology of St. Paul is Christ Himself (Col. 1:26): "The mystery which hath been hidden from ages and generations, but now is manifested to His saints, to whom God would make known the riches of the glory of this mystery among the Gentiles, which is Christ in you the hope of glory" (cf. Col. 4:3 f.; Rom. 16:25 f.). (d) The complex of ideas in the Epistle to Timothy is similar to that of the Epistle to the Hebrews. Against the Judaizing teachers who exalt the glory of the Mosaic cult, St. Paul opposes the higher glory of the Church. Against the shadows, types, figures, and promises of the Old Testament, the Apostle exalts the spirit and truth, the fulfillment and reality of the New Testament. Against the material and external splendor of the Temple of Jerusalem, he recommends the spiritual glory of the mystery of Christ.

The terms "pillar and ground of the truth," "house of God," "mystery of godliness," "appeared unto angels," contain allusions to the cult of the Temple in Jerusalem. With "pillar and ground of the truth" the Apostle alludes to the two columns erected by Solomon at the entrance of the Temple as symbols of the theocracy of the Old Testament, of truth and fortitude. These columns were destroyed together with the Temple, and so has passed the Old Testament. The New Testament, however, is the house of the living God which is eternal, never to be destroyed, from which God would never withdraw Himself. The Old Testament had also its mystery. The term "mysterium pietatis" alludes to it. This term can be translated: mystery of the cult, mystery of mercy. In the first meaning it implies the religion of men to God; in the second it implies the manifestation of the mercy of God toward men. Such a mystery was the manifestation of God over the propitiatory throne in the holy of holies, adored by the cherubim. This manifestation, however, of God was merely a figure, a symbol of the manifestation of God in the mystery of the Incarnation. Christ is the mystery of the mercy and loving kindness of God (cf. St. Augustine: "How wonderful the condescension of Thy mercy toward us. How incomparable the predilection of Thy love"). Christ is also the mystery of the perfect worship, the mystery of the worship in "spirit and in truth" in the Holy Eucharist, as the continuation and extension of the Incarnation.

With beautiful rhythms of an early Christian hymn to Christ triumphant, St. Paul specifies the mystery of godliness.[5] This hymn expresses the luminous center of St. Paul's theology in the words and tones of the charismatic enthusiasm of the apostolic Church. These verses unfold the mystery of the Incarnation in its phases, represent the whole dispensation exercised through the assumed humanity: the Nativity, Passion, Cross, Resurrection, and Ascension, Christ in His Church as principle of life, of the ever-growing mystical body.

[5] Prat, The Theology of Saint Paul (London, 1942), II, 429 f. Cf. J. M. Nielen, The Earliest Christian Liturgy, tr. by P. Cummins (St. Louis, 1941), p. 288.

(a) Christ was made manifest in the flesh by the Nativity (cf. John 1:14; Rom. 16:26; Col. 1:26; I Pet. 1:20); (b) Christ "was justified in the Spirit." The Spirit gave evidence about His being the Messiah, the Son of God (cf. Rom. 1:4), in the works which Christ wrought "in the Spirit," that the Spirit descended upon Him at the baptism in the Jordan. The miracles with which Christ was glorified upon the cross are a testimony of the Spirit, finally the Resurrection (Rom. 8:11), the descent of the Spirit on Pentecost (John 15:26). (c) "He appeared unto angels," who adored at His entering this world (Heb. 1:6), "and let all the angels of God adore Him," who ministered to Him and were witness of His resurrection and ascension (Phil. 2:10) "that in the name of Jesus every knee should bow, of those that are in heaven, on earth, and under the earth" (cf. Eph. 3:10; I Pet. 1:12); (d) "He was preached among the nations," "He was believed on in the world"; these verses delineate prophetically the mystical Christ, the glory of His ever-growing mystical body, Christ in the Church; (e) "Taken up in glory," by ascension. The verses are not in the chronological order of the events in the life of Christ. The lyrical and poetic character justifies the inversion of "was preached among the Gentiles, believed on in the world," and "taken up in glory," in order to conclude the hymn with a striking idea which may at the same time imply the ultimate glorification of Christ in His mystical body at the end of time.

The Intention of the Church

The words "mysterium fidei" of the Canon are an apposition to "chalice of the New Testament," and apply to the Eucharist in the specific significance of "the sacrament *katexochen*, the cult mystery."

The Eucharist is a mystery, it is a sacrament.[6] In the Holy Eucharist there is hidden not only the divinity, but also the humanity, the body and the blood. It is the most excellent sacrament, because it contains all the glory of the mystery of Christ spoken of in I Tim. 3:9, 16. The rest of the sacraments contain merely His power. The Eucharist is the mystery of faith, in a sense different from that which applies to the sacrament of baptism. Baptism is called mystery of faith ("quaedam fidei confessio"); the Eucharist is called mystery of faith (a) as object of faith: only by faith we know of the real presence of Christ, of the real presence of His body and blood. It is called mystery of faith (b) because the passion of Christ, represented in it, saves through faith. It is at the same time called the sacrament of love, with regard to what it signifies and what it effects.

In the hypothesis that the Church has added these words, some special reasons can be found for it. In the first place, we cannot regard as impossible such an insertion, which would make them a parenthesis within the words of consecration of the chalice. From the studies above we know that the scriptural reports about the consecration formulas have influenced the Canon. Such additions and accidental changes are: "enim" in the consecration of the host; the combining of "vobis et multis" in the consecration of the chalice. If, however, the Church has inserted the words "mysterium fidei," then there must have been an important reason, momentous motives. Although these words in that case would not be a part of the consecration formula, the mere fact that they were inserted within the words of consecration elevates them in their significance and dignity above the rest of the Canon, instituted by the Church, recited in the name of the Church.

[6] Cf. St. Thomas, *Summa theol.*, IIIa, q. 78, a. 3.

This apposition appears a very solemn statement, a high testimony, a pronouncement by the Church of the highest authority.

The primary motive on the side of the Church may have been the same as caused the insertion of "this most excellent" (chalice) into the words which introduce the formula of consecration of the chalice. It may have been the same motive as caused the recasting of the Canon: the doctrinal development of the constitutive elements of the Eucharist, of the consecratory power of the words of Christ against the tendencies (in the East), that only in conjunction with the epiklesis is consecration accomplished. These reasons have motivated the statement of the *De sacramentis* (IV, 4), which concludes: "Therefore the words of Christ accomplish this sacrament."

It may have been that the deacon who read a part of the diptychs before consecration, the other after consecration, interrupted the reading with the announcement "mysterium fidei" with which he called to attention and devotion for the most sacred moment. At the time the diptychs were inserted into the Canon, the words "mysterium fidei" were likewise inserted with the intention of proclaiming at this moment that the consecration is accomplished. That rather the words "mysterium fidei" instead of "mysterium pietatis" were inserted, is another reason to admit that these words were formerly pronounced by the deacon. That they were inserted before "qui pro vobis et pro multis effundetur," as an apposition to "calix novi testamenti," seems to exclude that any further act by any following prayer would be required, as an erroneous interpretation of the future tense of the "effundetur" could suggest.

In conclusion we may say: the words "mysterium fidei"

represent the immediate reaction of the Church at the moment of accomplished consecration. They represent a most solemn testimony of her belief that the words of Christ are consecratory. They are a testimony for the real presence of the mystery of Christ, of that cult mystery, described by St. Paul in such glowing colors. It is a silent association with the venerable hymn of the early Church, filled with the enthusiasm and glorified joy, full of admiration and gratitude.

CHAPTER XXIII

"Unde et memores" [1]

"WHEREFORE, O Lord, we Thy servants, and likewise Thy holy people, calling to mind the blessed passion of the same Christ Thy Son, our Lord, together with His resurrection from the grave, and also His glorious ascension into heaven, offer unto Thy excellent Majesty, of Thy gifts and presents, a pure Victim, a holy Victim, an immaculate Victim: the holy bread of eternal life, and the chalice of everlasting salvation."

The current interpretation of the Anamnesis can be summarized as follows: It is a commemorative prayer indicating that the Eucharistic sacrifice is the objective memorial of the passion of our Lord. The association of the mysteries of the [Nativity], Resurrection, Ascension, etc., is regarded as a mere subjective, mental, and oral commemoration. That is, the objective memorial of the death of our Lord in the consecration, and the following declaration about it in the Anamnesis, are the occasion of calling to mind also the historical events of the other mysteries.

The interpretation of the mystics of the Middle Ages, how-

[1] F. Cabrol, art. "Anamnese," *Dict. théol. cath.;* O. Casel, "Das Mysteriengedaechtnis der Mess Liturgie im Lichte der Tradition," *Jb. L.W.,* VI (1926), 113–204; Casel, "Neue Zeugnisse fuer das Kultmysterium," *Jb. L.W.,* XIII (1933), 99–171; J. Jungmann, "Praefatio und Stiller Kanon," *ZkTh,* LIII (1929), 91; J. Brinktrine, "Per la storia dell' Unde et memores," *Rivista liturgica,* IX (1922), 77; G. Morin, "L'anamnese de la messe romaine dans la premier moitié du Vᵉ siècle," *Rev. Bened.,* XXIV (1907), 404; J. Gassner, "Christ's Nativity Re-enacted in Sacrament," *Orate Fratres,* XX (1945), 69–80, 301–13; XXI (1947), 343–55.

ever, is different. They understand (cf. the visions of St. Hildegarde) the Eucharistic sacrifice as the re-enactment of the mysteries of the nativity, the death, the burial, the resurrection, and the ascension of our Lord, of which the Anamnesis is the explicit statement. This charismatic interpretation of the Eucharist, particularly of the Anamnesis, seems to be so full of wonders that we almost feel afraid all its charm and beauty will dissolve into mere pious symbolism and external analogies as soon as we ask about facts, about theological tradition, about its scriptural background and its dogmatic foundation. It is therefore a cause for both joy and gratitude that we are able to find a genuine tradition and a scriptural basis for it in the epistles of St. Paul and a dogmatic foundation in the writings of the holy Fathers of the Church.

THE ANAMNESIS AND I COR. 11:24–26

The Anamnesis, inspired by St. Paul, has incorporated the words of Christ, "Do this for a commemoration of Me," and the added declaration of St. Paul, "For as often as you eat this bread and drink the chalice you shall show the death of the Lord until He come." We shall analyze first the meaning of the command of Christ and of St. Paul's declaration, and then compare the Anamnesis with both.

The command of Christ refers to the ordination of the apostles as priests and as celebrants of the Eucharist.[2] Only St. Luke, the disciple and companion of St. Paul, and St. Paul himself record this command. St. Luke mentions it only once, after the consecration of the bread; St. Paul twice, after the consecration of each species. The second time St. Paul adds the specifying declaration: "For as often as you eat this bread and drink the chalice you show the death of the Lord

[2] Cf. Trent, Sess. 22, can. 2; *DB*, no. 949.

until He come." This declaration specifies the command in three respects: with the words "show," "death of the Lord," and "until He come."

The word "show" is a specification of "commemoration." "To do for a commemoration," or "to commemorate," refers to the celebration of the Eucharist and is equivalent to "offering the commemorative sacrifice." The word "show" indicates the specific manner of the Eucharistic celebration and alludes to the most prominent types of it in the Old Testament. "Show" with its equivalent terms (as found in the Anamneses of the Eastern liturgies), "show forth," "set forth," "announce," "proclaim," "declare," refers first of all to the words of consecration with their threefold significance. 1. Pronounced in the person of the priest in connection with the historical narrative of the institution, the words "This is My Body," "This is My Blood," commemorate historically the institution of the Eucharist. 2. Pronounced simultaneously in the person of Christ, they have pragmatic significance: they effect what they signify and are the "setting forth" of the Eucharistic memorial of Christ. 3. The pragmatic significance presupposed, they are a statement with logical significance, declaring the truth of the accomplished consecration. The command of Christ is fulfilled as soon as the words of consecration are pronounced. To pronounce them with their threefold significance is the declaration, the proclamation understood by St. Paul in the word "show." [3]

The phrase "death of the Lord" is a specification of the

[3] There is still another relation implied in the word "show." It connects the "proclamation" of the words of consecration with its type in the Old Testament. "Show forth" is a translation of the Hebrew "Haggadah," the name of the Jewish Passover rite, containing the ritual narrative of the Exodus (13:8, 14): "And thou shalt show thy son in that day saying: This is done because of that which the Lord did unto me when I came forth out of Egypt."

phrase "of Me" in Christ's command. The intention of the Apostle in this specification, and the intention of the declaration as a whole, is to inspire the Corinthians with due respect and reverence for the Eucharistic sacrifice. St. Paul does not record the institution of the Eucharist in this letter simply for the purpose of instructing the Corinthians about it. This he had done previously (I Cor. 11:23: "which also I delivered unto you"); they knew it, they celebrated it. His intention is to correct abuses which had crept into the celebration of the Eucharist at Corinth. He had heard that they behaved as if it were a banquet of common bread and common drink. He reproaches them and reminds them of the sacred character of the Eucharist. For this reason he mentions the words of Christ, and specifies the word "commemoration of Me" with the declaration that it is the "showing of the death of the Lord." The eating is an eating of the body of Christ, the drinking is the drinking of His blood, so really and truly that an unworthy behavior which does not distinguish this bread from common food, and the chalice from common drink, means an eating and drinking unto condemnation. Full of sorrow the Apostle adds: "not discerning the Lord's body . . . therefore are there many infirm and weak among you, and many sleep" (I Cor. 11:29). Because they were so forgetful and behaved so disrespectfully at the celebration of the commemorative sacrifice, which means the setting forth of Christ's death, they are visited with many afflictions, with premature death, perhaps even with eternal damnation.

Such is the meaning of St. Paul's declaration. It contains a specification of the Eucharistic memorial sacrifice and is at the same time a reproof: "You must be mindful [and behave accordingly] that you show the death of the Lord." St. Paul introduced I Cor. 11 with the words: "Now I praise you, brethren, that in all things you are mindful of me and keep my ordinances as I have delivered them to you." But in verse 17 he continues: "Now this I ordain, not praising you," etc., because they were not mindful of the instruction he had given them about the Eucharistic celebration.

The *Unde memores* of the Roman Canon and the Anamnesis in all liturgies is inspired by St. Paul and worded according to the declaration in I Cor. 11:23. The "therefore" connects the Anamnesis with both: with the command of Christ and with the declaration of St. Paul. It is an answer to the command of Christ and an assurance with the meaning: "O Lord, as Thou didst command us to do, we are doing. We offer the commemorative sacrifice, we set forth the sacrificial memorial." At the same time the Anamnesis replies to the admonition of St. Paul contained in his specific declaration, so that the "Unde memores . . . tam beatae passionis . . ." has the meaning: "We are mindful of the fact that we are setting forth the death of the Lord in this sacrificial memorial."

For a complete interpretation of the Anamnesis we should note that in most liturgies a double Anamnesis is found: one before the Canon or anaphora (sometimes within the anaphora immediately before consecration), the other after consecration. The preconsecratory Anamnesis in the Roman rite is the prayer *Suscipe Sancta Trinitas*. This preconsecratory Anamnesis indicates that the whole Eucharistic rite which follows is the execution of the commemoration commanded by Christ. The postconsecratory Anamnesis indicates that the command has been fulfilled. Although the verbs of both prayers are in the present tense, the "offerimus" of the first Ananmnesis refers to the consecration which follows, that of the second to the consecration accomplished. This is the interpretation proposed by Cardinal Bessarion (d. 1472) at the Council of Florence (1438–45), and accepted by the fathers of the Council more particularly in regard to the epiklesis. But this so-called "dramatic theory" applies equally to the Anamnesis.

Concluding the analysis of the fundamental idea of the Anamnesis, we may say: The whole Eucharistic rite is the execution in a wider sense of the "commemoration" commanded by Christ; in the strict sense and essentially the command is carried into effect in the central act of the consecration. The commemorative prayer after consecration, however, justifies its name of Anamnesis in a particular manner, because, inspired by St. Paul, it is a calling to mind of the significance of the consecration as a setting forth of the death of the Lord, and an exhortation to respectful behavior, to devout disposition. The Church is giving herself and her priests this admonition in order not to incur temporal punishment, affliction through sickness and premature death, and even dread judgment hereafter.[4]

THE MYSTERIES SPECIFIED

The declaration of St. Paul which has inspired the Anamnesis does not make mention of any other mystery besides the death of our Lord. Similarly, the description of the Eucharist by St. Justin Martyr (d. 167) speaks only of the Eucharist as the memorial of the passion of Christ. The Anamnesis of the euchologion of Serapion (toward the end of the

[4] The Eastern Anamneses have preserved more expressively the spirit of St. Paul with appropriate terms. E.g., the liturgy of the Armenians: "Commemorating and celebrating this great and fearful and holy and life-giving and divine mystery." Malabar liturgy: "We therefore . . . glorify, exalt, and venerate this memorial and sacrifice, this mystery, great, terrible, holy, and divine."

third century) likewise echoes the original formula as recorded by St. Paul.

On the other hand, beginning with the first complete anaphora extant, that of the *Traditio apostolica* of St. Hippolytus (ca. 220), practically all liturgies have added the resurrection: "Mindful therefore of His death and resurrection. . . ." The liturgy of the *Apostolic Constitutions* (VIII) has already included the ascension and the second coming. Some of the most important liturgies of the East (fragment of Deir-Balizeh, liturgies of St. James, Syrian, St. Mark, St. Basil) show moreover a significant new feature: they record the declaration of St. Paul (with the additional mention of the resurrection) in conjunction with the command of the Lord as if they were His words, and add the Anamnesis in identical terms. Thus the liturgy of St. Basil has: "Do this in remembrance of Me. For as often as you eat of this bread and drink this cup you declare My death and confess My resurrection." Then follows the Anamnesis: "Therefore, we also, O Master, remembering this saving passion, this quickening cross, the three-day burial, the resurrection from the dead, the ascension into heaven, the seating at Thy right hand, God and Father, and His glorious and terrible coming, offer. . . ." This formula suggests that the command of Christ, "Do this in commemoration of Me," contains implicitly the declaration of St. Paul; further, that the mystery of "the death of the Lord" implicitly includes the resurrection and ascension, etc. And in fact such is the case. Therefore we propose in the following to prove that in the mind of St. Paul the proclamation of the death of the Lord implicitly contains that of the resurrection and ascension, and so on, and we shall add reasons why the Apostle made explicit mention only of Christ's death.

THE "REDEEMING" DEATH

The central idea of St. Paul's teaching is Christ crucified and glorified. In his thought the resurrection of Christ is inseparable from His death: "He was delivered up for our sins and rose again for our justification" (Rom. 4:25). It is the idea of the "redeeming" death which connects the death of Christ with His glorification. The sacrifice of Christ requires for its efficacy as necessary extrinsic complement its acceptance by God. The passion is the "traditio" in the sacrifice of Christ, the glorification its "acceptatio." As in the case of the holocausts of the Old Testament the fire falling down from heaven upon altar and sacrifice revealed its acceptance by God, so the glorification of Christ by the fire of the divinity constitutes and reveals the acceptance of His sacrifice. By glorification the sacrifice of Christ is accepted, ratified, and made efficacious; the death is the "redeeming" death, His body and blood are life-giving and vivifying. This is the thought of St. Paul throughout his writings, especially in the Epistle to the Hebrews. At first sight it seems surprising to read that Christ became high priest by entering heaven, that He offered His sacrifice in heaven: "For if He were on earth, He would not be a priest" (Heb. 8:4); "By His own blood He entered into the holy place . . . to appear in the presence of God, by the sacrifice of Himself He appeared" (Heb. 9:12). The glorification is not an intrinsic element of the sacrifice of Christ, but its necessary extrinsic complement, its consummation which makes it efficacious. The resurrection is the descent of the glory of God, of the celestial fire upon the holocaust; the ascension is the raising up of the victim to God: they are the two stages of glorification.[5]

[5] Cf. Benedict XIV, *De sacros. sacrificio missae*, II, cap. 2, n. 5: "In the Jewish sacrifices the victim was burnt on the altar of holocausts, that any

The Eucharistic sacrifice is the memorial of the redeeming death of Christ. The Eucharistic sacrifice is valid, ratified, and accepted, because of the ratification and acceptance of the bloody sacrifice. Consecration is valid, efficacious, accomplished, on account of the communication of the fire of the glorified Christ. Therefore the Eucharistic sacrifice is the re-enactment of the passion and of the glorification.[6]

There are several reasons why St. Paul in his declaration makes explicit mention only of the death of our Lord, and why all liturgies, following his example, put the principal emphasis on the mystery of the death.

1. The passion of Christ is the essential sacrificial activity of Christ as offering priest; the glorification is the extrinsic complement of His sacrifice.

2. The death of Christ is visibly represented in the separated species; not so the glorification.

3. The death of Christ is re-enacted "vi verborum," the rest of the mysteries "per concomitantiam" (cf. Abbot Vonier's *Key to the Doctrine of the Eucharist*).

4. There is a final reason why St. Paul writing to the Corinthians mentions only the death. "I determined to know among you only Jesus Christ and Him crucified," he wrote in I Cor. 2:2, with reference to the special conditions obtaining at Corinth. He had found it necessary to impress on their minds

---

uncleanness therein might be consumed by the flames, and that the smoke might be wafted up to heaven in the odor of sweetness, as Holy Scripture says. In the New Law the victim was consumed by the resurrection and ascension of Christ. For by resurrection that which was mortal in Christ was swallowed up by life, as the Apostle says (II Cor. 5:4) and in the ascension of the victim was accepted by God in the odor of sweetness, and was placed at His right hand."

[6] The Council of Trent states (Sess. 13, c. 5; *DB*, no. 878): "It is most fitting that all Christians should be mindful and grateful to the common Lord and Savior for such an ineffable and fully divine benefit, by which the victory and triumph of His death is represented."

the mystery of the cross in all its stark reality. Further, he was accused of ignorance; in reply, he opposes to the wisdom of the Greeks the foolishness of the cross. A similar instance can be found in his letter to the Galatians: "O senseless Galatians, who hath bewitched you . . . before whose eyes Jesus Christ hath been set forth crucified among you?" (Gal. 3:1.) The reproof that he had to administer in I Cor. 11 urged him to emphasize the same idea, the death of Christ—re-enacted now in the Eucharist.[7]

THE NATIVITY

The text of St. Paul which inspired the fundamental idea of the Anamnesis presents likewise some general reason for the explicit commemoration of the Nativity found in some of the liturgies. St. Paul's declaration inculcates the reality of the sacrifice, the real presence of the victim, of the body and blood of Christ. The real presence of the body of Christ presupposes that by the Eucharistic proclamation He is really made present, introduced, presented into the hands of the priest upon the altar. Hence the emphasis in all the Anamneses upon the term "ejusdem Domini nostri Jesu Christi"; hence the multiplication of terms: "the same who was born of the Virgin, the same who was presented in the temple, the same who was delivered," etc. Basing ourselves therefore on the thought of the liturgies, we may conclude that the Eucharistic consecration is the pragmatic commemoration, the proclamation, of the Nativity as well.

There is furthermore a significant text in the Epistle to the Hebrews which more particularly inspired the explicit commemoration of the Nativity. "For it is impossible that with the blood of oxen and goats sin should be taken away. Where-

[7] Cf. F. Pratt, *op. cit.*, II, 15 f.

fore when He cometh into the world, He saith: Sacrifice and oblation Thou wouldst not: but a body Thou hast fitted to Me. Holocausts for sin did not please Thee. Then said I: Behold I come . . . that I should do Thy will, O God. . . . Then said I: Behold I come to do Thy will, O God. . . . In the which will we are sanctified by the oblation of the body of Jesus Christ once" (Heb. 10:4–7, 9, 10).

St. Paul introduces in this text a quotation from Ps. 39:7–9. The psalm is Messianic and the verses in question represent the Messiah declaring at the moment of His incarnation that all the ancient sacrifices were unpleasing to God, inadequate; that consequently a body had been prepared for Him by God the Father which should be the organ and instrument of a sacrifice of perfect obedience and absolute submission of His will to the divine will. The Hebrew text reads: "Ears thou hast opened for me," i.e., so that the will of the Father might be readily perceived and obeyed. St. Paul, however, adopted the version of the Septuagint, with the equivalent meaning that the body has been prepared to act, to carry out the divine will.[8]

In the declaration of I Cor. 11, St. Paul inculcated the central act of the sacrifice of Christ and its re-enactment in the Eucharist. This central sacrificial act is the essential act, because of the positive will of God. It is the climax in the consecration of the victim to God; but it is prepared, again because of the positive divine will, (a) by the substantial sanctification in the Incarnation, "per gratiam unionis," and (b) by the internal sacrifice of will and soul in the first moment of life in the flesh. In the first instant the most holy victim is sacrificed in "preparatione animi" by an act of charity and obedience. The redeeming death was prepared by this act of

[8] Cf. C. Callan, O.P., *The Epistles of St. Paul*, II, 422.

submission. The latter lasted throughout the life of the Savior, it informed, sanctified, consecrated all events of His life and prepared the victim for that great final act which, according to the will of the Father, should be the essential and consummative act: the passion crowned by death, the "consummatum est."

It is the teaching of the liturgies that the commemoration commanded by Christ in the term "of Me" applies to His sacrifice in the wider sense, as St. Paul likewise understood it: "In the which will we are sanctified by the oblation of the body of Jesus Christ once." It is the sacrifice comprising all the preparatory sanctifications and consecrations of the victim, together with all the consequent, externally consummative acts that surround the central essential act set forth visibly in the sacramental signs. The one single act of Eucharistic consecration is one "realiter," but manifold "ratione"; it presents all the many mysteries connected according to the will of the eternal Father with the redeeming death. The words of consecration, "This is My body," contain implicitly the words: "Behold, Thou hast prepared a body for Me. I come to do Thy will, O God."

None of the prominent Eastern liturgies make explicit mention of the Nativity in the postconsecratory Anamnesis. Several, however, refer to it implicitly, as, for instance, the liturgy of St. Chrysostom: "We, therefore, remembering this salutary precept, and all that happened on our behalf. . . ." Several liturgies do speak explicitly of the Nativity in the preconsecratory Anamnesis. Thus the Syrian liturgy: "We remember our Lord, God and Savior Jesus Christ, and all that He did for our salvation: His annunciation by an angel; His birth in the flesh, His baptism in the Jordan, His saving passion," etc. And practically all liturgies, beginning with the anaphora of the *Traditio apostolica,* mention the Incarnation and Nativity in their historical narratives of salvation that lead up to the consecration. As the Haggadah of the Pasch proclaimed the history of redemption in chronological order, so the Eucharistic anaphora in its turn narrates the history of salvation from the Incarnation until the Last Supper, climaxing in the words of consecration, and continuing, after the consecration, with the events that followed the Passion. Within the framework of this history in chronological order, the Incarnation and Nativity had their place, and still have their place in practically all liturgies before the consecration. As soon as the mediation of Christ is mentioned, the anaphora continues with the commemoration of the Incarnation and Nativity. As a rule the text of the commemoration of the Incarnation and Nativity is taken from the Epistle to the Hebrews, sometimes combined with a text from Ephesians.

The insertion of the mystery of the Nativity in the Roman Anamnesis took place probably sometime about the middle of the fifth century. Several causes may have contributed: the example of the East, the Christological heresies, the increasing prominence given to the celebration of Christmas in the Roman Church. It was the time of the controversies with Nestorius and Eutyches, the time of the great councils of Ephesus (431) and of Chalcedon (451). It was the time of the most noble and enthusiastic exponents of the mystery of the Incarnation, Pope Leo I and St. Peter Chrysologus, when the Christmas liturgy was beginning to develop into a great cycle with its Advent of preparation. Perhaps it was inserted by Pope Celestine I (422–33), who precisely on Christmas Day of the year 431 received the glad tidings of the successful conclusion of the Council of Ephesus and ordered the letter of announcement to be read publicly in the papal basilica immediately after the celebration of Mass, to the intense joy of the faithful. It may have been Pope Leo I, who in his epistle, *De Incarnatione contra Eutychen*, says so beautifully: "Filius Dei, de coelesti sede descendens et a paterna gloria non recedens, novo ordine, nova nativitate generatus," and exclaims: ". . . nativitas est mirabilis." (The same inspiring quotation from the Epistle to the Hebrews, incidentally, is alluded to in the definition of the Council of Chalcedon: "in novissimis autem diebus . . ."). Particular Churches of the West then followed the example of Rome. Milan, however, never did so.[9]

That the mystery of the Nativity was in some places never inserted (as at Milan) or in others removed (as at Rome) surely has its sufficient reason in the declaration of the apostles. It is only right and proper that emphasis and prominence be accorded to the central mystery of the redeeming death. Pope Benedict XIV sums it up neatly: "In this prayer the Greek Church mentions the Incarnation, the Nativity, the Passion, the Resurrection, the Ascension, and the descent of the Holy Ghost. If now the Roman Church speaks only of the Passion, the Resurrection, and the Ascension, the reason is that in these three mysteries, which are the principal parts of the sacrifice, the immolation and the consuming of the Victim are best represented."[10]

Such is the scriptural background of the Anamnesis. It is

---

[9] The Milanese practice found its advocate in Bernold of Constance (d. 1100): "Quid superfluum sit in Canone: Item ibi, Unde et memores Domine nos servi tui, Nativitatem Domini commemorant, cum juxta Apostolum in eiusmodi sacrificio non nativitatem Domini, sed morten eius annuntiare debeamus. Unde et sanctus Ambrosius in libris Sacramentorum: 'Quotiescumque, inquit, affertur sacrificium, mors Domini, resurrectio Domini, ascensio Domini significatur.'"

[10] *De sacros. sacrificio missae*, II, c. 11, n. 6.

a proclamation and a calling to mind of the enactment of the mysteries of the life of Christ mentioned therein. The Nativity, the Resurrection, and the Ascension are not mere mental associations, but a declaration that these mysteries are made present. This presence, however, is not to be understood as if by transubstantiation the mysteries of the life of Christ would be made present in their objective reality as the individual events.[11] What is made present in its individual, objective reality is *Christ*, "who was born of the Blessed Virgin, who died upon the cross, who rose from the dead, who ascended into heaven, who shall come again." Of the Passion as action there is in consecration, in the "mactatio mystica," the image, of Nativity, Resurrection, Ascension, there are analogies in transubstantiation by which Christ is made present upon the altar. The advent of Christ in sacrament is also a figure of His second coming, an analogy based on the causal relation between grace and glory of the redeemed: "gratia semen gloriae."

[11] J. B. Umberg, "Die These von der Mysteriengegenwart," *Zeitschrift fuer kath. Theologie*, LII (1928), 357–400.

CHAPTER XXIV

The Anamnesis

THE EUCHARIST A RE-ENACTMENT OF THE ENTIRE OPUS
REDEMPTIONIS; WITNESS OF THE FATHERS

THE Eucharistic theology of the Fathers is commonly
assumed to be undeveloped, incomplete, lacking exact terminology and systematic treatment. It is true, the Fathers of
the Church did not know of the many theories and disagree-
ments of the post-Tridentine theologians relative to the Eucharistic sacrifice; they did not write with strict scholastic
terminology; they did not propose a complete system concerning the Eucharistic mystery and its main aspects: the
real presence, transubstantiation, sacrifice, sacrament. At the
time of the Fathers no heresies directly opposed any of these
dogmas, and hence no systematic elaboration of doctrine was
called for. It was only later, in the Middle Ages, that difficulties arose directly out of Eucharistic questions: for instance, about the distinction between the historical and the
sacramental body of Christ (Rhabanus Maurus vs. Paschasius
Radbertus), and about the real presence (the Council of
Rome, 1079, vs. Berengarius). Against the Christological
heresies of their own times the Fathers had to explain the
Eucharistic mystery indirectly rather and incidentally, and
primarily they had to defend the fundamental dogma of the
reality of the body and blood of Christ.

Consequently we cannot expect to find in patristic literature a complete system about the Eucharistic sacrifice as reenactment of the different mysteries of our Lord's life, or about transubstantiation in its diverse aspects as Nativity, Passion, and glorification. Nevertheless there is contained in the writings of the Fathers an abundance of texts and statements which present the fundamental principle, so beautiful in its simplicity, so impressive in the unanimity with which it is accepted: the Eucharistic mystery is a continuation and extension of the mystery of the Incarnaton. There is further an abundance of texts which explain the Eucharistic sacrifice as the re-enactment of the Nativity, of the Passion, and of the glorification. Special emphasis, finally, is placed on the Eucharistic intervention of the Holy Spirit. We shall, in the following, consider each of these points in some detail.

THE EUCHARIST AS THE CONTINUATION OF THE INCARNATION

Leo XIII has concisely formulated the leading idea of the Eucharistic theology of the Fathers in his encyclical *Mirae Caritatis* (May 28, 1902): "The Eucharist, according to the testimony of the holy Fathers, must be regarded as a certain continuation and expansion of the incarnation. For by It the substance of the incarnate Word is united with individual men; and the supreme Sacrifice of Calvary is in admirable manner renewed."[1] It is a thought of infinite beauty and inexhaustible riches to conceive the "mystery of faith" (cf. the words of consecration) as the continuation of the "great mystery of godliness" (I Tim. 3:16). The Eucharistic the-

[1] "Eucharistia, Patrum sanctorum testimonio, Incarnationis continuatio quaedam et amplificatio censenda est. Siquidem per ipsam Incarnati Verbi substantia cum singulis hominibus copulatur; et supremum in Calvaria sacrificium admirabili modo renovatur."

ology of the Fathers considers and contemplates the Holy Eucharist not as something taken by itself, but in its dogmatic place within the organism of divine mysteries, within the luminous stream of communication and manifestation of the divine life, which originates in the Blessed Trinity from Father through the Son to the Holy Ghost, is poured out and made manifest *ad extra* in the mystery of Christ, and is communicated and continued through the Eucharist in the mystical body. Both mysteries—Incarnation and Eucharist—are sacred means, are great "sacraments" for the purpose of communicating the life of the Blessed Trinity to men.

On the basis of this principle, it is merely an analysis of details in the organic connection of these mysteries, if we state with the Fathers that whatever was visible in Christ has entered into the Eucharist, that all events enacted and suffered in the historical body of Christ are reflected in the sacramental body; what His coming "visibiliter" effected in the world, is now effected in man by His coming "sacramentaliter" in the Eucharist; what His passion "in specie propria" was for the world, that the Eucharist is "sacramentally" for man. Accepting the principle stated above, there is no longer any question of whether or not the full life of Christ, His whole work of redemption, is brought to us in the Eucharist; there is merely a question of how to grasp, how to explain and to define these wonderful facts with human concepts, how to put them into theological terms.

St. Justin (d. 167) was the first to introduce into patristic theology the parallelism of the Incarnation and the Eucharist: "For we do not receive these things as common bread or common drink; but as Jesus Christ our Savior, having been made flesh by a word of God, had flesh and blood for our salvation, so we have learned that the food, made a Eucharist by a word of prayer that comes from Him, from which our blood and flesh are nourished, by change are the flesh and blood of the incarnate Jesus." [2] The real presence of the body and blood of Christ and the analogy between the act of Incarnation and the act of transubstantiation, between the "word of God" and the "prayer that comes from Him," is what St. Justin set out to propound. But his method of explaining the Eucharist by means of the mystery of the Incarnation became the fundamental principle in the Eucharistic theology of the Fathers; so much so that occasionally, although without consequences upon tradition, it even led to certain exaggerations, e.g., in the writings of Theodoret (cf. below).

St. Irenaeus (d. 202),[3] likewise concerned with defending the reality of Christ's flesh and blood in the Eucharist, uses the same comparison. Thus he protests: "In the same manner in which you ascribe to the Eucharist only the value of a symbol, so also the Incarnation is reduced (by you) to mere appearance: there is not more flesh in the one than in the other. The Incarnation does not differ from the Eucharist."

St. Ambrose (d. 397) in turn positively sanctions this method. For he declares: "Let us use examples: with the example of the incarnation let us explain the truth of the mystery" (the Eucharist).[4]

St. Augustine (d. 430) [5] connects the two great "sacraments" of Incarnation and Eucharist on the basis of St. Paul's beautiful expression "Magnum est sacramentum pietatis"

[2] St. Justin Martyr, *I Apol.,* 66, 2; *PG,* 6, 427.
[3] St. Irenaeus, *Adv. haereses,* V, 2; *PG,* 7, 1124.
[4] St. Ambrose, *De mysteriis,* 9, 53; *PL,* 16, 424.
[5] St. Augustine, *In Jo.,* tr. 26, 13; *PL,* 35, 1613.

(I Tim. 3:16; note how significantly the Vulgate translated the Greek term "mysterion" with "sacramentum"). What St. Paul applies to Christ, "quod manifestum est in carne, justificatum est in Spiritu . . . assumptum est in gloria," St. Augustine predicates about the Eucharist (*In Joan.*, tr. 26, 13): "Unus panis unum corpus multi sumus (I Cor. 10:17). O sacramentum pietatis, O signum unitatis, O vinculum caritatis."

St. Cyril of Alexandria [6] (d. 444), the defender of the mystery of the Incarnation against Nestorius and the champion against Oriental rationalism, saw and proclaimed with great ingenuity the organic interrelation of the mysteries of Incarnation and Eucharist. A brilliant summary of his ideas is to be found in his commentary on St. John's Gospel. The most beautiful passage is the Eucharistic interpretation of the words of Christ: "And the glory that Thou hast given Me, I have given to them" (John 17:22). Great beauty and light are shed upon our understanding of the Eucharist, when St. Cyril reminds us that it is the same glory of which we read in the Prologue: "And we have seen His glory, the glory as it were of the only-begotten of the Father"; the same glory which appeared in Bethlehem and in the whole life of Christ, the glory of the Son of God shining through the humanity as through a veil (Eutymius), resplendent in His teaching, in His miracles, in Transfiguration, in Passion, Resurrection, and Ascension: the splendor of the glory and the figure of the substance of the Father.

St. Leo the Great (d. 461) summarized the relation between the Incarnation and the Eucharist in a famous and beautiful passage in his homily 74, 12: "What was visible in our Savior has entered into the sacraments." [7]

---

[6] St. Cyril of Alexandria, *In Jo.; PG*, 74, 474–608.
[7] St. Leo I, *hom.* 74, 2; *PL*, 54, 398.

Under pressure of the Christological heresies (Monophysitism and Nestorianism) the two mysteries of the Incarnation and the Eucharist were then considered and studied more intensively in their mutual relationship. To oppose the exaggeration of Monophysitism and likewise to defend the dogma of the two natures in Christ, a kind of exaggerated Dyophysitism was introduced by Theodoret (d. 458), which is reflected even in the writings of Pope St. Gelasius (d. 496).

St. Gelasius I [8] declares: "Certainly the image and likeness of the body and blood of Christ are celebrated in the action of the mysteries (the Eucharist). It is sufficiently evident that we have to admit in Christ God Himself what we confess, celebrate, and accept in regard to His image (the Eucharistic elements); as they are changed under the action of the Holy Spirit into the divine substance so that the two natures remain in their properties (permanentes tamen in sua proprietate naturae), so likewise do we have to understand the other principal mystery (Incarnation), whose efficacy and power these represent to us." The Pope speaks about the Incarnation and the Eucharist as of two mysteries that correspond to each other as principal mystery and its image and likeness. (Some commentators understand the phrase "permanentes tamen in sua proprietate naturae" of the accidents, and thus arrive at an orthodox interpretation.) Through the efforts of Leontius of Byzantium (d. 543), the teaching of St. Cyril of Alexandria emerged victorious.

EUCHARISTIC NATIVITY

The testimony for the real presence of Christ's body and blood in the Blessed Sacrament constitutes the starting point in the comparison the Fathers institute particularly between transubstantiation on the one hand, and annunciation and

[8] St. Gelasius, *Ep.* 27, 3; Thiel, *Ep. Rom. Pont.*, pp. 541 ff.

nativity on the other. They explain the Eucharistic consecration as the descent of the Word of God, as an overshadowing by the Holy Spirit; they compare the words of consecration with the activity of the Word of God forming for Himself a body in the womb of the Blessed Virgin. They institute a parallel between the petition for consecration in the Canon-prayer and the prayer of Our Lady for the coming of the Savior. In the words of consecration they see implicitly contained the words of Psalm 39: "Behold, I come to do Thy will, O God." The priest is compared to the angel Gabriel, the "Hosanna in excelsis" of the Canon to the hymn of the angels in Bethlehem. They state explicitly that the Christmas celebration is not a birthday celebration in memory only, but a making present of the mystery itself.

St. Athanasius (d. 373) in the *Fragmentum apud Eutychium:* "As soon, however, as the great prayers and holy petitions are said, the Word descends upon the bread and the chalice and they become His body."

St. Augustine [9] (d. 430) in *The City of God* most beautifully establishes the connection between the Nativity and the sacrifice of Christ, and understands both to be re-enacted in the Eucharistic sacrifice. It is he in particular who hears the echo of the words "Behold, I come to do Thy will, O God" (Ps. 39; cf. Heb. 10:5–9) in the words of consecration.

St. Leo (d. 461) considers the mysteries of the Incarnation and the Eucharist so closely connected with the mystery of grace that he says that the Christmas celebration is more than a date in our memories; it is a day on which Christ's birth is made present to us, for "the birthday of the Head is the birthday of the body." The birthday of Christ does not merely present an objective truth in which we believe, or a historical

[9] St. Augustine, *De civ. Dei,* 17, 20; *PL,* 41, 556.

date which we recall. Christ's nativity has entered and enters our lives anew with the newness of our incorporation into Him.

In homily 29, 1, he says: "Let us not be disturbed by our own inabilities. The Gospels and prophets will help us. They will set our hearts on fire and teach us that our Lord's birthday, when the Word was made flesh, is more than a date in our memories; it is a day we must look upon as present. Even now you may hear the angels' tidings brought to shepherds watching their flocks; for I have charge over the Lord's sheep, and in my heart I have kept the words I heard from heaven. Today, on this joyous feast, I can say to you: Behold, I bring you good news of great joy which shall be to all people; for there is born to you today in the town of David a Savior, who is Christ the Lord." This enthusiastic homily has filled and formed with its spirit the Postcommunion of the Mass at dawn: "May the birthday-newness of this Sacrament make us ever new, O Lord, whose unique nativity has banished human oldness."

St. Isidore of Seville [10] (d. 636) explains the Canon with reference to the particular circumstances of the nativity of Christ, and says that in the anaphora the heavenly powers are invited to join with the earthly creatures and to sing the "Hosanna in excelsis" as it was sung when our Savior was born.

St. John Damascene (d. 759) compares the Annunciation and the consecration: "Since we know that the Word has formed for Himself a body from His pure and immaculate Virgin Mother, is it therefore not conceivable that He can form for Himself a body from bread, and blood from wine? 'How shall this be,' said the holy Virgin, 'since I do not know man?' The archangel answered: 'The Holy Ghost. . . .' If you ask

---

[10] St. Isidore of Seville, De eccl. off., I, 18; PL, 83, 737–826.

the manner [of consecration], it shall suffice for you to know that it is done by the Holy Ghost, in the same way as the Lord formed for Himself flesh of the blood of the holy Mother of God." [11]

Paschasius Radbertus (d. 831): "It is the same Christ who by the Holy Ghost produced His flesh. Who else could create in the womb, so that the Word became flesh? In the same manner it is done [in the Eucharist], so we have to believe: that by the same power of the Holy Ghost through the word of Christ is effected His flesh and blood by an invisible action." [12]

We conclude this series of texts about the Eucharistic nativity with a passage from a letter of St. Hildegarde: "You are the angels of the Lord of hosts: because, as, at the words of the angel Gabriel, God became incarnate of the Virgin Mary in order by His nativity, passion and, ascension, to save man who was lost, so at your words the same body and the same blood of the same Son of God, with the representation of His nativity, passion and resurrection, is wrought for our salvation and for the salvation of all the faithful, both living and dead." [13]

THE EUCHARIST AND THE PASSION

It is superfluous to verify with a series of texts the teaching of the Fathers about the Eucharistic sacrifice as representation of the passion of Christ.

St. Justin (d. 167): "The Eucharist, the celebration of which our Lord Jesus Christ has prescribed in remembrance of the suffering which He endured." [14]

---

[11] St. John Damasc., *De fide orthodoxa*, 4, 13; *PG*, 94, 1139–42.
[12] Paschasius Radbertus, *De corpore et sanguine Domini*; *PL*, 120, 1297.
[13] St. Hildegarde, *Ep.* 47, Ad praelatos Moguntinenses; *PL*, 197, 224.
[14] St. Justin Martyr, *Dialogue with Trypho*, 41; *PG*, 6, 563.

St. Cyprian (d. 258): "And because we make mention of His passion in all sacrifices—for the Lord's passion is the sacrifice which we offer—we ought to do nothing else than what He did. As often, therefore, as we offer the cup in commemoration of the Lord and of His passion, let us do what it is known the Lord did." [15]

St. Gregory Nazianzen (d. 390) analyzed the transubstantiation as incarnation and immolation simultaneously, saying: "Do not hesitate, O priest, to pray and to practice the mission for us, when with a word thou attractest the Word, when thou art cutting with unbloody immolation the body and blood of the Lord, using a word instead of a sword." [16]

St. Gaudentius Brixenensis (d. 410): "The labors of the passion of Christ we offer in the figure [sacrament] of His body and blood."

St. Gregory Nazianzen's thought is preserved most beautifully in the Ethiopian Missal:

May there be opened the doors of light,
May there be opened the doors of glory,
May the veil be lifted from the face of the Father,
May the Lamb of God descend,
May it be placed upon the priestly table before me, a sinful servant,
May the song (the sung words of consecration) be sent, the fiery
    terrible sword,
May it appear upon this bread and the chalice,
And sever this oblation.[17]

THE CONSECRATION, GLORIFICATION

The Eucharistic sacrifice is, according to the Fathers, the celebration also of the Resurrection, the re-enactment of the

[15] St. Cyprian, Ep. 63, 17; PL, 4, 398.
[16] St. Gregory Naz., Ep. 171; PG, 37, 279.
[17] Cf. P. Chaine, La consecration et l'epiclese dans le missel éthiopien (Rome, 1940), p. 31.

manifestation of the risen Lord. The prayers of the Canon are a petition for glorification, a calling down of the fire of glory, as Elias called down fire from heaven upon his sacrifice. Holy Communion is a drinking of the cup filled with the fire of glory, it is a being touched with the live coal (cf. Isa. 6), a glowing in the fire of the Holy Spirit. "Anthrax" (live coal) as a name for the Eucharistic body occurs often in the Eastern liturgies and likewise in the writings of the Fathers, and by means of it they explain the effect of Holy Communion.

St. Cyprian explains the difference between the custom of celebrating the Eucharist in the morning, and Christ's own celebration of the Last Supper and the institution of the Eucharist in the evening: "But still it was not in the morning, but after supper, that the Lord offered the mingled cup. . . . It behooved Christ to offer about the evening of the day, that the very hour of sacrifice might show the setting and the evening of the world. . . . But we celebrate the resurrection of the Lord in the morning." [18]

St. Ephraem (d. 373): "Fire fell once upon the sacrifices of Elias and consumed them. For us the fire of mercy became the sacrifice of life. Fire at one time consumed the sacrifice; but Thy fire, O Lord, we eat at Thy sacrifice." [19]

Cyrillonas (Syrian poet at the end of the third and beginning of the fourth century): "Drink of the cup of fire, the blood which inflames all that partake of it."

St. Cyril of Alexandria (d. 444) celebrates the Eucharist as a re-enactment of the manifestation of the risen Lord: "It surpasses all understanding; we close the doors [of the church], but then Christ joins us, and appears to all of us, invisibly and

[18] St. Cyprian, *Ep.* 63, 16; *PL*, 4, 397.
[19] St. Ephraem, *De incomprehensibilitate filii*, 4.

visibly at the same time. . . . He permits and presents His sacred body to be touched."

In the controversy with Nestorius, who denied the Eucharist to be the Son of God, St. Cyril as the defender of the faith spoke clearly of the vivifying and sanctifying flesh and blood of Christ in the Eucharist: "The flesh became spiritual after resurrection in order to communicate to us the energy for our resurrection." [20]

In the same writing against Nestorius, and in a special scholion "De carbone" St. Cyril explains the "live coal" as the incarnate Word present in the Eucharist with His humanity "transformed into His divine glory and activity."

St. John Damascene (d. 754): "Let us draw near to Him with ardent desire and receive the divine coal, so that in the fire of our desire and in the heat of the received coal our sins may be burnt and our hearts illuminated, and we may become so much inflamed in the exchange (ignis commercio) of fire as to become gods." [21]

The Roman Pontifical calls the Eucharistic sacrifice a holocaust, consumed by the fire of the Holy Spirit to an odor of sweetness (De cons. altaris): "Domine sancte Pater omnipotens aeterne Deus . . . preces nostrae humilitatis exaudi et respice ad huius altaris holocaustum, quod non igne visibili probetur, sed infusum Sancti Spiritus tui gratia in odorem suavitatis ascendat."

EUCHARISTIC INTERVENTION OF THE HOLY GHOST

The same divine Spirit who formed the body of Christ in the womb of the Virgin, by whom Christ offered Himself upon the cross, and who awakened Him in the tomb to life

[20] St. Cyril of Alexandria, *Adv. Nestorium*, 7, 3.
[21] St. John Damasc., *op. cit.*, 4, 13; *PG*, 94, 1140–45.

and glory, this same Holy Spirit vivifies, sanctifies, and glorifies the Eucharistic body of Christ. And because it is the same divine Spirit, whose activity transcends space and time, therefore the Fathers are able to understand and to explain that the very body that was born of the Virgin, that was crucified and pierced with the lance, and that is risen and is seated at the Father's right hand, is now made present, offered, and given in the Holy Eucharist; therefore, too, in the consecration there is re-presented the Nativity, the Passion, and the glorification, because all this is wrought by the sanctification of the Holy Spirit, whose activity reaches from the eternal "hodie" into all places, unto all times, uniting events and deeds.

Gaudentius Brixinensis (d. 410): "Do not think that this is earthly which has become something heavenly by Him who entered it and made it His body and blood. But believe that it became what it is announced to be, by the fire of the divine Spirit."

St. Fulgentius Ruspensis (d. 535): "When could holy Church ask more fittingly for the coming of the Holy Ghost (epiklesis) than for the consecration of the sacrifice, since she knows that her Head was born according to the flesh by this same Holy Ghost? For Mary was told by the word of the angel: 'The Holy Ghost shall come upon thee and the power of the Most High shall overshadow thee.' " [22]

St. Gregory the Great (d. 604) is reported by Paul the Deacon (d. 780) to have said: "With the same power with which our Creator has created everything out of nothing and has built for Himself a body from the flesh of the Virgin, He changes bread and wine through the sanctification of His Spirit into flesh and blood."

[22] St. Fulgentius, Ad Monimum, 1, 2; PL, 65, 187.

St. Fulbert of Chartres (d. 1028): "It is the same flesh, the one assumed from the Virgin, and the other consecrated from material and virginal creature; it is one and the same artist, namely, the Spirit, who by invisible action transforms it into the substance of true flesh. It is not the symbol of an empty mystery, but the true body of Christ built by the Holy Ghost." [23]

St. Peter Damian (d. 1072): "The body of the Lord, which is consecrated on the sacred altar, . . . conceiving the power of the Holy Ghost is vivified and sanctified, so as to be able to vivify and sanctify us." [24]

Rupert of Deutz (d. 1135): "Because the Virgin conceived Him by the Holy Ghost, who is the eternal fire, and because He has offered Himself by the same Holy Ghost as a living oblation to the living God—as the Apostle says (Heb. 9:14): 'qui per Spiritum aeternum semetipsum obtulit immaculatum Deo')—therefore it is done in the fire of the altar: by the activity of the Holy Ghost, namely, bread becomes the body, wine becomes the blood of Christ." [25]

St. Hildegarde: "The same power of the Most High which effected the body in the womb of the Virgin, transforms upon the altar at the words of the priest the oblation of bread and wine into the sacrament of flesh and blood. Therefore appear also the nativity, the passion, the burial, the resurrection, and the ascension of the Son of the heavenly Father in the same sacrament." [26]

[23] St. Fulbert of Chartres, *Ep.* 1; *PL,* 141, 195. Cf. *Ep.* 5; *PL,* 141, 202.
[24] St. Peter Damian, *Liber qui appellatur Gratissimus,* 9; *PL,* 145, 110.
[25] Rupert of Deutz, *In Ex.,* 2, c. 10; *PL,* 167, 617.
[26] St. Hildegarde, *Ep.* 43. Responsum Hildegardis de corpore et sanguine Domini; *PL,* 197, 213.

St. Thomas and the Patristic Tradition

Not as a special question, but by way of an appendix which will summarize the patristic tradition as explained above, we shall add a few quotations from St. Thomas. In his Eucharistic theology St. Thomas has preserved and transmitted to us faithfully and completely the tradition of the Fathers: in the whole structure of his treatise, in the order of the questions, in the quotations and authorities to whom he refers, in the principles applied, in the conclusions deduced, everywhere we find patristic thought presented in systematic form and uniform terminology.

The Eucharist as the Continuation of the Incarnation

No theologian could express more concisely and more beautifully the relation of these two mysteries than does St. Thomas: "Because in this sacrament is comprised the entire mystery of our salvation, therefore it is enacted with greater solemnity than the other sacraments." [27] To grasp the full import of this statement, we have to remember that according to St. Thomas: all the events of the life of Christ in His humanity, in His body, have redemptive value; even the events in His dead body are "sacramenta salutis"; the Eucharist is so much the perfection, consummation, and end of the other sacraments that these latter are somehow merely an anticipation of an effect of the Eucharist. (Scheeben in his *Mysteries of Christianity* also develops this point eloquently.)

"All actions and sufferings of Christ operate instrumentally in the power of the divinity unto the salvation of men." [28]

[27] St. Thomas, *Summa theol.*, IIIa, q. 83, a. 4.
[28] *Ibid.*, q. 48, a. 6.

"Whatever happened in the flesh of Christ, even after the soul had left, has been redemptive in virtue of the divinity united to the body." [29]

"What Christ has acted or suffered in His humanity is redemptive for us in virtue of His divinity, . . . [in virtue of] the divine power which reaches presently (praesentialiter) all places and times." [30]

"Like the rest of His deeds and words [so the words of consecration likewise] have instrumentally redemptive power." [31]

Salvation of man by incorporation into Christ is accomplished by means of the sacraments: "per substantiam Christi" in the Eucharist, "per virtutem Christi" in the rest (cf. *Summa theol.*, IIIa, q. 62, a. 1: "per sacramenta novae legis homo Christo incorporatur").

EUCHARISTIC NATIVITY

Referring to a statement of St. Cyril of Alexandria, St. Thomas compares the historical advent and nativity with the sacramental Christmas and comes to the conclusion: As the visible coming of Christ brought the life of grace to the world, so His sacramental coming effects the life of grace in man: "Christus . . . qui sicut in mundum visibiliter veniens contulit mundo vitam gratiae, secundum illud Jo. 1, 17: 'Gratia et veritas per Jesum Christum facta est,' ita in hominem sacramentaliter veniens vitam gratiae operatur, secundum illud Jo. 6, 58: 'Qui manducat me, vivet propter me.' Unde et Cyrillus dicit: Vivificativum Dei Verbum uniens seipsum pro-

[29] *Ibid.*, q. 50, a. 6.
[30] *Ibid.*, q. 56, a. 1.
[31] *Ibid.*, q. 78, a. 4.

priae carni, fecit ipsam vivificativam. Decebat enim eum nostris quodammodo uniri corporibus per sacram eius carnem et pretiosum sanguinem, quae accipimus in benedictionem vivificativam in pane et in vino." [32]

The Eucharist and the Passion

"The effect which the passion of Christ had (in specie propria) in the world, this the sacrament effects in man." [33]

The Eucharist and Glorification

Following an idea of St. Cyril of Alexandria (cf. above), St. Thomas [34] compares the preconsecratory invocation of the Canon (*Quam oblationem*) with the petition for glorification in the high-priestly prayer of Christ.

And quoting a text from St. John Damascene, he explains the "live coal" of Isa. 6:6 as a figure of the causality and effect of the Holy Eucharist. [35]

Eucharistic Intervention of the Holy Ghost

Again quoting St. John Damascene, St. Thomas [36] makes the statement that transubstantiation is brought about "sola virtute Spiritus Sancti." He compares it to the formation of the body of Christ in the womb of the Virgin, and concludes that the action of the Holy Ghost in producing the same effect does not exclude the cooperation of an instrument, i.e., of the humanity of Christ as an organic instrument and of the priest as "causa ministerialis."

[32] *Ibid.*, q. 79, a. 1.
[33] *Ibid.*
[34] *Ibid.*, q. 83, a. 4 ad 7.
[35] *Ibid.*, q. 79, a. 1 ad 2.
[36] *Ibid.*, q. 78, a. 3.

CONCLUSION

These texts from the Church Fathers and from St. Thomas give evidence that the commemoration of the Nativity, Resurrection, and Glorification of Christ means more than mere mental associations. It would, however, be an exaggeration to understand the "enactment of the opus redemptionis" as a making present of the mysteries of Passion, Nativity, Resurrection, as the individual actions in their objective reality. Such a making present of the mysteries of the life of our Lord is unthinkable for philosophical and theological reasons. St. Thomas, the faithful interpreter of patristic thought, says explicitly: "The celebration of this sacrament is an image representing Christ's passion." Of the mysteries of the life of Christ as actions, we may see in the Eucharist analogies, based on causal relations. Such an interpretation does not detract in the least from the great reality and presence of the body and blood of our Savior, of "Christus passus et glorificatus." We do not detract in the least from the wonderful reality of transubstantiation as the action by which "Christus passus et glorificatus" is made present. There exist wonderful analogies between transubstantiation and the events of the life of Christ, between our incorporation into Christ by Holy Communion and the nativity and resurrection of the Savior, just as there are causal relations between the mysteries of Incarnation, Holy Eucharist, and grace.

This is the thought of the Church Fathers and of St. Thomas about the enactment of the "opus redemptions" by the sacred liturgy. In this way is re-enacted the "great Sacrament," the one reality, which is ever the same and ever new, comprising in itself all reality and actuality of the mystery of which St. Paul says (I Tim. 3:16):

"And manifestly great is the mystery of godliness:
which was manifested in the flesh,
was justified in the spirit,
appeared to angels,
was preached to Gentiles,
believed in the world,
taken up in glory."

THE PROSPHORA

"We . . . offer unto Thy excellent Majesty, of Thy gifts
and presents, a pure Victim, a holy Victim, an immaculate
Victim: the holy bread of eternal life, and the chalice of
everlasting salvation."

About this prayer, called the prosphora (oblation), Cardinal Schuster says: "After the anamnesis . . . there follows
at once the offering up of the victim himself to the Father at
the hands of the priest. This is indubitably one of the most
important and solemn moments of the liturgical actio." In
the opinion of this author transubstantiation merely constitutes the host an actual victim, and the Prosphora is the
actual sacrificial oblation.

Since, however, the essence of the Eucharistic sacrifice
consists in consecration, and the actual oblation of the victim
is an essential element of the sacrifice, we have to say: the
relation of the prosphora to the consecration is analogous to
the relation of the Anamnesis to the consecration. The Eucharistic sacrifice is essentially a memorial; the subsequent
Anamnesis is a calling to mind of the significance of the consecration as a setting forth of the death of the Lord. Likewise
is the prosphora a calling to mind of the significance of the
consecration as sacrificial oblation.

As long as the separated species remain on the altar, the
Eucharistic sacrifice is virtually continued, and consequently

the act of offering is virtually continued, so that we may say, that at the prosphora the Eucharistic sacrifice is offered, because with it the oblation made by the consecration is virtually continued.

"Of Thy presents and gifts," could be a remembrance of I Par. 29:14: "All things are Thine, and we have given Thee what we received of Thy hand." "The pure host, the holy host, the immaculate host" contains an allusion to the prophecy of Malachias (1:11): "And there is offered to My name a clean oblation." Because of the aspect of sacrament, there is added "the holy bread of eternal life and the chalice of everlasting salvation."

CHAPTER XXV

The Postconsecratory Invocations

THE three postconsecratory invocations (Supra quae, Supplices te rogamus, per quem haec omnia) constitute the most intricate problem in the interpretation of the Canon. It is a historical and theological problem, and a question of art. There is no agreement among the authors about the origin of these invocations. Moreover, there are so many theories about the original form of them that it seems to remain an insoluble question. From the theological point of view, one thing is certain: they are not part of the consecratory formula. For the rest the opinions are most divergent with regard to the object of these invocations. In the present chapter on these invocations generally, we list first the series of various opinions; secondly we sketch the historical development. A review of the invocations in the different liturgies together with a study of the doctrine of the Fathers of the Church on the consecration and its causes, will help to formulate certain principles to be followed in the interpretation of these invocations.

VARIOUS OPINIONS

These series of opinions can be classified into two groups: the one group explains the invocations as petitions for the

effect of the sacrifice and the sacrament; the other group explains them as petitions for consecration and for the effects
of the consecration. We propose the different opinions in
systematic order, beginning with those that admit the least,
and then proceed to the exaggeration which has construed
of these invocations a point of dogmatic difference between
Rome and the Eastern Orthodox Church.

All interpreters admit that the postconsecratory invocations contain a petition for the effect of the Holy Eucharist.
But there are many authors who maintain that these invocations originally and in their present form are exclusively
petitions for the effect of the sacrifice and the sacrament.
Cardinal Schuster [1] can be considered the most recent representative of this opinion, who presents a dogmatical and
historical reason for his view. A petition for consecration
after the words of our Lord could not be reconciled with the
faith of the Church,[2] that consecration is accomplished with
the words of Christ. Even if the postconsecratory invocations are not given consecratory power, the mere petition
for consecration after consecration has already been accomplished would imply a contradiction in the intention of the
Church. Secondly, the postconsecratory invocation of the
anaphora of the *Traditio apostolica* of St. Hippolytus which
the Cardinal regards as the original Roman Canon, is an
invocation for the effect of the Eucharist. He concludes:
"Unlike the Eastern liturgies, which at this point have so
distorted the primitive invocation of the Paraclete as to turn
it into an epiklesis, that is, a sacramental formula of transubstantiation, the Roman Canon on the contrary retains its original meaning as a prayer in preparation for Communion."
The same opinion was held by John Torquemada at the

[1] *Op. cit.*, I, 283 f.
[2] *DB*, no. 874; cf. no. 698.

Council of Florence (1438–45): [3] "Oratio illa non est, ut conficiatur quod confectum est, sed ut consequamur effectum Sacramenti." This opinion was adopted by De Lugo, Vasquez, Billuart, Bellarmine, Suarez.[4] This theory is further developed in most of the devotional literature on the Eucharistic sacrifice. It is understood as a petition for the change of the faithful into the mystical body of Christ, especially with reference to the prayer Supplices te rogamus. Such is also the opinion of St. Thomas,[5] who understands the verb "transferri": not about the body of Christ, but about our union with the Church triumphant, our union with God through Holy Communion. According to St. Thomas the invocations before the consecration ask for transubstantiation, the invocations after the consecration are petitions for transubstantiation into the mystical body by Holy Communion.

A modification of this view includes in the object of invocation not only the mystical body, but also the body of Christ inasmuch as we offer it (Hoppe, Le Brun, Oswald, Bossuet). N. Gihr: "To these sacrificial gifts which are to be carried up from the earthly to the heavenly altar, belongs not only the mystical body of Christ, that is, the faithful with all they are and have—with their prayers and concerns, labors and sufferings, struggles and combats—but also the Eucharistic sacrificial body and sacrificial blood of our Lord, inasmuch as we offer them."

The second group of authors understand consecration as the object of these invocations, in one or the other way. Pope Innocent III [6] was already concerned about the apparent contradiction, that in these invocations is asked for conse-

[3] Cf. Harduin, Conc., IX, 978.
[4] Cf. S. Salaville, "Epiclese eucharistique," Dict. théol. cath.
[5] Summa theol., IIIa, q. 84, a. 4 ad 9.
[6] PL, 217, 888.

cration after consecration has been already accomplished. He says: "It is evident . . . that this chapter 'Qui pridie quam pateretur' should be put at the end of the Canon, because in it the consecration is accomplished. But because it would have interrupted the historical order, in so far as at the end of the Canon would be commemorated what historically took place in the center, the provident composer of the Canon was forced as it were, in order to preserve the historical order, to locate the chapter 'Qui pridie quam pateretur' like the heart of the Canon in the center; so that what follows is to be understood to precede according to that figure of language, which is used many times, that in the narrative follows what logically is previous." According to this Pope the intention to preserve the historical order (Last Supper, Resurrection, Ascension, Descent of the Holy Ghost) the invocation of the Holy Ghost which should precede the formula of consecration, is displaced.

Of primary importance for a satisfactory solution of the problem is the so-called "dramatic theory" of Cardinal Bessarion.[7] The Cardinal solemnly declared at the Council of Florence in his own name and in the name of all the fathers representing the Eastern Church: "Because we have heard from all the holy doctors of the Church, especially from the most blessed John Chrysostom, who is best known to us, that the words of the Lord are the words which change and transubstantiate bread and wine into the true body and blood of Christ; and that these divine words of the Savior have all power of transubstantiation, therefore we follow by necessity the same most holy doctor and his sentence." In Bessarion's thought it does not imply a contradiction that the invocation of the Holy Ghost follows the

[7] PG, 161, 494–526.

consecration already accomplished. The Blessed Trinity brings about in one action the transubstantiation in response to all the invocations which in a human way is extended in time. Not to invert the theological order of the divine persons, the invocation of the Holy Ghost follows the invocation of the Second Person, and the consecration. Therefore the invocation of the Holy Ghost does not refer to the time "in quo" it is pronounced, but to the time "pro quo," i.e., to the time before the consecration.

With reference to the present form of the Roman Canon, Scheeben [8] has modified the opinion of Bessarion. Scheeben understands the invocation of Christ as angel of sacrifice. For the rest, his opinion coincides with Bessarion's opinion, inasmuch as he says that the chapter is the petition of the Church to Christ the high priest, an expression of the intention of the Church she had when the words of consecration were pronounced: "The Church acting in her own name, turns to the heavenly high priest and angel of the testament, in order to accomplish through Him her sacrifice upon the heavenly altar, just as in the Mosaic sacrifice the lay folk turned to the priest, that he might carry their gifts upon the earthly altar and through the sacrificial fire send them up to God."

Dom Cagin has contributed much to a clarification of the problem with his studies on the Trinitarian structure of the Canon and of the liturgy of other sacraments. With many parallel texts from the liturgies of East and West, Cagin has illustrated that the Canon commemorates the work of the Father in creation and conservation until the Sanctus; from the Sanctus to the epiklesis the Canon commemorates the redemptive work of the Son; the epiklesis itself represents

[8] *Handbuch der kathol. Dogmatik*, III, 421.

the commemoration of the Holy Ghost. He has called attention to the fact that in the liturgy of the other sacraments,
e.g., baptism, holy orders, there are also pronounced invocations after the sacrament has already been accomplished.
The shortcoming of human language makes it impossible
to pronounce simultaneously all these invocations, for which
the sacrament is the response.

S. Salaville [9] deserves much praise and thanks for his profound and comprehensive study of the history and literature
of the epiklesis. He inspired renewed studies of the scriptural
background of the invocation of the Holy Ghost, he noticed
the influence of the dogma of the Trinity and its development
upon the development of the invocations, especially "that
every action ad extra" (the consecration included) is the
common work of the Blessed Trinity; (b) the doctrine of the
"appropriation" of certain actions to certain divine persons,
particularly the consecration to the Holy Ghost.

De la Taille [10] emphasizes the explanatory character of
the prayers after the consecration: Anamnesis, prosphora,
epiklesis are the oral and explanatory supplement of the pragmatic Anamnesis, prosphora, and epiklesis which are implied in the act of consecration. He has given to some terms
of Cagin a more precise definition, e.g., to the petition for
acceptance of the sacrifice as extrinsic supplement of the
sacrifice, which makes it efficacious, for which we may ask
fittingly after the consecration has been accomplished. He
did not, however, penetrate the full import of the Trinitarian
structure of the Canon.

The exaggerations of the Eastern Orthodox Church about
the postconsecratory invocations were introduced by Nikolas

[9] S. Salaville, *Echo d'Orient*, 1908–11.
[10] *Mysterium fidei*, pp. 438–53.

Cabasilas [11] (d. 1363) and by Simeon of Thess.[12] These authors understood the postconsecratory invocations not only as invocations of the Holy Ghost to consecrate, but also of consecratory power. According to their opinion, the words of our Lord taken by themselves, have merely a historical, recitative value; only in conjunction with the invocations do they have consecratory, sacramental power. The main error of this interpretation consists in the statement that it constitutes the genuine, patristic tradition.

That this opinion contradicts the faith of the Church and adulterates patristic tradition, was the unanimous declaration of the fathers of the East and the West assembled at the Council of Florence. Yet there were presented by Le Quien and by Dom Touttée [13] opinions which show a leaning toward such ideas. These authors admit that the words of Christ are consecratory, but their consecratory power is conditioned on the surrounding prayers. This opinion exaggerates the value of the Canon as a sacramental.

HISTORICAL DEVELOPMENT OF THE POSTCONSECRATORY INVOCATIONS

The starting point in the development of all invocations of the Canon was the blessing of our Lord in the narrative of the institution of the Holy Eucharist. St. Cyril of Alexandria testifies to this fact: "Jesus gives thanks, turns in the form of a prayer to His Father in order to associate Himself with His father in the gift He is about to make for us by the vivifying eulogy. All grace and every perfect gift descend upon us from the Father through the Son in the Holy Spirit.

[11] N. Cabasilas, *Liturgiae expositio; PG,* 150, 425–40.
[12] *Expositio de divino templo; PG,* 155, 733–40.
[13] Dom Touttée, *De doctrina S. Cyrilli hieros.,* Paris, 1720. *PG,* 33, 238.

This act of Christ was therefore for us a model of supplication which we must address in the moment of the offering of the mystery of the holy and vivifying oblation. That is what we are used to do." [14]

The greatness of the majesty of God who is invoked, further the greatness of the object asked for, justify the multiplication of these invocations. The special problem is the differentiation of them, particularly the distinction of the postconsecratory from the preconsecratory. There is found here and there in the different liturgies that distinction between the invocations before the consecration and those after the consecration, that in the first is asked for consecration, in the latter for the effects and fruits of sacrifice and sacrament. This is no problem. The problem of the epiklesis consist in this, that there are found postconsecratory invocations which ask evidently not merely for the effect of sacrifice and sacrament, but for consecration. It is a puzzling phenomenon that consecration is asked for after consecration has already been accomplished. This antinomy finds its solution, if we note that, besides the object for which petition is made, there is another principle of differentiation between the preconsecratory and postconsecratory invocations: the distinction of the divine persons to whom the invocations are addressed. This principle of distinction is likewise alluded to in the words of St. Cyril, so far as he says: "All grace and all perfect gifts descend, namely, upon us from the Father through the Son in the Holy Spirit." It is the purpose of the present chapter to give evidence for these principles of differentiation with texts from different liturgies and from the teaching of the holy Fathers of the Church.

[14] PG, 72, 908; 72, 452.

LITURGICAL TRADITION ABOUT THE POSTCONSECRATORY
INVOCATIONS

The postconsecratory invocations of the *Traditio apostolica* ask certainly for fruitful Holy Communion, probably
also for consecration. The invocation is addressed to the Father to send the Holy Spirit: "And we beg that Thou send
Thy Holy Spirit upon the oblation of holy Church, gathering into one all the saints who partake that they may be
filled with the Holy Spirit unto the strengthening of their
faith in truth." Most of the authors agree that this invocation in which the Holy Spirit is explicitly mentioned asks
merely for the effect of the Holy Eucharist. According to the
interpretation of Cardinal Schuster, the following effects may
be distinguished: "We beg that Thou send Thy Holy Spirit
upon the oblation of holy Church, gathering into one": this
is the first fruit of the Eucharist, Catholic unity; "that they
may be filled with the Holy Spirit": the nourishing of the interior life according to the promise (who eats Me shall live
because of Me): this is the second fruit; "unto the strengthening of their faith in truth": this is the third fruit of Holy
Communion, inasmuch as it strengthens the faith which is
sincere. One could maintain that this invocation is merely
for the effect of the Holy Eucharist. But if we compare this
text with other invocations, it could be understood as an invocation for both, for consecration and fruitful Communion:
for consecration, "upon the oblation of holy Church"; for
salutary effect of Holy Communion, (a) gathering into one
all the saints, (b) that they may be filled with the Holy
Spirit, (c) unto the strengthening of their faith in truth.

There is no doubt that in the invocations of the anaphora
of Serapion the object of invocation is twofold: consecration

and fruitful Communion: "May it come, O God of truth, Thy holy Word upon this bread, that it may become the body of the Word, and upon this chalice, that it may become the chalice of the blood of truth; and bring about that all communicants may receive the remedy of life," etc. It is a so-called Logos-epiklesis, since it asks for the descent of the divine Word. The fragment of Deir-Balizeh had very probably also a postconsecratory invocation; but the manuscript ends just too soon.

The *Apostolic Constitutions*, and all great Eastern liturgies ask distinctly for both objects: "Send down upon this sacrifice Thy Holy Spirit, the witness of the Lord Jesus' sufferings, that He may show this bread to be the body of Thy Christ, and the cup to be the blood of Thy Christ, that those who are partakers thereof may be strengthened for piety . . . may be filled with the Holy Ghost," etc. The words "that He may show" are equivalent to the words "witness of the Lord Jesus' suffering." This is proof that it is a petition for consecration: for the words "show" and "show forth" mean, in the language of St. Paul which is alluded to in this text, "to consecrate."

The liturgy of St. James asks distinctly for both, for consecration and communion: "Have mercy upon us, O God, according to Thy great mercy, and send forth on us, and on these offered gifts, Thy all-holy Spirit . . . that descended on Thy apostles in the form of tongues of fire in the upper room . . . this thine all-holy Spirit, send down, O Lord, upon us, and upon these offered gifts, that coming by His holy and good and glorious appearing, He may sanctify this bread, and make it the holy body of Thy Christ. Amen. And this cup the precious blood of Thy Christ; that they may be to all that partake of them for remission of sins, and for life everlasting, for the sanctification of souls and of bodies, for bearing the fruit of good works, for the establishing of Thy holy Catholic Church." In the liturgy of St. Mark the epiklesis is this: "Send down upon us also, and upon this bread and upon this chalice, Thy Holy Spirit, that by His all-powerful and divine influence He may sanctify and consecrate them, and make this bread the body. Amen. And this cup the blood of the new testament, of the very Lord and God, and Savior, and universal King Christ Jesus."

The liturgy of St. Basil: "We draw near with confidence to Thy holy altar and, offering the antitypes of the sacred body and blood of Thy Christ, we pray Thee and implore Thee, O saint of saints, through a favor of Thy goodness, that Thy Holy Spirit may come over us and over these offerings, that He may bless and sanctify them, and make this bread the precious body of our Lord God and Savior, Jesus Christ, and this chalice the precious blood of our Lord God and Savior Jesus Christ, which was shed for the life and the salvation of the world."

The liturgy of St. John Chrysostom: "Thus we offer unto Thee this reasonable and unbloody sacrifice; and we pray and beseech and implore Thee, to send down Thy Holy Spirit upon us and upon these gifts . . . and make this bread the precious body of Thy Christ . . . and that which is in the chalice the precious blood of Thy Christ . . . changing them by Thy Holy Spirit."

In most of the liturgies cited above, God the Father is asked to send, either the Word (Logos-epiklesis) or the Holy Spirit to consecrate. There are some invocations in which the entire Trinity is invoked as the cause of consecration, as in the liturgy of St. James: "God and Father of our Lord and God and Savior Jesus Christ, the glorious Lord,

Thou hast accepted the gifts, offerings, and fruits brought unto Thee as an odor of a sweet spiritual fragrance, and hast been pleased to sanctify them, and make them perfect, O good one, by the grace of Thy Christ, and by the presence of Thy all-holy Spirit."

INTERPRETATION BY THE HOLY FATHERS OF THE CHURCH

The Fathers' interpretation of the postconsecratory epiklesis is in close adherence to liturgical texts. With reference to texts in which consecration is asked from the Blessed Trinity, they emphasize the unity of action "ad extra" common to all three persons; they ascribe consecration to the Holy Ghost in the way of appropriation of sanctifying activity to the third divine person; throughout all the explanation about the meaning of these invocations appears the great concept of the Fathers about the analogy between the mystery of Holy Eucharist and the mystery of the Incarnation, and about the relationship of both these mysteries to the mystery of the Blessed Trinity. They do not neglect the differences between the mystery of the Holy Eucharist and the mystery of the Incarnation. These differences appear in passages where the Fathers ascribe the consecration to Christ the high priest, to Christ and His words, to the words of Christ and the Holy Ghost together. Most of the texts have already been discussed in the question about the Anamnesis and the doctrine of the Fathers about the Eucharist as the re-enactment of the nativity, passion, and glorification of Christ. In the present place they are discussed from the particular viewpoint as postconsecratory invocations with the special emphasis on the Holy Ghost as the principle of consecration.

The consecration is ascribed to the Blessed Trinity by St. Irenaeus,[15] so far as he says that the consecration is accomplished upon the invocation of God. The same idea is expressed by St. Gregory of Nyssa [16] who ascribes the consecration to the omnipotence of God. The three divine persons are specified in the words of St. Cyril of Alexandria: "All grace and all perfect gifts come to us from the Father, through the Son, in the Holy Ghost." St. Cyril of Jerusalem [17] attributes the consecration to the "invocation of the holy and adorable Trinity."

The consecration is ascribed to Christ, to the words of Christ; to Christ and His words together. St. Cyprian: "If Jesus Christ, our Lord and God Himself is the high priest of God the Father, and if He offered first Himself as sacrifice to the Father and if He has ordered to be offered in His commemoration, then that priest truly acts in the place of Christ, who imitates what Christ did, and he offers them a true and full sacrifice in the Church to God the Father, if he begins to offer in the way he knows Christ has offered." [18] St. Cyril of Alexandria: "The oblations made in the Churches are sanctified, blessed, and consecrated by Christ." [19] St. Ambrose: "The blessing of Christ and the consecration by the words of Christ." St. John Chrysostom: "It is not the man who works it that the oblations become the body and blood of Christ, but Christ Himself, crucified for us. The priest here represents Him and pronounces the words, but the power and the grace are from God. This is My body, says

[15] *PG*, 7, 580.
[16] *PG*, 45, 84.
[17] *PG*, 23, 1072.
[18] *PL*, 4, 385.
[19] *PG*, 72, 1396.

he (the priest in the name of Christ). This word transforms the oblation." [20]

The Holy Ghost is understood to be the principle of Eucharistic consecration in the *Didascalia:* "The thanksgiving (eucharistia) is sanctified by the Holy Ghost." [21] St. Cyprian says: "The oblation cannot be sanctified where the Holy Ghost is not present." [22] Son and Holy Ghost are called the principle of consecration in a passage of St. Basil: "Son and Holy Ghost are the fountain of all sanctification." [23] St. Ambrose: "It is not sanctified to be such a great mystery except through the invisible activity of the Holy Ghost." [24]

That it is no contradiction to ascribe the consecration on the one hand to the words of Christ, on the other hand to the Holy Ghost, it was pointed out with all theological clarity by Paschasius Radbertus, whom St. Thomas followed faithfully, adding his terminology. Paschasius Radbertus: "It is not consecrated except in the word of the Creator and in the power of the Holy Ghost. In such a way, therefore, we have to believe about this mystery, that through the same power of the Holy Ghost by the word of Christ in an invisible activity is produced His flesh and blood." [25] Again: "In the word and through the power of the Holy Ghost a new thing is produced." St. Thomas has added the distinction between principal and instrumental cause: "And by that, what is said that only through the power of the Holy Ghost such a change is accomplished, an instrumental power is not excluded."

[20] *PG,* 49, 380.
[21] *Didascalia,* 6, 21.
[22] *PL,* 4, 392.
[23] *PG,* 32, 249.
[24] *PL,* 42, 873.
[25] *PL,* 70, 1279.

Development of the Roman Epiklesis

Most of the interpreters of the Roman Canon admit that the Roman liturgy also had at one time an epiklesis of the Holy Ghost. This is deduced from two texts of Pope Gelasius, from a passage found in St. Ambrose, and from the fact that the invocation of the Holy Ghost is found regularly in the consecratory anaphoras adopted in the various sacraments.

Pope Gelasius, *Epist. ad Elpidium:* "Bread and wine become the divine substance, the Holy Ghost working this." [26] Again: "How shall the heavenly Spirit, being invoked, come to the consecration of the divine mystery, if the priest who prays Him to be present, is condemned as being full of evil deeds?" [27] St. Ambrose: "How should the Holy Ghost not have everything that belongs to God, who (Holy Ghost) with the Father and the Son is mentioned by the priests in baptism, and is invoked in the oblations?" [28]

About the original place of the invocation of the Holy Ghost in the Roman Canon, Cardinal Schuster [29] maintains that the natural and traditional place for this epiklesis is before the consecration. Later, he says, the traditional form underwent a change in the East, especially at the time of the Macedonian controversies regarding the divinity of the Holy Ghost. Most of the interpreters, however, basing their opinion on a study of the original texts of Eastern liturgies, admit that the Roman Canon had likewise a postconsecratory epiklesis. The analysis of the two prayers, *Supra quae propitio* and *Supplices te rogamus*, suggest that they are the remnants of the original Roman epiklesis. If we admit that with the

[26] Cf. Thiel, *Ep. Rom. Pont.*, I, 542.
[27] Thiel, I, 486.
[28] *PL*, 16, 837.
[29] *Op. cit.*, I, 284.

rearrangement of the Roman Canon the postconsecratory epiklesis of the Holy Ghost was suppressed, nevertheless this reform was done with great discretion, so as not to eliminate the idea of the postconsecratory epiklesis. But, as A. Fortescue [30] cautions, no argument for the opinion, that the rearrangement was for the purpose of suppressing the epiklesis of the Holy Ghost, can effect more than probability. All attempts of reconstruction of the original Roman epiklesis are most problematic and to a great extent subjective. The only reason deserving serious consideration is the insistence of the Latin Fathers of the fourth and fifth century on the words of Christ as a consecratory formula. This insistence was provoked by these utterances, that the words and the invocation would consecrate. St. Ambrose, the *De sacramentis*, St. Augustine, Caesarius of Arles, and St. Isidore of Seville can be referred to with explicit statements, to prevent any misinterpretation, as if besides the words of Christ any other prayer would have consecratory power, and be a part of the formula of consecration. It is the special merit of the Fathers of the Latin rite, to have clearly distinguished between invocation and sacramental consecratory formula. This distinction is, however, not new; it is contained in the universal faith of the Fathers of East and West, that the words of Christ consecrate. Abstracting from the causality of the words of Christ, considering precisely the divine power by which the consecration is accomplished, one may answer with the words of the different invocations: the omnipotence of God, the Blessed Trinity, the Father, the Word of God, and the Holy Ghost.

[30] Fortescue, *op. cit.,* p. 139.

CHAPTER XXVI

The Individual Postconsecratory Invocations

T O the three postconsecratory invocations applies the general liturgical principle: prayers are multiplied in order to express: human insufficiency; greatness of the work of transubstantiation; awe before the divine omnipotence, which accomplishes transubstantiation.

There is, however, more than merely numerical distinction between these three prayers. There are, besides, other reasons which led to the separation of the two prayers *Supra quae* and *Supplices te rogamus,* which in the older form of the *De sacramentis* are still one prayer, and to the addition of the third: *Per quem haec omnia.*

Both prayers, *Supra quae* and *Supplices te rogamus,* are united to one prayer and connected with Anamnesis and prosphora in the *De sacramentis:* "Therefore mindful . . . we offer to Thee . . . and we ask and pray that Thou mayest accept this oblation upon Thy altar on high through the hands of Thy angels, as Thou hast deigned to accept the gifts of Thy just Abel and the sacrifice of our patriarch Abraham, and what the high priest Melchisedech offered to Thee." In this old form there appears a perfect parallel between the Eucharistic sacrifice and the sacrifices which are types of it. In the new form of the two prayers the Eucharistic sacrifice is singled out and with a new action "perferri in sublime altare tuum" considered exclusively, which does not apply to the types. This is the main difference between the two prayers: (a) the Old Testament sacrifices were acceptable and accepted because of the devotion, disposition ("ex opere operantis") of those who offered them. The New Testament sacrifice is acceptable and accepted because of its own dignity; (b) the typical sacrifices were never really carried upon the heavenly altar, except symbolically; the New Testament sacrifice is really carried up to heaven, accepted in heaven, made divine. To this main difference we may add minor reasons of distinction: in the composition of these two consecutive prayers appears a certain dramatic progress: the first prayer uses a figure of an action previous in time to the action of the second prayer. The good pleasure of God on the sacrifice appears first in the "propitio ac sereno vultu respicere digneris." This good pleasure of God is followed by the action "carry up." The separation of these two prayers was most probably influenced by the memory of the miraculous events which happened in the Old Testament sacrifices to which the figures of the words "look down" and "let to be carried up" refer: "look down" refers to the miraculous fire falling down from heaven and consuming the sacrifices; "carry up" refers to the ascending of the victim in the form of smoke "to the odor of sweetness."

"Supra quae propitio"

The colorful scriptural background breathes into this prayer a very profound and exultant devotion. The great figures of Abel, Abraham, and Melchisedech, the pontifical blessing of the Mosaic liturgy, the allusions to the Benedictus of Zachary and the Magnificat of the Blessed Virgin in ideas, terms, and structure, are inspiring features in the majestic grandeur of this prayer. The disputed nature of the post-consecratory invocations, besides the fact that the Eucharistic sacrifice is much more excellent than all the sacrifices of the Old Testament, led St. Thomas [1] to say: "Although this sacrament is in itself preferable to all the sacrifices of the Old Testament, nevertheless the ancient sacrifices were very acceptable to God because of the devotion of those who offered them. Therefore the priest asks in this prayer, that this sacrifice may be accepted by God because of the devotion of those who offer it, just as they (the sacrifices of the Old Testament) were accepted by God." Again he says: "In the Canon of the Mass the offerings of Abraham and Abel are remembered more because of the devotion of those who offered them than because of the typical relation of the offerings." On the basis of our conclusions of the preceding chapter about the postconsecratory invocations generally, we have to say that the *Supra quae* is a petition for consecration and acceptance of the Eucharistic sacrifice, that again may be fulfilled what was prefigured in the sacrifices of Abel, Abraham, and Melchisedech. The allusions to the Benedictus and to the Magnificat bring the Eucharistic consecration again in relation to the mystery of the Incarnation.

The pronoun "quae" refers to the object for which the acceptance by God is prayed for: the Eucharistic sacrifice. The phrase "do Thou deign to regard with gracious and kindly attention and hold acceptable" is equivalent to the phrase "accept and bless" of the first preconsecratory invocation, with the difference that the expression "to bless" is replaced by the figure of "to regard with gracious and kindly at-

[1] St. Thomas, *Summa theol.*, IIIa, q. 83, a. 4 ad 2.

tention." This phrase is used because of the scriptural text about the sacrifice of Abel (Gen. 4:4): "And the Lord had respect to Abel and to his offerings."

The formula of blessing "look down with gracious and kindly attention" is found many times in the psalms, e.g., Ps. 66:2: "May God have mercy on us, and bless us, and may He cause the light of His countenance to shine upon us, and may He have mercy on us." This blessing is derived from the priestly blessing ordained by God (Num. 6:23): "Say to Aaron and his sons: Thus shall you bless the children of Israel, and you shall say to them: The Lord bless thee, and keep thee. The Lord show His face to thee, and have mercy on thee. The Lord turn His countenance to thee, and give thee peace. And they shall invoke My name upon the children of Israel, and I will bless them." Obeying the command of God, Aaron invoked the blessing upon the people of Israel (Lev. 9:22): "And stretching forth his hands to the people, he blessed them. And so the victims for sin and the holocausts and the peace offerings being finished, he came down." To this blessing and the divine promise is likewise referred II Par. 30:27: "And the priests and the Levites rose up and blessed the people; and their voice was heard." It is a blessing after the sacrifice was offered, and a blessing invoked upon the people for whom the sacrifice was offered as a result of its acceptance by God. The original function of this pontifical blessing suggests that this postconsecratory invocation includes in analogy a petition for consecration and acceptance of the mystical sacrifice as a result of the Eucharistic sacrifice, and as such a petition for the effect of the Eucharistic sacrifice. It is, however, not the only object asked for, as the further analysis of the three following types reveals.

It is the characteristic note of the First Gospel to demonstrate that Christ is the Messiah foretold in the prophecies of the Old Testament. Regularly the argumentation concludes with a reference to the respective prophecy (e.g., Matt. 2:2). The Magnificat, which is alluded to in the terms and in the structure of the *Supra quae,* concludes with such a reference to the prophecy (Luke 1:46–55): "My soul doth magnify the Lord . . . because He has regarded the humility of His handmaid. . . . He has received Israel His servant, being mindful of His mercy: as He spoke to our fathers, to Abraham and to his seed forever." A similar reference is contained in the Benedictus (Luke 1, 68–79): "Blessed be the Lord God of Israel, because He hath raised up a horn of salvation to us, in the house of David His servant as He spoke by the mouth of His holy prophets . . . the oath which He swore to Abraham our father." The *Supra quae* does not refer to a verbal prophecy, but to types with the same intention however, to demonstrate and to instruct that the Eucharistic sacrifice is the fulfillment of the prophecy contained in these sacrifices of the Old Testament.[2]

SELECTION OF THE FIGURES

In the Epistle to the Hebrews which has immediately inspired this prayer, and in the Eastern liturgies, many more types are mentioned. St. Paul mentions Abel, Henoch, Noe, Abraham, Sara, Isaac, Jacob, Joseph, Moses, Gedeon, Barac, Samson, Jephte, David, Samuel, and the prophets. In the Eastern anaphoras we find added: "the incense of Zachary, the alms of Cornelius," etc. The reasons for the selection of the three types is obvious: St. Paul does not enumerate merely examples that refer to sacrifices; the Eastern liturgies

[2] Cf. Council of Trent; *DB,* no. 939.

use this invocation many times as a blessing for incense, therefore fittingly the name of Zachary was inserted. With the accommodation of the invocation to the Eucharist, those types had to be selected which recommended themselves as prominent figures of the Eucharistic sacrifice. Such are the sacrifice of Abel, of Abraham, and of Melchisedech. The sacrifice of Abel is the first sacrifice recorded in Holy Scripture. The sacrifice of Abraham has prominence, because he was chosen by God to be the father of all the faithful, and then because of the nature of his sacrifice; the prominence of Melchisedech as a type of the priesthood of Christ is the special subject of the Epistle to the Hebrews.

"THE OFFERINGS OF ABEL THY JUST SERVANT"

The purity of intention, the nature of the priesthood and of the sacrifice of Abel are of typical significance for the priesthood and for the sacrifice of Christ, for the priesthood and the sacrifice instituted by Christ. This type is introduced with the charming term "Thy servant." This is a prophetic name of Christ, derived from Isa. 42:1, quoted from this text by Matt. 12:18, in the Acts 3:13; 4:27, words sanctioned by the heavenly Father on the occasion of the baptism in the Jordan (Matt. 3:17).

Isa. 42:1: "Behold My servant, I will uphold him; My elect, My soul delighteth in him." Matt. 3:17: "And behold a voice came from heaven, saying: This is My beloved Son, in whom I am well pleased" (cf. II Pet. 1:17). The addition of the attribute "Thy servant," which is a prophetic attribute of Christ, is added to Abel because of his typical relation to Christ.

The second attribute "just" Abel is given by our Lord Himself (Matt. 23:35): "That upon you may come all the just blood that hath been shed upon the earth, from the blood of Abel the just. . . ."

Abel is given both these attributes as a type of Christ in two ways: because of the purity of intention with which he offered the sacrifice (Gen. 4:4), and because of his martyrdom, to which Christ refers particularly in Matt. 23:35. God was pleased with the sacrifice of Abel, because He was pleased with the intention and devotion, with the faith of Abel (Heb. 11:4): "By faith Abel offered to God a sacrifice exceeding that of Cain, by which he obtained a testimony that he was just, God giving testimony to his gifts; and by it he being dead yet speaketh." According to the common opinion of the Fathers, the sign with which God declared His good pleasure on Abel and his sacrifice was the fire that fell from heaven and consumed the sacrifice of Abel.[3] The words Gen. 4:4, "And the Lord had respect to Abel and his offerings," may therefore be translated, as we find it in Theodotian: "God sent fire over Abel and his sacrifice." The same idea is expressed in the words of St. Paul (Heb. 11:4): "by which he obtained a testimony that he was just" according to the interpretation of St. Jerome (*In Gen.* 4:4): "Whence could Cain know that the gifts of his brother were accepted by God, and his own rejected, if not in the way Theodotian understood? Namely: God sent fire over Abel and his sacrifice" (cf. Elias: III Kings 18; Gedeon: Judges 6:21; Manue: Judges 13:20; David: I Par. 21:26; Solomon: II Par. 7:1; Nehemias: II Macch. 1:32).

Abel is a type of the Eucharist with his victim also (cf. Rupertus Deutz, *In Gen.*): "Abel was with his sacrifice a type of the sacrifice of Christ in the Eucharist. Because the sacrifice which Jesus Christ instituted in that night, although

[3] John Hennig, "Abel's Place in the Liturgy," *Theological Studies,* VII (1946), 126–41.

it is in its external appearance bread and wine, in truth is the Lamb of God, the first-born of all lambs or sheep, which belong to the pasture of Paradise."

"The sacrifice of Abraham our patriarch"

Abraham is father and patriarch of the Israelites for two reasons: natural generation; his priesthood. Abraham is called in liturgy "our patriarch" because of his being the "father of all the faithful," and because of the nature of his sacrifice.

Abraham is called "our father"; (Luke 1:55): "As He spoke to our fathers, to Abraham and his seed forever." (Luke 1:73): "The oath which He swore to Abraham our father, that He would grant to us." (John 8:56): "Abraham your father rejoiced that he might see My day." Abraham was not only father and patriarch of the Israelites by natural generation, but also by his priesthood, as it appears in the text of St. Paul (Heb. 7:9): "And as it may be said even Levi who received tithes in Abraham, paid tithes in Abraham: for he was yet in the loins of his father when Melchisedech met him." All priesthood is derived from the priesthood of Abraham, so far as the heads of the families were priests. God ordained later, because of the unity of the nation, that one family, the family of Levi and Aaron, should exercise the priesthood for the rest.

Abraham is "our patriarch" because of the great promises made to him as father of all the faithful; (Gen. 17:5): "Neither shall thy name be called any more Abram; but thou shalt be called Abraham: because I have made thee a father of many nations." To these promises St. Paul refers; (Heb. 11:17): "and he that had received the promises," etc.

Abraham is a type of Christ particularly with his sacrifice with which he represents in the *Supra quae* all sacrifices of the state of the law of Moses, as Abel represents all sacrifice of the state of the law of nature. The sacrifice of Abraham is the most perfect type for the sacrifice of Christ, (a) because he is in an eminent way the typical representative of mankind which is longing and striving for the blessing of God, chosen by God and well pleasing to Him, although only as a lay offerer. No one before Christ had in offering such universal significance as Abraham with his sacrifice; (b) because his sacrifice is the most perfect type of the sacrifice of Christ in the idea of sacrifice: his sacrifice as a moral act from the side of men by which the divine blessing is requested and acquired, is the most perfect act of sacrificial intention as unconditional obedience and unreserved self-denial; (c) because the victim of the sacrifice of Abraham was a human being, representing most perfectly himself; it was the most valuable object on his side, the best gift he could present to God. Heb. 11:19: "By faith Abraham, when he was tried, offered Isaac . . . accounting that God is able to raise up even from the dead. Whereupon also he received him for a parable." Faith inspired Abraham to obey, otherwise he would have said: It is impossible: on the one hand Thou hast promised (Gen. 21:12), "In Isaac shall thy seed be called"; and on the other hand Thou commandest me to sacrifice him. Abraham trusted in the promise of God, that it would be true, even if it would be necessary that God should raise Isaac from the dead (cf. v. 19). Thus Abraham is the most lively figure of the sacrifice of self-denial, compared with which only the sacrifice of Christ is higher.

"Thy high priest Melchisedech"

The epistle to the Hebrews is the theology of the priesthood of Christ as antitype of the priesthood of Melchisedech. This is the scriptural background of these words of the prayer.

Melchisedech is the first to be called priest in Scripture (the patriarchs were not given this name); he is appointed by God as a special type of Christ. He is a type of Christ in a higher sense than Abraham: while Abraham as lay offerer is more a type for the sacrifice of the Blessed Mother (as "ministra" of the sacrifice of Christ), Melchisedech is in the same complex of ideas the type of the priesthood of Christ, of the hierarchical priesthood.

Melchisedech is a type of Christ by his name ("king of justice"; Christ is truly King of justice; cf. Heb. 7:1; Isa. 9:7; Ps. 71:1–3; 84:10; Zach. 9:9; Mal. 4:2), by his office and state (king of Salem; cf. Heb. 7:1 f.), by his generation (being introduced in Scripture without a father, without mother, without a wife; now, Christ as man has no father, Christ as God has no mother), by his age and the duration of his priesthood (without beginning and without end [Heb. 7:3]: "Without father, without mother, without genealogy, having neither beginning nor end of life, but likened unto the Son of God, continueth a priest forever"), by his priesthood and pontificate, in so far as he is the first and the last priest of his kind. There is then the superiority of the priesthood of Melchisedech over the priesthood of Abraham, because he received tithes from Abraham and in his turn blessed Abraham, so that virtually through Abraham were given tithes to Melchisedech by Aaron, and Aaron also was blessed by Melchisedech (Heb. 7:2): "To whom also Abraham divided the tithes of all: who met Abraham returning from the slaughter of the kings, and blessed him." Heb. 7:6: "But he whose pedigree is not numbered among them, received tithes of Abraham, and blessed him that had the promises."

Lastly, there is the type in the host offered: bread and wine. Now, the order, the rite, and the species of priesthood depend on the object which is offered: it is the same object (in the external appearance) offered by Christ and by the Church.

Melchisedech is called in the prayer "high priest." In the Epistle to the Hebrews the text reads (Heb. 7:1): "For this Melchisedech was king of Salem, priest of the most high God" (as in Gen. 14:18: "But Melchisedech the king of salem, bringing forth bread and wine, for he was the priest of the most high God"). According to A. Baumstark,[4] it is an error by a translator that the attribute of God is referred to the priesthood of Melchisedech.

According to B. Botte,[5] this is a hypothesis without any basis, since Melchisedech is called "high priest" already in the *Apostolic Constitutions* (8, 12).

The pronoun "Thy" sums up the superiority of the priesthood of Melchisedech above the priesthood of Abraham and any other priesthood (except the priesthood of Christ, for which he is the type). He is the priest of God as hierarchical priest, appointed priest and mediator by God, the royal representative of God.

This is the spirit of the *Supra quae*. The innocence and charm of Abel, offering the first fruits in the springtime of mankind, his face still radiant from the beauty of Paradise, himself a martyr, is able by his devotion to inspire to devotion. The faith of Abraham, his confidence in the promises of God, his personal sacrifice, his obedience and self-denial, reveal the ideal attitude of a priest. And then there is the man of God with consecratory power, with superhuman dignity, the representative of the hierarchical priesthood: what he blesses is blessed, what he consecrates is consecrated; the

---

[4] A. Baumstark, *Liturgia Romana e liturgia dell' Esarcato* (Rome, 1904), pp. 166–68.
[5] B. Botte, *Le Canon de la messe romaine.* Louvain, 1935. Cf. G. Bardy, "Melchisedeciens," *Dict. théol. cath.*

true representative of God, the mediator, the dispenser of the mysteries of God: he calls to our mind the dignity of the hierarchical priesthood of the New Testament, on the dignity of the priests "according to the order of Melchisedech." Conscious of this dignity, the priest of the New Testament will bless, give thanks, sanctify, consecrate.

CHAPTER XXVII

Supplices te rogamus

It is a very beautiful and very mysterious prayer, of which Florus Diaconus [1] says: "These words of the mystery are so profound, so wonderful and inconceivable, that we ought rather to revere them with humility and a holy awe than attempt to interpret them."

"We humbly beseech Thee, Almighty God, command these to be carried by the hands of Thy holy angel to Thine altar on high, in the presence of Thy divine majesty, that as many of us as shall, by partaking of this altar, receive the most sacred body and blood of Thy Son, may be filled with all heavenly blessing and grace. Through the same Christ our Lord."

The prayer consists of two parts: (a) command these to be carried by the hands of Thy holy angel to Thine altar on high; (b) that as many of us as shall . . . may be filled with all heavenly blessing. In the first petition we may distinguish three questions: what is to be understood by "these," to be carried to the heavenly altar; who is the angel of sacrifice; what is "the altar on high"?

The same difference of opinions referred to in the previous prayer as to the "Upon which do Thou vouchsafe to look" is met with in the present prayer. According to one group of interpreters the petition refers to the mystical body, to the

[1] Florus Diaconus, *De expositione missae*, 66; *PL*, 119, 58.

352

prayers for the effect of Holy Communion, by which the faithful are incorporated into the sacrifice of Christ, carried up to the altar on high; the second group of interpreters understands the prayer as a petition for the Eucharistic consecration.

Ballarmine [2] declares: "We admit that it would be most absurd to say that the body of Christ should now first be taken bodily into heaven by angels." The petition refers therefore to our prayers to be carried up to heaven, to be heard, prayers for fruitful Communion. This interpretation is suggested also by the special rubric in some Missals of the Middle Ages, indicating that in this place the priest may pray by himself whatever he desires.

Cardinal Schuster says: "It begs God to grant that the earthly liturgy may be ratified in heaven so far as regards the personal fruit of the sacrament and its substantial efficacy. Since in Holy Scripture it belongs to the ministry of the angels to present to God the prayers and the merits of the saints, we pray that they may perform the same office for the sacrifice which we offer upon our altars, so that it may abundantly bless all such as participate in it through Holy Communion. Unlike the Eastern liturgies, which at this point have so distorted the primitive invocation of the Paraclete as to turn it into an epiklesis,—that is, a sacramental formula of transubstantiation—the Roman Canon retains its original meaning as a prayer in preparation of Communion." [3]

N. Gihr: "By the word 'haec' evidently nothing else is to be understood than what we met with in the immediately preceding word 'quae'; each time reference is made to the

[2] Bellarmine, *Disputationes de controversiis christianae fidei* (Rome, 1838), III, 805.
[3] Schuster, *op. cit.*, I, 296 f.

same object offered. To these sacrificial gifts, which are to be carried up from the earthly to the heavenly altar, belongs not only the mystical body of Christ, that is the faithful with all they are and have,—with their prayers and concerns, labors and sufferings, struggles and combats—but also the Eucharistic sacrificial body and sacrificial blood of our Lord, inasmuch as we offer them." [4]

As a consequence of the chapter on the postconsecratory invocations generally, this prayer has to be interpreted as a prayer for consecration like the preceding prayer, continuing, intensifying, and specifying the invocation with reference to the "angel of sacrifice" as mediator.

The Angel of Sacrifice

In the interpretation of "the angel of sacrifice," there are presented three different opinions: (a) it is an angel in the proper sense, namely, a created spirit, and may refer as a collective singular to the angelic ministry generally, or to a particular angel; (b) Christ is Himself the angel of the sacrifice; (c) the Holy Spirit is the angel of sacrifice.

We review these three interpretations as to the scriptural background and as to liturgical texts and patristic tradition, and add some considerations from the context and the structure of the Canon.

An Angel in the Proper Sense

The proximate scriptural source of the prayer "command these to be carried by the hands of Thy holy angel to Thine altar on high, in the presence of Thy divine majesty" is found in Apoc. 8:3 f.: "And another angel came and stood before the

[4] Gihr, *The Holy Sacrifice of the Mass* (St. Louis, 1924), p. 661.

altar, having a golden censer; and there was given to him much incense, that he should offer of the prayers of all the saints upon the golden altar, which is before the throne of God." The angels offer to God the prayers of men as their guardians, patrons, and advocates; not in order to manifest them to God, since nothing is hidden in the sight of God, but in order to beseech God at the same time for them, and make their prayers efficacious, so that they may obtain the desired effect, to impetrate what they petition.

To the ministry of the angel at the sacrifice several texts of the Old Testament refer: Gen. 22:11: "And behold an angel of the Lord from heaven called to him, saying: Abraham, Abraham: and he answered: Here I am. And he said to him: Lay not thy hand upon the boy, neither do thou anything to him." To the liturgical ministry of the angels the vision of Jacob also refers (Gen. 28:12): "And he saw in his sleep a ladder standing upon the earth, and the top thereof touching heaven: the angels also of God ascending and descending by it. . . . And when Jacob awaked out of sleep, he said: Indeed the Lord is in this place, . . . this is no other but the house of God and gate of heaven." The sacrifice of Gedeon had the special ministry of an angel (Judges 6:21): "The angel of the Lord put forth the tip of the rod which he held in his hand, and touched the flesh and the unleavened loaves, and there arose a fire from the rock and consumed the flesh and the unleavened loaves: and the angel of the Lord vanished out of his sight." Still more specific as to the idea of an angel carrying up the sacrifice to heaven is a text about the sacrifice of Manue (Judges 13:20): "Then Manue took a kid of the flocks and the libations, and put them upon a rock, offering to the Lord, who doth wonderful things: and he and his wife looked on. And when the flame from the altar went up toward heaven, the angel of the Lord ascended also in the flame."

Liturgical tradition seems to favor the interpretation of this text as referring to the ministry of the angels; the anaphora of St. Mark asks God to receive the oblation "by angelic ministry" and by "Thy archangelic ministry." The Coptic liturgy asks for acceptance "through the ministry of Thy holy angels and archangels." The most decisive text is that of the *De sacramentis,* which has "by the hands of Thy angels."

Certain scriptural texts would suggest that it is a particular angel. Some interpreters refer to the angel Raphael because of Tob. 12:12: "When thou didst pray with tears, and didst bury the dead . . . I offered thy prayer to the Lord. . . . For I am the angel Raphael, one of the seven who stand before the Lord." Cornelius a Lapide [5] refers to the angel Gabriel because of Luke 1:12: "And there appeared to him an angel of the Lord, standing on the right side of the altar of incense." Dionysius the Carthusian [6] identifies the angel with St. Michael, who as the angel of the Church militant is also to be honored as the guardian angel of the Holy Eucharist. St. Ambrose refers likewise to the angel Gabriel: "There appears conveniently an angel in the temple (when Zacharias offered the sacrifice of incense), because the advent of the true priest was already announced, and the heavenly sacrifice was prepared in which angels should minister." [7] Hildebert of Tours (d. 1134) [8] identifies the angel with the guardian angel of the priest.

[5] Cornelius a Lapide, *In Lucam,* 1:12.
[6] Dionysius the Carthusian, *In Apoc. Enar.,* VIII, 8.
[7] St. Ambrose, *In Lucam,* 1:12.
[8] Hildebert of Tours, *De mysterio missae; PL,* 171, 1188.

Some authors referring to the opinion of St. Thomas [9] mis-represent his teaching. Once he is quoted as favoring the opinion that the angel is to be understood as a created spirit, a second time in favor of the opinion that it is Christ. St. Thomas, however, does not limit the interpretation exclusively to one significance, but admits both: the interpretation in the sense of a created spirit, and of Christ: (a) the priest asks that the angel who assists at the divine mysteries may present to God the prayers of the priest and of the faithful, according to Apoc. 8:4: "And the smoke of the incense, which came with the prayers of the saints, ascended up before God out of the angel's hand." Then St. Thomas adds: "The angel can also be understood as Christ Himself, who is the angel of the great council, unites His mystical body with God the Father and with the Church triumphant."

CHRIST AS THE ANGEL OF SACRIFICE

Scripture and tradition present arguments in favor of the interpretation of Christ as the angel of sacrifice.

There are two prominent texts of Scripture, in which Christ is called "angel of the great council," and "the angel of the testament." The first text is contained within the great Messianic prophecy (Isa. 9:6): "For a child is born to us, and a son is given to us, and the government is upon his shoulder: and his name shall be called wonderful, counselor (Septuagint translates: angel of the great council), Mighty God, the Father of the world to come, the prince of peace." In the term "wonderful Counselor" is contained an allusion to the angel of sacrifice in Judges 13:18: "And he said to him: What is thy name, that, if thy word should come to pass,

---

[9] *Summa theol.*, IIIa, q. 83, a. 4 ad 9. Cf. B. Botte, *L'ange du sacrifice*, etc. (Louvain, 1929), pp. 207–21.

we may honor thee?" And he answered him: "Why askest thou my name, which is wonderful?" When Manue offered thereupon a sacrifice, this angel ascended with the rising flames into heaven (Judges 13:20): "And when the flame from the altar went up toward heaven, the angel of the Lord ascended also in the flame." St. Augustine understands this angel as Christ and explains the text in connection with Isa. 9:6. He comes to the conclusion that the angel ascended with the flames to heaven in order to indicate that Christ Himself would be the sacrifice.

To the second text, in which Christ is called "angel of the testament," our Lord Himself refers in connection with the prophecy about the precursor: Matt. 11:10: "For this is he of whom it is written: Behold I send my angel before thy face, who shall prepare thy way before thee." Our Lord refers to the prophecy of Mal. 3:1: "Behold I send my angel, and he shall prepare the way before my face. And presently the Lord, whom you seek, and the angel of the testament, whom you desire, shall come to His temple." The angel of the testament "whom you desire" is the Messiah. He is called "angel" because He descended from heaven to announce the Gospel, and He ascended into heaven, like the angel of Manue, in order to open heaven for us. He is called angel "of the testament" in the same sense as St. Paul (Gal. 3:19) speaks of Christ as mediator of reconciliation: "Why then was the law? It was set because of transgressions, until the seed should come, to whom He made the promise, being ordained by angels, in the hand of a mediator."

The Canon of the *Traditio apostolica* has this passage: "We render thanks unto Thee, O God, through Thy beloved Son Jesus Christ, whom in these last times Thou didst send to us a Savior and Redeemer and the angel of Thy will." The term "angel of Thy will" reveals the influence of St. Paul (cf. Eph. 1:5: "That He might make known to us the mystery of His will, according to His good pleasure"; Eph. 1:11: "In whom we also are called by lot, being predestinated according to the purpose of Him who worketh all things according to the counsel of His will").

The *Apostolic Constitutions* (8, 12) has the term "angel of the great council": "Who didst bring all things out of nothing into being by Thy only-begotten Son, but didst beget Him before all ages by Thy will, Thy power, and Thy goodness . . . God the Word, the living Wisdom, the first-born of every creature, the angel of the great council and Thy high priest."

The Roman liturgy knows likewise the term "angel of the great council." It is found in the Introit of the third Christmas Mass with the text of Isa. 9:6 in the Vulgate translation.

The interpretation of Christ as the angel of this prayer was preferred by commentators since the twelfth century.

It is a variation of this interpretation in the way J. M. Scheeben [10] understands Christ as angel of the sacrifice: "The prayer *Supplices te rogamus* is not merely an accommodation of Apoc. 8:3 to the Eucharist, with which the angel assisting at the sacrifice is addressed to carry up the prayers of the priest and congregation to the heavenly altar, but with this idea is connected and interwoven a type of the Old Testament for the priesthood of Christ: the Mosaic priest as angel of sacrifice and of the testament carrying the gifts of the people of God to the altar and by means of the fire of the altar up to heaven represented as type the Son of God who by His sacrifice is the true angel of the testament." This variation is based on texts of the Old Testament in which

[10] J. M. Scheeben, *Handbuch der kathol. Dogmatik*, III, 451.

Moses, and the priest generally, is called "angel" (Mal. 2:7): "For the lips of the priest shall keep knowledge, and they shall seek the law at his mouth: because he is the angel of the Lord of hosts."

St. Thomas admitted this interpretation, saying: "The angel can also be understood as Christ Himself, who is the angel of the great council, who unites His mystical body with God the Father and with the Church triumphant."

THE HOLY GHOST AS ANGEL OF SACRIFICE

The interpretation of the angel of sacrifice as the Holy Ghost has its basis in the Eastern epiklesis with its explicit invocation of the Holy Ghost.

Nowhere in the Scripture is the Holy Ghost called "holy angel." It is on the other hand rather an exception that an angel is given the attribute "holy," being a created spirit, e.g., Acts 10:22: "received an answer of a holy angel." There is, however, no other prayer of the Canon to which would apply what St. Paul says about the sacrificial intervention of the Holy Ghost (Rom. 15:15 f.): "that the oblation of the Gentiles may be made acceptable and sanctified in the Holy Ghost"; Heb. 9:11: "But Christ, being come a high priest of the good things to come, . . . how much more shall the blood of Christ, who by the Holy Ghost offered Himself unspotted unto God, cleanse our conscience from dead works, to serve the living God? And therefore He is the mediator of the new testament."

Although not frequently, there occur some liturgical texts with the Holy Ghost called "angel." So in the Missale Gothicum in the blessing of the font, the Holy Ghost is invoked as "angel of truth": "Bless, O Lord our God, this creature of water, and may Thy power descend upon it;

infuse from above Thy Spirit, the Holy Paraclete, the angel of truth." Likewise in the Mozarabic liturgy are found invocations of the Holy Ghost as angel. A sacramentary of Ratold has this prayer "In fractione": "Deign, O Lord, to send Thy holy angel upon the sacred and immortal mystery, namely, upon Thy body and Thy blood."

THE "ANGEL OF SACRIFICE" IN THE CONTEXT

From the point of view of dogmatics, any of the interpretations explained may be admitted. Since the prayer is a petition for consecration, it may refer to any of the causes of it: it may refer to the ministry of a created spirit, it may refer to Christ as the principal priest, it may refer to the Holy Ghost, through whom Christ is offering His sacrifice. In a prayer for consecration all these causes in the respective order are implied, one directly, the rest indirectly. If we understand the angel as Christ, than the rest are asked for "in actu exercito," i.e., indirectly, because Christ consecrates under the ministry of the angels, through the power of the Holy Ghost.

We may add special reasons from the context of the prayer and from the structure of the Canon, which would confirm the interpretation of the angel of sacrifice primarily as a created spirit.

In the context of the three postconsecratory invocations can be noticed a certain progress and specification, according to the causes which are invoked to accomplish the consecration: the first invocation, *Supra quae,* refers primarily to the ministry of the human priest offering the sacrifice together with the congregation. The second prayer, *Supplices te rogamus,* refers fittingly to the ministry of the angels. The third prayer, *Per quem haec omnia,* refers evidently to the priesthood of Christ. Now, should it be that the second prayer, *Supplices te rogamus,* would refer to Christ, then it would be incongruous to conclude it with the phrase "through Christ our Lord"; further, the third prayer would not have any distinction from the second, both referring to the priesthood of Christ.

Considering finally the *Supplices te rogamus* in the entire structure of the Canon, as a prayer which has its symmetric counterpart before consecration, then we have to say that it corresponds to the Sanctus of the angels. Just as in the Sanctus heaven and earth are united in the hymn of praise and thanks, so are the human priest and the heavenly spirits united in the two prayers *Supra quae* and *Supplices te rogamus,* as they concur with the activity of the principal priest Christ, "per Christum Dominum nostrum."

The fact that the second prayer refers primarily to the ministry of the angel, does not exclude the idea that the consecratory activity of Christ and of the Holy Ghost be contained as connotation. Since there is no consecration without Christ, every prayer and petition for consecration necessarily has the connotation of the causality of Christ. Since Christ consecrates through the power of the Holy Ghost, the Holy Ghost is correspondingly also petitioned by connotation. Considering the Trinitarian structure of the Canon, the invocations after the consecration are primarily to be understood on the luminous background of the activity of the Holy Ghost. The Holy Ghost is not mentioned in the Roman Canon. But as there is a third group of prayers, this group represents the activity of the third person of the Blessed Trinity. In this way the Holy Ghost, not mentioned by name but merely signified with the structure of the Canon, is the luminous background, the heavenly fire within which Christ as high priest and angel of the sacrifice, assisted and surrounded by the ministering angels, is standing at the altar, ascending into heaven to offer His sacrifice upon the heavenly altar, before the throne of His heavenly Father.

"THY ALTAR ON HIGH"

The words "Thy altar on high" form one phrase with "command these to be carried by the hands of Thy holy angel" and have to be explained in connection therewith, just as the passage of the Apocalypse which is the immediate source of the entire phrase (Apoc. 8:3): "And another angel came and stood before the altar, having a golden censer; and there was given to him much incense, that he should offer of the prayers of all saints upon the golden altar, which is before the throne of God." The manifold meaning of the term "golden altar," "heavenly altar," in Scripture and in liturgical tradition, adds a particular brilliance to the prayer, since each meaning of the "altar on high" differentiates likewise the meaning of the action of the words "to be carried by the hands of Thy holy angel."

Berengardus, *In Apoc.* 6:9, says: "The altar of God is Christ; the altar is the Church; the altar is the saints and perfect men, who are members of the Church." St. Bernard (*Serm. in festo omnium Sanctorum*): "The heavenly altar under which St. John heard the voices of the saints, . . . nothing else than the very body of our Lord and Savior." St. Thomas understands as altar of the *Supplices te rogamus* the Blessed Trinity and the Church triumphant; he admits, however, also that Christ is our altar (*Summa theol.,* IIIa, q. 83, a. 4 ad 9): "Altar on high is called either the Church triumphant, into which we ask to be transferred, or God Himself, the participation of whom we petition; about this altar says Exod. 20:26: Unto My altar thou dost not ascend by steps, i.e., in the Trinity there are not distinguished degrees." Again in Ia IIae, q. 102, a. 4 ad 7: "The reason of these precepts (about Exod. 22 and Deut. 16:2) was the typical significance: because in Christ, who is our altar, we have to believe the true nature of flesh so far as His humanity is concerned; this means to make an altar from earth. So far as His divinity is concerned, we have to believe His equality with the Father, and this is the meaning, that there are no degrees in the Trinity, that one has not to ascend to the altar by steps."

THE HEAVENLY ALTAR IN SCRIPTURE

The golden altar of the Apocalypse (8:3) is a fusion of the ideas of the altar which appeared in the vision of Isaias with the altars of the Temple in Jerusalem, with the golden altar of the holy place, and with the propitiatory throne in the holy of holies. There exists, therefore, a parallelism between the structure of the Sanctus and the structure of the *Supplices te rogamus.*

The altar of the vision of Isaias appeared in the symbolism of the altar of incense in the holy place in Jerusalem (Isa. 6:6): "And one of the seraphim flew to me, and in his hand was a live coal, which he had taken with the tongs off the altar."

The altar of incense was ordained by God (Exod. 30:1–9; 37:25–28): "Thou shalt make also an altar to burn incense, of setim wood. It shall be a cubit in length, and another in breadth, that is, foursquare, and two in height. Horns shall go out of the same. And thou shalt overlay it with the purest gold, as well as the grate thereof, as the walls round about and the horns. And thou shalt make to it a crown of gold round about, and two golden rings under the crown on either side, that the bars may be put into them, and the altar be carried. And thou shalt make the bars also of setim wood, and shalt overlay them with gold. And thou shalt set the altar over against the veil that hangeth before the ark of the testimony before the propitiatory wherewith the testimony is covered, where I will speak to thee. And Aaron shall burn sweet incense upon it in the morning. When he shall dress the lamps, he shall burn it. And when he shall place them in the evening, he shall burn an everlasting incense before the Lord throughout your generations." This altar, called "the golden altar," stood in the middle before the inner curtain. The ritual of the offering of incense was as follows: A priest took some glowing charcoal from the altar of holocausts and carried it in a golden vessel into the tabernacle, while another carried the incense. The first priest scattered the charcoal on the altar, and the second laid the incense upon it. Meanwhile the people stood in the court, where they were engaged in prayer, and then they received the priests' blessing.

The altar in the highest sense was the propitiatory throne in the holy of holies. It was ordained by God (Exod. 25:10–22; 37:1–9). There was first the ark of the covenant, or of the witness. It was a chest of acacia wood, covered with gold both inside and outside. Its length was 2½ cubits, its width and height 1½ cubits. Round the middle of it ran a garland of pure gold. At the four corners were golden rings, through which gilded poles were passed along the shorter side to enable the ark to be carried; these poles were never to be removed. Inside the ark was nothing but the two stone tables, on which the Ten Commandments were inscribed (Exod. 25:16; Deut. 10:4 f.). According to Heb. 9:4, beside the ark were kept Aaron's rod and a vessel of manna. In Deut. 31: 25 ff. we read that the book of the law also lay beside the ark.

Over the ark was the kapporeth (i.e., the cover of pure gold). It was not merely to be the cover of the ark, but it had a far higher purpose. This is implied by the fact that it was of solid gold, whereas the ark was only of wood, overlaid with gold. Its true purpose is suggested by the holy of holies being called the house of the kapporeth, i.e., expiation. The kapporeth may be explained as God's resting place. At each end of it, and inseparable from it was a cherub of beaten gold, with wings stretched inward over the ark, forming the throne of God.

The propitiatory throne was altar in the highest sense. This is expressed in the solemn offering on the day of atonement, when the high priest brought the blood into the holy of holies, poured it out seven times on the floor before the throne and once on the throne itself. This scene is described in the Apocalypse (5:6 f.), where the Lamb ascends the throne and receives the book: "And I saw, and behold in the midst of the throne and of the four living creatures, and in the midst of the ancients, a Lamb standing as it were slain, having seven horns and seven eyes: which are the seven spirits of God, sent forth into all the earth. And He came and took the book out of the right hand of him that sat on the throne." The propitiatory throne is in this scene an altar in the highest sense, uniting into it the altar of light and the altar of incense.

The meaning of the altar of incense, so far as it appears in the Apocalypse as distinct from the propitiatory throne, signifies the sacrifice of the saints, distinct from the sacrifice of Christ.

CHRIST AS ALTAR

The altar is the dwelling place of the divinity. Now, no place is more appropriate to God than the body of the Word, in which dwells the divinity by a sanctification not merely accidental, but substantial. So we have to say: By the Incarnation, Christ was anointed both as priest and as altar. Scheeben explains: The same divine principle which, as spiritual unction, consecrates Christ in His human soul as most high priest, consecrates Him likewise as most high altar, to carry His victim. Both dignities—priest and altar—belong in Christ to the humanity but as anointed by the divinity. Since the altar is the visible representative of God, those who desired to offer sacrifices had to do so through an altar. But Christ, having the altar in Himself, approached to God through Himself (Heb. 9:24): "For Jesus is not entered into the holies made with hands, the patterns of the true; but into heaven itself, that He may appear now in the presence of God for us."

These relations were expressed in the symbolism of the propitiatory throne: the holy of holies signified the heaven of the glorious divinity, where God appears to the angels and to the blessed in His glory and beatitude on the throne of His majesty. The ark of the covenant, of incorruptible wood, signified the body of Christ. Covered with gold, it signified the glorious body of Christ after the Resurrection. The propitiatory, which was of pure gold, signified the throne of the divinity, sitting as it were upon the humanity, or as preceding the humanity of Christ, with the assistance and ministry of the cherubim and all the angels.

Scripture testifies to the concept of Christ as altar. Our Lord rebuked the scribes and Pharisees (Matt. 23:17–19):

"Ye blind, for whether is greater, the gift or the altar that sanctifieth the gift." According to this word, the sanctity of the victim has its cause in the sanctity of the altar. From the sanctity which the altar has from the contact, so to speak, of the presiding and indwelling divinity, it communicates to the victim placed upon it. Christ applies these ideas to Himself (John 2:19) when He says: "Destroy this temple, and in three days I will rebuild it." St. Augustine explains (*Quaestiones Evangeliorum*): "Seeing that the Lord said: whether is the greater, the gold, or the temple which sanctifieth the gold? and also said: whether is the greater, the gift, or the altar which sanctifieth the gift, we must interpret both temple and altar as Christ Himself."

In John 2:21 our Lord announced a future substitute for the Temple, having a perfect spiritual worship, resplendent with the beauty and the glory of a celestial victim: "In these days I will rebuild it"—a changed structure, a house which is God's very own, being the sanctuary of the new and eternal testament, the tabernacle and altar of the true sacrifice, a center of worship never to be profaned, namely, His body. In virtue of the power of eternal life, a body raised from the dead, to be a vessel of universal propitiation, and ark and temple that will remain forever.

CHRIST THE GOLDEN ALTAR

Christ is a golden altar because of the spiritual worship accomplished upon it by the power of the divinity; He is a golden altar because in Him reside all sacrificial and sanctifying power; He is a golden altar because not visible to the senses, but only accessible by faith, like the golden altar in the holy of holies; He is a golden altar in the glory of the Resurrection. This last reason makes Christ also the heavenly altar.

That Christ after His resurrection fulfills the function of heavenly altar, is a consequence of His rising as Temple. Besides, the text of St. Paul (Heb. 13:10) states expressly this truth: "We have an altar whereof they have no power to eat who serve the tabernacle." Now, it is this text which has inspired the second part of the *Supplices te rogamus,* namely, the petition for Holy Communion: "that as many as shall by partaking at this altar, receive the most sacred body," etc.

The Concept of Heavenly Altar in the Liturgy

The attributes of the altar, which in the Roman Canon is called "the altar on high," are various in the Eastern liturgies: propitiatory altar; holy, mystical altar; stainless altar in heaven; holy, heavenly, reasonable altar; altar of forgiveness, set up by Thy mercy and in which Thy glory dwells. These attributes combine the features of the propitiatory altar in the holy of holies, the throne of God, with the altar of incense in the holy place. "To carry up to the altar" signifies: (a) transubstantiation into the body of Christ; (b) special emphasis on transubstantiation into the glorious body, i.e., glorification. This idea is particularly revealed with the altar of incense: the victim laid upon it is glorified by its fire, the fire of the glowing coals is communicated to the victim; (c) acceptance by God.

The *Apostolic Constitutions* speaks of Christ as heavenly altar (8,13): "Let us further beseech God through His Christ, and let us beseech Him on account of the gift which is offered to the Lord God, that the good God will accept it, through the mediation of His Christ, upon His heavenly altar, for a sweet-smelling savor."

The liturgy of St. James speaks of "the altar above the skies," of the "holy and spiritual altar above the skies," of

"His altar that is holy and above the heavens, spiritual and rational." "Let us pray: that the Lord our God, having graciously received them to His altar that is holy and above the heavens, rational and spiritual, for the odor of a sweet spiritual savor." This altar particularly includes the ideas of the Apocalypse, with the vision of Isaias, as it is apparent in the prayer before Holy Communion: "The Lord bless us and make us worthy with the pure touching of our fingers to take the live coal, and place it upon the mouths of the faithful for the purification and renewal of their souls and bodies, now and always."

The idea of the propitiatory throne is expressed in the prayer of the great entrance and in the prayer of the veil: "God Almighty, Lord great in glory, who hast given to us an entrance into the holy of holies, through the sojourning among men of Thy only-begotten Son, our Lord. . . . We thank Thee, O Lord our God, that Thou hast given us boldness for the entrance of Thy holy places, which Thou hast renewed to us a new and living way through the veil of the flesh of Thy Christ."

The Liturgy of the Holy Apostles Addai and Mari, or the Chaldean liturgy, understands the celebration of the Eucharist as enacted "before the glorious throne of Thy power, the unattainable seat of Thy majesty, the great place of Thy burning love, the altar of forgiveness, which is set up by Thy mercy, and in which Thy glory dwells." At the beginning of the liturgy of the faithful we read: "The glorious and holy and life-giving and divine mysteries are set and ordered upon the propitiatory altar."

From this review of the scriptural texts and of the various liturgies we see that we may interpret the "altar on high" either as Deity or as Christ. If we understand the altar as the Deity, then the "carry up to the altar on high" implies simply acceptance of the sacrifice by the Deity. If we understand the altar as Christ, then it means transubstantiation; the sanctity of the altar is communicated to the oblation. If we conceive the altar as Christ, the golden altar, then transfiguration, glorification is emphasized. If in the postconsecratory invocation we attend to the connotation of the consecration of the mystical body, then we may speak of the altar of the Church triumphant in heaven, that altar of incense which in the Apocalypse is seen distinct from the throne of God.

We may interpret consecration with the symbolism of the vision of Isaias: the oblation is laid upon the altar of incense, i.e., the glorified Christ. From the glowing charcoal the fire of glory is transfused to the oblation, it is becoming glorious, transfigured. If we explain the consecration with the symbolism of the Apocalypse (the Lamb ascending upon the throne of God, a Lamb as it were slain, with seven eyes), then the consecration is an immolation, a sprinkling of the sacrificial blood upon the propitiatory throne, at the same time a sacrifice of light, and the oblation is transformed into light, spiritualized, divinized.

Summarizing we may say: the angel deputed by God to assist at the Eucharistic sacrifice ministers to it by his intercession with our invocation for the consecration.

"Partaking at This Altar"

This part of the *Supplices te rogamus* is clearly a prayer for the effects of sacrifice and sacrament, a prayer of preparation for Holy Communion. It is an invocation for the consecration of the mystical body and emphasizes in the terms employed the incorporation into Christ, the partaking of the heavenly altar as an extension and continuation of the Incarnation.

HISTORICAL DEVELOPMENT

Although this petition is not found in the *De sacramentis,* it is one of the most ancient elements of the Eucharistic anaphora, substantially found in the prayer of the *Didache,* explicitly pointed out in the Canon of the *Traditio apostolica:* "Mayest Thou grant to all who partake, to be filled with the Holy Ghost." The *Apostolic Constitutions* has this invocation: "That those who are partakers thereof may be strengthened for piety, . . . may be filled with the Holy Ghost." The idea of Holy Communion as an extension of the glorification of Christ, is the point of the preconsecratory invocation of the fragment of Deir Balizeh: "Fill us also with Thy glory which is with Thee." The liturgy of St. James continues with the symbolism of the altar in the vision of Isaias: "The Lord bless us and make us worthy with the pure touching of our fingers to take the live coal, and place it on the mouth of the faithful for the purification and renewal of their souls and bodies." The Byzantine liturgy, just as the Roman Canon, connects the petition for Holy Communion with the petition for consecration: "That our Lord, the lover of men, receiving the same on His holy, heavenly, and mystical altar for a perfume of spiritual sweetness, will send down again upon us His divine grace and the gift of the Holy Spirit."

SCRIPTURAL BACKGROUND

The Roman phrase does not pray for the descent of the Holy Ghost. It does not ask for glorification. It has substituted for these ideas the words "may we be filled with all heavenly blessing and grace." Evidently the idea of the "blessed" of the narrative of the institution is once more taken up, and continued. The attributes "all" and "celestial" recall the words of St. Paul (Eph. 1:3): "Blessed be the God and Father of our Lord Jesus Christ, who hath blessed us with spiritual blessings in heavenly places in Christ." This unusual phrase occurs three times in the Epistle to the Ephesians. In a beautiful connection of ideas in Eph. 2:5 f.: "But God . . . hath quickened us together in Christ (by whose grace you are saved), and hath raised us up together, and hath made us sit together in the heavenly places, through Christ Jesus." This is what the invocation of the Canon asks, this blessing in "supercoelestibus." It is the intimate union with Christ, to become companions with Christ in His life, in His resurrection, in His ascension, in His sitting upon heavenly thrones. In the prophetic nature of St. Paul's words, in the certainty of being redeemed, redemption being accomplished, St. Paul sees already its effects and fruits accomplished in the past tense of the words: "hath quickened us together, . . . hath raised us together, . . . hath made us sit together in the heavenly places." Holy Communion appears as an extension of the events of the life of Christ, an extension, a continuation of the mystery of the Incarnation.

Both terms, "blessing and grace," complete the idea of continued Incarnation. These terms are contained in the angelic salutation to the Blessed Virgin "full of grace, . . . blessed art thou." It is as if the angel of sacrifice, having carried up the victim to the heavenly altar, would turn round and repeat his joyful salutation, "you shall be filled with all heavenly blessing and grace."

THE PHRASE WITHIN THE STRUCTURE OF THE CANON

Authors who think that this phrase was added at the last rearrangement of the Canon, find it awkwardly joined to the first part of the *Supplices*. They think that the phrase "from this altar" refers to the earthly altar, whereas in the first part it is the heavenly altar, Christ.

But no difficulty is presented by including in "this altar" the idea of the heavenly altar of the first part of the prayer. Further, considered within the entire structure of the Canon, the petition for Holy Communion is the symmetrical counterpart of the conclusion of the preconsecratory invocation "that it may become for us the body and the blood of Thy most beloved Son Jesus Christ." This part of the *Quam oblationem* certainly contains the connotation of a petition for the effects of the Holy Eucharist. To this connotation we see the corresponding postconsecratory element in the invocation "that we may be filled with all heavenly blessing and grace."

As the "that it may become for us the body and the blood of Thy most beloved Son" recalls the humble and at the same time exultant answer of Mary, "Be it done unto me according to thy word," so we may hear it from the heart and the soul of the faithful. And thus the invocation finishes in the rhythms of the Magnificat.

CHAPTER XXVIII

"Per quem haec omnia, Domine"

"By whom, O Lord, Thou dost always create, sanctify, vivify, bless, and bestow upon us all these good things."

This third postconsecratory invocation is separated from both the others through the intercessory prayers. So far as its origin is concerned, there is no connection at all between this last invocation and both the others. In its present state it does not have much of an invocation: all the verbs are in the indicative ("Thou dost create, sanctify, vivify," etc.). Only the five crosses suggest the impetratory character. These epikletic blessings caused many difficulties to the interpreters of the Middle Ages. St. Peter Damian [1] (d. 1072) said: "There arises the question not to be passed over, why over the blessed and completely consecrated host still the sign of a blessing is made. Moreover, things are added in the Canon (after the consecration), which seem to indicate that the consecration is not yet accomplished." Innocent III [2] had the same difficulty. He refers to the words of St. Peter Damian and adds: "In this question I prefer rather to be instructed than to instruct, and only mention than propose an opinion. Truly, since I did not find anything definite said about this question," etc. The opinion of St. Thomas we have referred to above. He understood the crosses not as blessings, but as

[1] St. Peter Damian, *Expositio Canonis*, no. 9; *PL*, 145, 885.
[2] Innocent III, *De mysterio missae*, V, c. 2; *PL*, 214, 887.

375

commemorative signs of the power of the passion of Christ. Robert Paululus [3] formulated the same idea with these words: "The signs of the cross before the consecration are a petition for consecration; afterwards . . . they testify that it is accomplished." The Council of Trent [4] made some efforts to explain the meaning of these crosses, and, as we find in its records, many thought the crosses over the consecrated host should not be made, in order not to give the impression that something is wanting to the consecration.

ORIGIN

Cardinal Bona [5] had already suggested what later under the authority of Duchesne was almost generally accepted: that this prayer was originally a blessing of the fruits of the earth, which took place here at every Mass. When this custom disappeared, the prayer remained and was understood of the Eucharist itself.

In the Gelasian sacramentary it is connected with a blessing of beans on Ascension Day: "On the ascension of the Lord, the following blessing. Bless, O Lord, also these new fruits of beans . . . in the name of our Lord Jesus Christ, through whom," etc. In the Leonine sacramentary it is the clause of a blessing of water, honey, and milk in the first Mass of Whitsunday. A similar blessing of grapes was customary on St. Sixtus day (August 6). On Holy Thursday in this place we still have the blessing of the holy oils. The words "all these" referred, therefore, originally to the fruits of the earth. Cardinal Schuster [6] calls it a kind of parenthesis in the Canon and says: "This 'haec omnia creas, sanctificas, vivificas, bene-

[3] Robertus Paululus, De offic. eccl., II, c. 32.
[4] Le Plat, Monumenta, V, 432.
[5] Cardinal Bona, Rerum lit., II, 14; p. 455.
[6] Schuster, op. cit., I, 303; cf, Duchesne, Origines du culte, pp. 174 f.

dicis et praestas nobis' has nothing to do with the sacred Eucharistic species, to which, moreover, it would hardly be feasible to allude again in so abrupt a manner, but refers to the fresh produce of the earth, to the oil for the sick and to the fresh first fruits which had just been presented on the altar in order to receive the blessing of the priest. Only of these can it be said, 'All these things dost Thou create, hallow, quicken, bless, and bestow upon us,' language which would be, at the least, strange and incomprehensible, if it were meant to be applied to the Blessed Sacrament." According to this opinion, the prayer is a historical remnant, at present merely a repetition of the previous invocations, without any specific differentiation.

R. Buchwald [7] does not agree with the opinion that the whole reason for the introduction of this prayer was the rather irrelevant blessing of first fruits. He maintains that it is a relic of a former Logos-epiklesis. He supposes an invocation of the Logos, now missing from the introduction of this prayer in the Leonine and Gelasian sacramentary. In both sources the wording is this: "Bless, O Lord, likewise these creatures." These words suppose that a blessing has immediately preceded. In his opinion the original form would have been: "Bless, O Lord, these creatures of bread and wine . . . in the name of our Lord Jesus Christ, through whom," etc. He thinks that Leo I adopted the epiklesis of the Holy Ghost, removed the older Logos-epiklesis, which remained in the Canon merely as a remnant. (The Missale Ambrosianum has a Logos-epiklesis with our prayer as a clause: "We do this, we celebrate these, O Lord, in order to comply with Thy precepts. . . . It is for Thee, almighty Father, to send now Thy only-begotten Son . . . that Thou mayest now

[7] R. Bushwald, *Die Epiklese*, pp. 51–53.

give us His body for salvation, as Thou hast given to mankind redemption through His passion.") The opinion of Buchwald, although it explains the origin of the prayer differently, does not give to the present prayer more significance than the previous opinion.

An essay of Dom Joseph Kreps [8] connects this prayer with the final doxology. He says with much reason that it is incongruous to limit the significance of this prayer in the present Canon to a historical remnant. This would not justify its presence as a regular part of the liturgy, while formerly it had rather been an exceptional blessing. It has to be understood, so the author concludes, as a kind of summary (together with the following doxology) of the whole significance and efficacy of the Eucharistic sacrifice.

THE "PER QUEM HAEC OMNIA" IN THE STRUCTURE OF THE CANON

Only a broader view which considers this invocation in connection with both the other postconsecratory invocations, then in connection with the final doxology, finally within the structure of the entire Canon, as it corresponds to a preconsecratory element, will give a satisfactory solution and reveal the intention of the Church.

As compared with both the preceding postconsecratory invocations, it has its specific feature as the invocation for consecration through Christ's priesthood. The first invocation, *Supra quae*, refers to the ministry of the human priest with the faithful, the second invocation, *Supplices te rogamus*, refers to the ministry of the angels, the third, *per quem haec omnia*, refers to the priesthood of Christ.

[8] J. Kreps, "La Doxologie du Canon," I; *Cours et conférences des semaines liturgiques* (Louvain, 1929), pp. 223–30.

The words "all these" takes up again, after the interruption by the intercessory prayers, the idea of the invocations. This pronoun refers to the same object as the pronouns in the *Supra quae* and in "jube haec" of the *Supplices te rogamus*.

The connection with the final doxology is evident from the external grammatical parallelism. We may observe a tripartite structure of the doxology, which serves to augment its solemnity: The first element is the clause of the *Nobis quoque peccatoribus*, "Per Christum Dominum nostrum"; the second is an amplified form, "Per quem haec omnia"; the third is the doxology itself, "Per ipsum," etc. In the first element the priesthood of Christ is confessed generally; in the second element the mediation is specified primarily from God to men; in the third element, in the doxology the primary end of all mediation concludes solemnly the specific greatness of Christ's priesthood: the glory of the Father in the Holy Ghost.

Finally, we have to consider the prayer in the entire structure of the Canon, as the symmetrical element of a prayer before consecration. The symmetrical element in the preconsecratory Canon is the passage about the mediation of Christ in the first preconsecratory invocation: "through Jesus Christ Thy Son," partly also in the coordinated passage in the beginning of the Preface: through the priesthood of Christ the heavenly Father is given praise and thanks by men in communion with the angels; He is invoked to consecrate through the priesthood of Christ; likewise in the Canon after the consecration the human priest with the faithful, in communion with the angel of the sacrifice, invoke the acceptance of the sacrifice through the priesthood of Christ.

The universality of the mediation and priesthood of Christ is noted with three groups of terms: "all these," "always," the five verbs (create, sanctify, vivify, bless, bestow). These three terms recall similar ideas in the Canon before the consecration: the object of thanksgiving through Christ was creation, the acts of providence, redemption, "all these things"; the thanksgiving was specified as being due always and everywhere, according to the benefactions of God through Christ which continue "always and everywhere." Finally, the five verbs, although partly synonymous, refer to the benefactions of God in creation, redemption, sanctification.

The phrase "through whom all these" alludes to the passage in I Cor. 8:6: "Yet to us there is but one God, the Father, of whom are all things, and we unto Him; and one Lord Jesus Christ, by whom are all things, and we by Him." For us Christians, who know that God is the first principle and the last end of all things, there is only one God, from whom all things proceed as from the first cause, and to whom we tend as our ultimate end (Rom. 11:26). Furthermore, for us who know that Lord means Him on whom all things depend, there is only one Lord, Jesus Christ, by whom as the exemplar and efficient cause all things were made (John 1:3) and through whom as God incarnate we Christians have been redeemed (Eph. 4:5 f.).

The "always," which has its parallel also in the prophecy of Malachias, includes likewise the advice of St. Paul (Heb. 13:15): "Through Him, therefore, let us offer the host of praise always to God."

In the five verbs, which are partly synonymous, the abundance, the universality, of the mediation of Christ is expressed in the first place. Then some differentiation can be seen also: the three terms "sanctifies, vivifies, blesses," to which correspond three signs of the cross, contain an allusion to the Blessed Trinity. Between the first term and the rest we can distinguish the work of creation from the work of redemption. While, regarding the mediation of Christ in the work of creation, we may recall the word of St. John (John 1:3): "All things were made by Him, and without Him was made nothing that was made," for the universality of the priesthood of Christ in the redemption, we remember Heb. 7:25: "Whereby He is able also to save forever them that come to God by Him"; and Heb. 10:14: "For by one oblation He has perfected forever them that are sanctified." The two last terms, "blesses and bestows," may refer the one to the Eucharistic consecration, the other to Holy Communion.

The *Per quem haec omnia"* is without Amen. Although these different Amens, except the one which concludes the final doxology and goes back to apostolic times, all of them are of later origin. However, the fact that the *Per quem haec omnia* was left without Amen, indicates its connection with the final doxology.

CHAPTER XXIX

Memento of the Dead [1]

"Remember also, O Lord, Thy servants and hand-maids, N. and N., who have gone before us with the sign of faith, and sleep the sleep of peace. To these, O Lord, and to all who rest in Christ, grant, we beseech Thee, a place of refreshment, of light, and of peace. Through Christ our Lord. Amen."

Historical Development

The practice of the Church to remember the departed in the holy sacrifice is as old as the liturgy itself. The holy Fathers of the Church and the liturgies give evidence to this. There is, however, no uniform tradition as to the point at which they are to be remembered. Since it was originally a part of the "Prayer of the faithful," the Memento of the dead was said wherever the "prayer of the faithful" was located. At Alexandria it was recited at the beginning of the Mass of the faithful, in the liturgy of Antioch at the end of the anaphora as part of the great intercession. The mention of certain names may have been introduced in the middle of the fourth century.

St. Justin (d. 167) knew the "prayer of the faithful," which

[1] E. Bishop, *Liturgica historica* (Oxford, 1918), p. 113.; M. Andrieu, "L'insertion du Memento des morts au canon romain," *Revue de sciences relig.*, I (1921), 151–54; F. J. Doelger, *Sphragis* (Paderborn, 1912), pp. 99–104; A. M. Schneider, *Refrigerium I. Nach lit. Quellen und Inscriften.* Freiburg i. B., 1928.

from the beginning probably included the memento of the dead. Tertullian (d. 222) speaks of the prayer for the departed. St. Cyril of Jerusalem says: "Afterwards we remember those who died, first the patriarchs, ... generally for all who died from among us." [2] St. Chrysostom ascribes this custom to an ordinance of the apostles: "Not without reason the apostles have ordained that at the celebration of the tremendous mysteries the departed shall be commemorated. They knew very well that to them great help is given therein." [3] St. Augustine [4] says that supplications for the souls of the departed should not be omitted; the Church has made a practice of offering these supplications for all who died in Christian communion, even without pronouncing their names within the general commemoration.

In the *Traditio apostolica* the prayer of the faithful was said before the anaphora. The *Apostolic Constitutions* has the Memento after the epiklesis: "We further offer to Thee also for all those holy persons who have pleased Thee from the beginning of the world, . . . with all whose names Thou knowest. . . . Let us pray for those that are departed in faith." The prayer book of Serapion has this memento: "Let us pray also for all the departed, of whom there is the memory. Sanctify these souls; Thou knowest all of them. Sanctify all who died in the Lord and join them to all Thy saints and give them a place and dwelling in Thy kingdom." The liturgy of St. James: "Remember, O Lord God, the spirits and all flesh, of whom we have made mention and of whom we have not made mention, who are of the true faith, from righteous Abel unto this day: unto them do Thou give rest there in

[2] *Cat. myst.*, V, 9.
[3] *Hom. 3 in Ep ad Phil.*, n. 4.
[4] St. Augustine, *De virginitate; PL*, 40, 423.

the land of the living, in Thy kingdom, in the joy of paradise, in the bosom of Abraham and of Isaac and of Jacob, our holy fathers; whence pain and grief and lamentation have fled: there the light of Thy countenance looks upon them, and enlightens them forever." An example of the Memento at the beginning of the anaphora is found in the liturgy of St. Mark: "O Lord our God, give peace to the souls of our fathers and brethren who have fallen asleep in Jesus, remembering our forefathers of old, our fathers, patriarchs, prophets, apostles, martyrs, confessors, bishops, and the souls of all the holy and just men who have died in the Lord."

The division of the Mementos, one to be said before the consecration, the second after the consecration, is peculiar to the Roman liturgy, as we have said above. Abbot Cabrol and Cardinal Schuster maintain that in Rome the diptychs were read originally at the Offertory; St. Leo I [5] (440–61) mentions the reading of the diptychs at Rome. The division into two prayers is, according to these authors, a consequence of being written on two tablets, one with the names of the living, the other with the names of the dead.

According to V. L. Kennedy, C.S.B.,[6] the Memento of the dead as part of the Canon is the result of the reform of the Canon by Pope Gelasius: when the prayer of the faithful was suppressed, the intercessions within the Canon developed; the memento of the dead was added, but limited to Masses for the dead and only for private Masses. This is the reason why it is not found in the Canon of the Gelasian Sacramentary. As a regular part of the Canon it was introduced in Gallican and Irish Churches in the seventh century with the introduc-

[5] St. Leo I, *Ep.* 70; *PL*, 54, 914.
[6] V. L. Kennedy, *The Saints of the Canon of the Mass.* Citta del Vaticano, 1938.

tion of the Roman Canon there. Eventually the practice was adopted in Rome.

INTERPRETATION

The general character of the Memento of the dead is thoroughly Roman. It is the same spirit as is found in the Roman Christian epigraphy of the fourth and fifth centuries.

"Remember also." This also connects the Memento of the dead with the Memento of the living, an evidence that formerly they were somehow united. The prayer consists of two parts, one before, the other after the names. Two conditions are mentioned for names to be read: (a) they must have received "the sign of faith," i.e., baptism (character of baptism), and (b) they must have departed in peace with the Church, "sleep the sleep of peace." The tender expression "sleep the sleep of peace" is a biblical expression (Matt. 9:24: "He said: Give place, for the girl is not dead, but sleepeth"), which has inspired the terms "Koimeterion," "dormitorium," "cemetery": place to sleep. The second part of the prayer is for all "who rest in Christ." The expressions "to rest" and "to die in the Lord" are from Scripture (Apoc. 14:13): "And I heard a voice from heaven, saying to me, write: Blessed are the dead who die in the Lord. From henceforth now, saith the spirit, that they may rest from their labors." To rest in Christ means to be in the grace of God, in the communion of life and love with Christ.

The object of the prayer is expressed with three terms: "place of refreshment," "place of light," and "place of peace." The first term expresses the happiness of the blessed in opposition to the punishment of the senses; both the other terms refer to the beatific vision and its consequence upon the appetite.

The term "place of refreshment" alludes to the Gospel of St. Luke 16:23 f.: "And lifting up his eyes when he was in torments, he saw Abraham afar off and Lazarus in his bosom: and he cried and said: Father Abraham, have mercy on me and send Lazarus, that he may dip the tip of his finger in water to cool (refresh) my tongue: for I am tormented in this flame."

The contrast to the heat and the thirst of hell is likewise expressed in Apoc. 7:16 f.: "Neither shall the sun fall on them, nor any heat; the Lamb shall lead them to the fountain of the waters of life."

"Place of light" means heaven, the beatific vision (Apoc. 21:25): "And the gates thereof shall not be shut by day: for there shall be no night there." "And the city hath no need of the sun nor of the moon to shine in it. For the glory of God hath enlightened it, and the Lamb is the lamp thereof." "And night shall be no more. And they shall not need the light of the lamp nor the light of the sun, because the Lord God shall enlighten them."

"Place of peace." Peace is the consequence of the beatific vision in the appetite (Tob. 13:18): "Blessed are all they that love Thee, and that rejoice in Thy peace." Isa. 66:12: "For thus saith the Lord: Behold I will bring upon her as it were a river of peace, and as an overflowing torrent the glory of the Gentiles." So touching in their simplicity are the inscriptions on Christian epitaphs: "Vale in pace"; "In pace Domini dormias"; "Pax cum angelis"; "In pace delicium"; "Tecum pax Christi."

"Nobis quoque peccatoribus"

"To us sinners also, Thy servants, hoping in the multitude of Thy merices, vouchsafe to grant some part and fellowship with Thy holy apostles and martyrs: with John, Stephen, Matthias, Barnabas, Ignatius, Alexander, Marcellinus, Peter, Felicitas, Perpetua, Agatha, Lucy, Agnes, Cecilia, Anastasia, and with all Thy saints, into whose company we pray Thee admit us, not considering our merit, but of Thine own free pardon. Through Christ."

Origin

According to V. L. Kennedy (*op. cit.*), the addition of the *Nobis quoque peccatoribus* is another element of the reform of the Canon by Pope Gelasius (although not in its final shape which was given by Pope Gregory I). M. Maranget expressed the opinion that both prayers, the *Communicantes* and the *Nobis quoque peccatoribus,* may have been inserted by Pope Symmachus (498–514), of whom the *Liber pontificalis* says, that his devotion to the apostles and saints was very great.

It is common to most liturgies to continue the prayer for the dead with a petition for the priests and clerics assisting at the altar. In the liturgy of St. James we read after the memory of the dead: "But for us, O Lord, direct Christian and well-pleasing and sinless ends of our lives in peace, gathering us under the feet of Thine elect, when Thou wilt and as Thou wilt, only without shame or sin." Likewise in the liturgy of St. Mark: "Rest their souls and grant them the kingdom of heaven, but to us vouchsafe Christian and well-pleasing and sinless ends of our lives and give us a share and a part with Thy saints." The *Breviarium in Psalmos,*[7] attributed to St. Jerome, quotes part of the *Nobis quoque peccatoribus:* "Ad capescendam futuram beatitudinem cum

---

[7] *Breviarum in Psalmos; PL,* 26, 1094. Cf. G. Morin, *Anecdota Maredsolana,* I, 3.

electis eius, in quorum, nos consortium, non meritorum inspector sed veniae largitor, admittat Christus Dominus noster. Amen."

INTERPRETATION

The first three words of the prayer *Nobis quoque peccatoribus* are said aloud, because in early times the subdeacons remained bowed during the Canon up to this point. Later, when the Canon was no longer recited aloud, these words were pronounced so as to be heard as a sign especially for the subdeacons that the priest had reached this point in the Canon.

"In the multitude of Thy mercies" is a remembrance of Ps. 50:1 f.: "Have mercy on us, O God, according to Thy great mercy. And according to the multitude of Thy tender mercies, blot out my iniquity."

"Some part and fellowship with Thy holy apostles and martyrs." These words occur first in a letter of St. Polycarp to the Philippians written about 107, which were probably taken from the apostolic liturgy: "God give you a portion and a share with His saints." A similar phrase is found in Ps. 72:26: "For Thee my flesh and my heart hath fainted away. Thou art the God of my heart, and the God that is my portion forever." In the Epistle to the Colossians, St. Paul uses a similar expression (Col. 1:11): "Giving thanks to God the Father who hath made us worthy to be partakers of the lot of the saints in light." The words "with Thy holy apostles and martyrs" seem to be a general allusion to the *Communicantes*.

List of Saints by St. Gregory I

1 St. John (the Baptist) corresponds to the position of the Blessed Virgin in the *Communicantes*

7 martyrs: Stephen, first martyr

Matthias, apostle (omitted in the *Communicantes*)

Barnabas, apostle, companion of St. Paul

Ignatius, bishop

Alexander, priest or bishop

Marcellinus, priest

Peter, exorcist

7 women saints (arranged according to countries):

Africa: Felicitas

Perpetua

Sicily: Agatha

Lucia

Rome: Agnes

Cecilia

Orient: Anastasia

St. Gregory I arranged the list of saints in hierarchical order, just as he did with the list of the saints of the *Communicantes*. St. John the Baptist was the first to be inserted, together with St. Stephen from the Alexandrian rite, by Pope Gelasius. The Congregation of Rites declared (March 27, 1824) that it is St. John the Baptist. This declaration was withdrawn in 1898. But it seems to be St. John the Baptist for several reasons: (a) St. John the Evangelist was mentioned in the *Communicantes*; (b) in the Byzantine rite the order is: Our Lady, St. John the Baptist, the apostles; (c) the Alexandrian rite, whence the insertion came, has without doubt St. John the Baptist. St. John the Baptist is given a position similar to that of the Blessed Virgin in the *Communicantes* with regard to the words of our Lord (Matt. 11:11): "Amen I say to you, there hath not risen among them that are born of women a greater than John the Baptist."

St. Stephen was held in great veneration after the finding of his relics in 415. He was given the name "martyr" by St. Paul (Acts 22:20): "And when the blood of Stephen Thy witness was shed, I stood by and consented."

St. Matthias was inserted because of his being an apostle. There was no cult of his in Rome until the ninth century. We see here again the tendency to bring the names in hierarchical order, to fill the list of the apostles.

St. Barnabas was a companion of St. Paul. There are many reasons to admit that he was an apostle in the strict sense: St. Paul and St. Barnabas were ordained together with prayers and the imposing of hands. They were to complete the Apostolic College and to take the place of the two saints (James the elder, who had suffered martyrdom, James the younger, whose activity was restricted to the care of the mother Church in Jerusalem).

St. Ignatius (d. 107) was regarded by the early Christians as a disciple of St. Peter. He was ordained bishop by him and martyred in Rome under Trajan (98–117). His letters were looked upon almost as canonical writings.

St. Alexander I (109–19), pope and martyr, buried on the Via Nomentana, was inserted not much before the time of St. Gregory I. The problematic nature of this identification appears in the light of the facts, that there are three groups of martyrs at Rome containing an Alexander or a saint buried in the Cemetery of Ficulea.

About St. Peter and St. Marcellinus from the suburbicarian district of Rome, buried at Silva Candida, we have the inscription of Damasus:

"Marcelline tuos pariter Petre nosse triumphos
percussor retulit Damaso mihi cum puer essem."

The executioner himself told Pope Damasus when he was a boy, the story of these two saints. Their cult originated probably at the time of Pope Damasus. They were probably inserted by Pope Gelasius.

Perpetua and Felicitas, who were martyred about 202 or 203, were Carthaginians. The acts of their martyrdom (*Passio S. Perpetuae*) is a historical document of primary importance. A mosaic in the archiepiscopal palace in Ravenna shows probably both these saints. Their names were inserted by Pope Gelasius, who was "natione Afer." (Note. In some documents the names are separated; hence it could be that Felicitas is not the African martyr, but a Roman saint: the mother of the seven martyrs of July, who enjoyed a great cult in Rome. In that case her name could have been inserted early in the sixth century. The first name inserted was that of Felicitas. The name of Perpetua was at first a marginal addition.)

About the insertion of the names of St. Agatha and St. Lucy we have the testimony of St. Aldhelm (d. 709): "Sanctae Agathae rumores castissimae virginis Luciae praeconia subsequantur, quas praeceptor noster Gregorius in canone cotidiano quando missarum solemnia celebrantur pariter copulasse cognoscitur hoc modo in catalogo martyrum ponens: Felicitate, Anastasia, Agatha, Lucia." St. Agatha was martyred in the year 251 in Catania. Her cult was introduced in Rome at the end of the fifth century. Pope Gregory I had a devotion to this saint and probably founded a monastery in Sicily (SS. Maximini et Agathae) in her honor. St. Lucy, who was martyred in the year 304 in Syracuse, has a very legendary *Passio*. St. Gregory probably founded another monastery in her honor (SS. Andreas et Lucia).

St. Agnes, who was martyred at the tender age of thirteen

years, enjoyed a cult in Rome from the first time of such a cult. St. Damasus, St. Ambrose, and Prudentius testify to its popularity. If there arose any idea of inserting women saints into the Canon, then St. Agnes was the first to be inserted in a list of the Roman liturgy.

St. Cecilia, who was martyred probably in the middle of the third century and was buried in the crypt next to that of the popes at St. Callistus, was identified with the foundress of the "Titulus Ceciliae." Her cult spread at the end of the fifth century.

St. Aanastasia, who was identified with the martyr of Sirmium, was venerated in Rome under the influence of the Byzantine Empire (536–68). Her name was inserted in the Canon for similar reasons about the same time.

DOXOLOGY [8]

It is the sacred art of the psalms to conclude with a doxology. This practice was continued by the apostles in epistles, instructions, and prayers. Then there is the doctrine of St. Paul about the reconciliation of the universe in Christ contained in this solemn conclusion, and at the same time, with the words "forever and ever," an allusion to the consummative sacrifice in heaven, to this never-ending canticle of the Lamb, to the eternal hymn of praise and thanksgiving.

SCRIPTURAL BACKGROUND

It is a text from the Epistle to the Romans that has primarily inspired the final doxology (Rom. 11:36): "For of Him and by Him and in Him are all things: to Him be glory forever.

[8] Cabrol, "La doxologie dans la priere chretienne des premier siècles," *Recherches de science rel.*, XVIII (1928), 9–30; J. A. Jungmann, *Die Stellung Christi im lit. Gebet* (Muenster i. W., 1926), pp. 178–82; A. Kleber, "The Conclusion of the Orations," *The Homiletic and Pastoral Review*, 1943.

Amen." "Of Him," i.e., all things depend upon Him as upon their cause and creator; "by Him," i.e., they are sustained by Him; "in Him," i.e., unto Him as to their last end. The sacerdotal mediation of Christ is expressed in the words of the Epistle to the Hebrews (2:10): "For it became Him, for whom are all things, who had brought many children into glory, to perfect the author of their salvation, by His passion. For both He that sanctifieth and they who are sanctified are all of one." Of some influence upon the doxological conclusion of the orations, has been the text of the Epistle of St. Jude (Jude 25): "To the only God our Savior through Jesus Christ our Lord, be glory and magnificence, empire and power, before all ages, and now, and for all ages of ages. Amen."

INTERPRETATION

For the interpretation of the doxology we have to consider the text itself, then the context, i.e., its connection with the conclusion "per Christum Dominum nostrum" of the *Nobis quoque peccatoribus,* then with the "Per quem haec omnia."

For the interpretation of the text itself the double nature of Christ is the directive principle: through Christ as the mediator infinite glory is given to the Father and the Holy Ghost in two ways: (a) so far as He offers Himself; (b) so far as through Him all homage and adoration of all creatures ascend to God as a pleasing sacrifice. With Him, the Father and the Holy Ghost jointly receive all honor and glory, since Christ is God, a Person of the Blessed Trinity, to whom the Eucharistic sacrifice is offered. In Christ are honored the Father and the Holy Ghost; because of the unity of essence the divine persons are eternally in each other ("perichoresis").

Through Christ, our head and mediator, we render to God all honor and glory inasmuch as we offer the Eucharistic sacrifice "through Him and with Him" as His priests, ministering unto His high priesthood. Further, we give all glory and honor to the Father and the Holy Ghost inasmuch as "in Him" we are included in the victim which is the mystical body, and are jointly offered with Him.

AMEN [9]

The most important Amen of the Canon, which was originally the only one, may be traced back to the Epistle of St. Paul to the Corinthians (I Cor. 14:16): "Else if thou shalt bless with the spirit, how shall he that holdeth the place of the unlearned say Amen to thy blessing?"

This Amen is found in the *Didache* (10): "If anyone is holy, let him come; if anyone is not so, let him repent. Maranatha. Amen." It is recorded by St. Justin (*I Apol.*, 65): "When he has ended the prayers and thanksgiving, all the people present cry out, saying Amen." The Greek liturgy still preserves the people's answer after each consecration. The original Amen expresses the union of the faithful with the hierarchical priest, ratifying the sacred action. It is the assent, a testimony, a confession of faith in the redemptive mysteries celebrated in the sacramental mode of the Eucharistic sacrifice. It is also a testimony that the Holy Eucharist is the sacrifice of Christ in His Church.

[9] P. Salmon, *Les Amen du canon de la messe.* Citta del Vaticano, 1938.

Index

Aaron, priesthood, of, 114

Abel: "*Supra quae propitio*," 345; type of Christ's priesthood, 17

Abraham: "*Supra quae propitio*," 347; type of Christ's priesthood, 17

"Accept" compared with "bless," 197

Acceptance of sacrifice; *see* Redeeming death

Actio, name of Eucharist, 47

Agatha: insertion of name, 234; in list of saints, 391

Agenda, name of Eucharist, 47

Agnes, in list of saints, 391

Aldhelm, in list of saints, 49

Alexander I (pope): insertion of Passion, 241; in list of saints, 390

Alexandrian liturgy, *Nobis quoque peccatoribus,* 215

"All of this," origin, 245

All Souls Day, three Masses, 275

Altar on high: Christ as altar, 367; Christ the golden altar, 368; heavenly altar in liturgy, 369-72; heavenly altar in Scripture, 364-66; origin of the phrase, 363; "partaking of the altar,' 372-74

Ambrose, St.: angel of sacrifice, 356; Eucharist and Incarnation, 307; names of Canon, 48; Roman epiklesis, 338; words of consecration, 362

Amen, 394

Analogy between transubstantiation and mysteries of Christ, 266

Anamnesis: commemoration of Nativity, 298; compared with command of Christ, 290-92; compared with declaration of St. Paul, 292; insertion of Nativity, 301; interpretation of mystics, 289

Anamnesis (*continued*)
mand of Christ, 290-92; compared with declaration of St. Paul, 292; insertion of Nativity, 301; interpretation of mystics, 289

Anaphora, name of Canon, 49

Anastasia: insertion of name, 234; in list of saints, 392

Ancient liturgies, words of consecration, 241

Angel of sacrifice: angel in the context, 361-63; angel in the proper sense, 354-57; angel of sacrifice in Scripture, 355; Christ as the angel, 357-60; different opinions, 354; Holy Ghost as the angel, 360-62

Angelic choirs, in *Traditio apostolica,* 127

Angels, concelebration of Church with, 148

Anthrax, Eastern term for Eucharist, 130, 314

Antichrist, abolishing the perpetual sacrifice, 276

Antiochian rite: place of diptychs, 228; place of intercession, 214

Apocalypse
Eucharistic canticle of, 36
illustrations in mosaics, 38-40
influence on mosaics and Canon, 261
liturgy of, 81-87
reference to canticle of Moses, 57
reflecting apostolic liturgy, 145
Sanctus of, 144, 149-59
and theophanies, 144-58